PENGUIN CANADA

PROGNOSIS

JOHN LAWRENCE REYNOLDS is the author of twenty fiction and non-fiction works, including *When All You Have Is Hope*, co-authored with Frank O'Dea. His book *Free Rider: How a Bay Street Whiz Kid Stole and Spent $20 Million* won the National Business Book Award and was optioned as a motion picture. *Shadow People*, his study of secret societies throughout history, was published in more than a dozen countries. A two-time winner of Arthur Ellis Awards for Best Mystery Novel and winner of a National Magazine Award, Reynolds lives in Burlington, Ontario.

Also by John Lawrence Reynolds

Non-Fiction

When All You Have Is Hope (with Frank O'Dea)

The Naked Investor:
Why Almost Everybody But You Gets Rich on Your RRSP

Shadow People: Inside History's Most Notorious Secret Societies

Straight from the Top (with Robert Milton)

All in Good Time (with Brian Tobin)

Money Management for Canadians (contributor)

Free Rider: How a Bay Street Whiz Kid Stole and Spent $20 Million

Mad Notions

RRSPs and RRIFs for Dummies

Ballroom Dancing: The Romance, Rhythm and Style

Fiction

Haunted Hearts

Solitary Dancer

Gypsy Sins

Whisper Death

And Leave Her Lay Dying

The Man Who Murdered God

PROGNOSIS

THE CURRENT STATE AND SHAKY FUTURE OF CANADA'S HEALTH SYSTEM

JOHN LAWRENCE REYNOLDS

PENGUIN
CANADA

PENGUIN CANADA

Published by the Penguin Group

Penguin Group (Canada), 90 Eglinton Avenue East, Suite 700, Toronto, Ontario, Canada M4P 2Y3 (a division of Pearson Canada Inc.)

Penguin Group (USA) Inc., 375 Hudson Street, New York, New York 10014, U.S.A.
Penguin Books Ltd, 80 Strand, London WC2R 0RL, England
Penguin Ireland, 25 St Stephen's Green, Dublin 2, Ireland (a division of Penguin Books Ltd)
Penguin Group (Australia), 250 Camberwell Road, Camberwell, Victoria 3124, Australia (a division of Pearson Australia Group Pty Ltd)
Penguin Books India Pvt Ltd, 11 Community Centre, Panchsheel Park, New Delhi – 110 017, India
Penguin Group (NZ), 67 Apollo Drive, Rosedale, North Shore 0632, Auckland, New Zealand (a division of Pearson New Zealand Ltd)
Penguin Books (South Africa) (Pty) Ltd, 24 Sturdee Avenue, Rosebank, Johannesburg 2196, South Africa

Penguin Books Ltd, Registered Offices: 80 Strand, London WC2R 0RL, England

First published 2008

1 2 3 4 5 6 7 8 9 10 (RRD)

Author representation: Westwood Creative Artists
94 Harbord Street, Toronto, Ontario M5S 1G6

Manufactured in the U.S.A.

ISBN-13: 978-0-14-305093-3
ISBN-10: 0-14-305093-1

Library and Archives Canada Cataloguing in Publication data available upon request.

Visit the author's website at www.wryter.ca

Visit the Penguin Group (Canada) website at www.penguin.ca

Special and corporate bulk purchase rates available; please see www.penguin.ca/corporatesales or call 1-800-810-3104, ext. 477 or 474

For Nan and Gord Roeder
and to the memory of Lisa

Healing is a matter of time,
but it is sometimes also
a matter of opportunity.

—HIPPOCRATES

CONTENTS

PROGNOSIS

INTRODUCTION
HOCKEY, MARK TWAIN, AND McLUHAN

Hockey may be Canada's national passion, but analyzing the country's health care system is its national pastime. We discuss it everywhere—in the newspapers, at the water cooler, in Tim Hortons, over lunches and dinners, and on the internet. Our obsession with the topic recalls Mark Twain's comment about the weather: *Everybody talks about it but nobody does anything about it.*

People elsewhere in the world might question our endless complaints. Canadians, statistics tell us, enjoy among the highest life expectancies and lowest infant mortality rate of all industrialized nations, including the United States, yet we spend far less per capita on caring for our citizens than our wealthier neighbour. We value our health care system above almost every other national concern, and the overwhelming majority of us like to believe it reflects two quintessentially Canadian values: fairness and pragmatism. But the criticism continues, often punctuated with raised voices and fists.

Few Canadians talked and wrote more about the health care system in recent years than former Saskatchewan premier Roy Romanow. His Royal Commission report on health care, issued with great fanfare on

November 28, 2002, was greeted with huzzahs for the author's hard work and wisdom, and was praised for its comprehensive approach and firm recommendations. Public health care, Romanow trumpeted, was "a right of citizenship," and Canadians viewed health care as "a moral enterprise, not a business venture."

Four years later, a review of the report and its impact revealed the following:

- The proposal by the Royal Commission on Health Care to include home care among five specific areas of special funding, as recommended by Romanow, was later deleted in direct contradiction to the Romanow Report's recommendations.
- No changes had been made to the Canada Health Act.
- The Health Council of Canada, yet another government-funded body, had been established with a mandate and budget so confusing in their articulation that it is difficult to define either its goals or its cost to taxpayers.
- Federal and provincial governments continued to skirmish over who decides what to do, and for whom, and how much to pay for it.
- Canada's most widely circulated English-language magazine devoted virtually an entire issue to attacking the concept of Canada's publicly funded health care system, praising the merits of private enterprise and, in a manner worthy of any small-town chamber-of-commerce effort to promote local industry, printing a "Complete User's Guide to Private Medical Care in Canada."[1]
- As dedicated, comprehensive, and detailed as the Romanow Report may have been, it suffered from the same problem all government reports encounter: it wasn't read by the people most affected by its findings. Those employed within the health care system digested its contents and debated its findings. Those outside the system—the consumers of health care services in Canada—relied for the most part on media reports that treated the Romanow Report as though it were any other news story, meaning it was crowded off the pages

and television screens by urgent headlines dealing with wars, murders, assaults, and the weekend antics of movie stars. Meanwhile, horror stories of extended wait times and the health care system's escalating costs remained a hot topic among columnists and the hosts of radio call-in programs, whose lamentations continued to drown out the Romanow highlights.

At times, it appears that the only subject of any dialogue concerning our health care system is the public-versus-private-funding debate, an exchange that remains as polarized and vehement as any evenly matched Stanley Cup playoff game. The funding question dominates the discussion not because it is fundamental but because the choices are easily defined (even if the relative benefits remain vague), and the proponents tend to divide along political left-right lines, producing an innate resistance to compromise and rapprochement.

Challenges to the health care system extend beyond the manner of funding. What's more, while the public-versus-private barrage gives no hint of an early ceasefire, no matter how many targets are demolished (and quickly restored) by both sides, everything else continues apace. In fact, at times the flurry of exchanges between funding competitors risks being left behind by the engines of change and the hard hammers of reality, until both sides appear like medieval scholars duelling over the number of angels pirouetting on the heads of pins. For, no matter how the funding question may be posed, other challenges and opportunities loom. Five to ten years from now, the funding debate will likely be continuing but the challenges and promises will be at our feet—or, in many cases, at our bedside. They include these:

- *The question of aging,* not only of the general population but of physicians and nurses who are growing old and whose numbers are thinning out in lockstep with the increasing need for their services. This problem is a global concern, not merely a Canadian predicament, and the scope of the challenge should not be underestimated. Consider these statistics:

AVERAGE AGE OF PHYSICIANS, 2000–2005

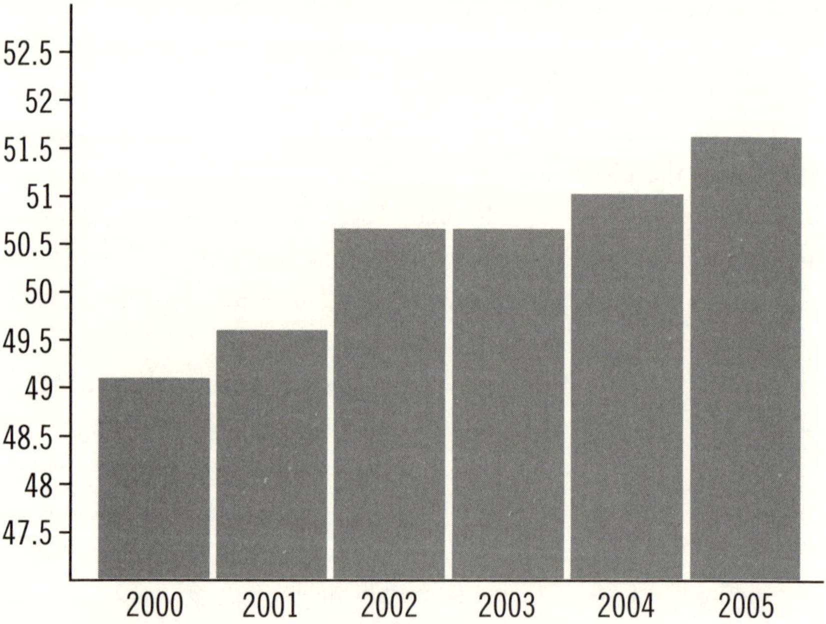

SOURCE: CMA SURVEY *ACCESS CHALLENGES AHEAD*, JULY 2006

The average age of a Canadian physician in 2000 was 49.1. By 2005 this had climbed to 51.7 despite the retirement of physicians at the top end of the age scale and the influx of newly graduated and licensed doctors at the low end. In 2006, it was projected that almost 60 percent of all physicians in Canada would be 55 or over in fewer than 10 years. With that in mind, consider this:

GPs/FPs ACCEPTING NEW PATIENTS

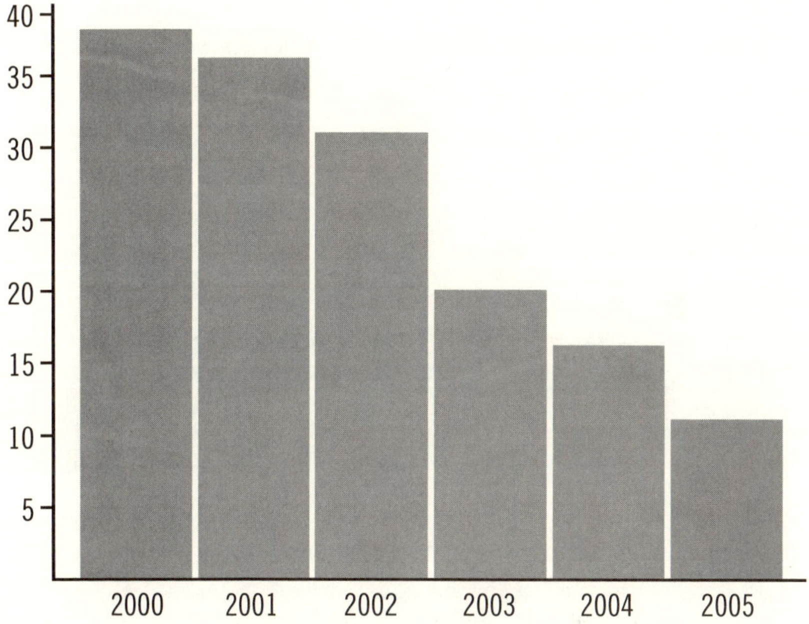

SOURCE: CMA SURVEY *ACCESS CHALLENGES AHEAD*, JULY 2006

In 2000, 38.4 percent of physicians in general practice/family practice were accepting new patients. Five years later, the percentage had dropped to 11.4.

- *The impact of globalization on medical care.* Can international corporations influence a sovereign nation's policies of caring for its citizens? Don't bother asking—they already do.
- *The promise of technology.* We are rightly leery of daily "breakthroughs" in medical research and therapy, yet we all hope to benefit from promised incremental improvements in health care, many of them from sources other than clinics and laboratories. How much of this promise will become reality?

- *The changing approach to maintenance of good health.* A gram of prevention is worth a kilo of cure. Should we be spending more on prevention?
- *The state of mind of physicians, nurses, and other health care providers.* If they are as overworked and underpaid as some claim, what impact does their dissatisfaction have on the quality of the care we receive?
- *The lessons of industry.* Banks do not function today as they did in our grandparents' time, so why does the health care system? Can the manufacturing industry teach hospitals to save lives?
- *The limits of funding.* An MRI clinic on every corner would be a benefit to every Canadian, but so is practicality after all.
- *The apparent fecklessness of governments to tweak the system in response to criticisms and concerns.* When the federal government responded to public outcries about waiting times for five targeted procedures by providing economic rewards, resources poured in to improve access to those procedures at the expense of treatment for hysterectomies, colonoscopies, and gallbladder surgeries. Should governments keep their hands off and permit the system to heal itself?
- *The (perhaps) growing inevitability of inadequate resources.*
- *The ability of private citizens—consumers of products and services supplied by the country's largest industry—to change the system with their own initiative.* During the 1970s, observers predicted that Canada was facing a serious shortage of hospital beds as a result of an expanding aging population. Many implored governments to invest hundreds of millions of dollars in building new hospitals and launching major expansion programs for existing facilities. Thirty years later, statistics showed that the number of days spent in hospitals by Canadians had declined a dramatic 66 percent. While some of this decline was the result of new technology such as minimal-invasive surgery procedures leading to shorter post-operative hospital care, much of it was attributed to changing lifestyles producing generally healthier citizens.[2] Eradicating smoking, controlling

obesity, reducing alcohol consumption, and promoting physical activity would almost certainly result in a similar reduction today.

These subjects and their implications too often are swamped by the rhetoric of crisis, yet they continue to evolve along with our perception of them.

DOES THE COUNTRY NEED ANOTHER BOOK ON THE SUBJECT? AN AUTHOR'S REPLY

It seemed to me that Canada did not need another tract dealing exclusively with the funding question. Our library and bookstore shelves bend with the weight of tomes on the subject, most of their content linked more closely to handicapper reports in racing forms than to hard facts. Other things were happening, many of them off the centre stage of the funding debate and critical to the unfolding of the main plot, yet few people were assessing them. Most discussions on the impact of technology, the concern over globalization, and the restructuring of hospital administration, to name just three, occurred among health professionals while consumers fretted over wait times and the rarity of MRI scanners. If doctors, nurses, and administrators weren't communicating these developments to the public, perhaps it was time others did, even if they lacked specific links to the system. Thus this book.

This will undoubtedly raise eyebrows and prompt expressions of concern in some quarters. How accurately can an outsider evaluate the implications of change within a culture as deep and wide-ranging as health care? The immediate answer: Perhaps as much as the end-users of the health care system can, which is really the point of this book.

My interest in Canada's system of medical care and treatment is identical to that of everyone else, including those who rely directly on its economic, social, and cultural factors: I want to live as long, as energetically, and as free from discomfort as possible, and at the lowest practical cost. So I want to know what is happening that will assist me to enjoy good health over whatever number of years remain for me, and how many barriers must be removed or hurdled to do it. A neurosurgeon, a paramedic, or a deputy minister of health is not needed to tell these tales. In fact, perhaps it's better if people like that step aside.

"We don't know who discovered water," Marshall McLuhan observed, "but we're certain it wasn't a fish."[3] It takes someone from a different environment to fully appreciate various qualities both subtle and significant, which is my justification for exploring specific directions in which Canada's health care system appears to be taking us.

Note the qualifier "specific." This is not a comprehensive examination of Canada's health care system. To achieve that goal requires a multi-volume encyclopaedia that would be substantially out of date at the moment of its release. *Prognosis* deals with selected developments chosen according to their current timely concern, likely future impact, accessibility of information, and degree of comprehension by people like me and you—the ones, we should remind ourselves, to whom the system is or should be dedicated to serve.

The most commonly applied single-word description for Canada's health care system in recent years has been "crisis." Yet a prevalent sense of crisis in itself creates a crisis. We are not facing a crisis in our health care system. We are facing problems that we can all address and help to solve. We can do this by choosing to relieve pressure on the system; by placing as much emphasis on *system* as we do on *health*; by understanding that all systems require management and maintenance; and by recognizing repeated crisis headlines in the mass media for what they are: not evidence of the crumbling of public health care, but warnings that the system deserves our attention.

John Lawrence Reynolds
September 2007

1

PHYSICIANS AND SURGEONS
A MATTER OF MONEY AND STRESS

Orthopaedic surgeon Gary Coulter breaks an old but still frequently held stereotype of doctors. Many Canadians over the age of fifty, those who draw on the majority of health care services, idealize physicians as bespectacled white males wearing steel mirrors on their foreheads and echoing the wisdom of Olympus. Today's medical practitioners are less likely to be either white or male, and more likely to be outspoken and frustrated.*

Dr. Coulter clearly matches this latter description. The walls of his cramped office in Mississauga, Ontario, display neither diplomas nor charts of skeletal-muscular diagrams. Instead, they are hung with posters of popular baseball, hockey, basketball, and football stars, many accompanied by team jerseys, all signed in dedication to the surgical skills of the tenant.

This surgeon carries himself more like Tiger Woods than Dr. Kildare. Lean, athletic, and constantly in motion, he might be more comfortable in a gym or sports bar than in a clinic or operating room. It is easy to imagine him bantering with friends about the merits of the Blue Jays, Oilers, and Roughriders, colouring his conversation with mild expletives. Instead, between examining an apparently unending stream of patients suffering

*A pseudonym

pain from damaged joints, he decries with deep passion the state of Canada's health care system generally and orthopaedic surgery specifically.

His complaints are part philosophical, part economic. Coulter pioneered the use of extracorporeal shock-wave therapy (ESWT) in Canada. Developed for treatment of joint ailments such as tennis elbow, plantar fasciitis, and Achilles tendinitis, known commonly as painful heel, the technique has proven remarkably effective as a cure for these debilitating and common disorders. Tennis elbow often has little to do with swinging a racquet; carpenters, dentists, window cleaners, musicians, and others suffer from its agonizing symptoms. Plantar fasciitis, an inflammation of the connective tissue on the bottom of the foot, strikes at any age.

In the past, both ailments were treated by surgery with variable, sometimes disastrous, results. Foot surgery to correct Achilles tendinitis could cause damage to the Achilles tendon, leading to permanent crippling. Coulter's application of ESWT manages to reduce or eliminate pain in about three out of four patients suffering from Achilles tendinitis, significantly higher than routine procedures. He performs the technique in his own clinic, without invasive surgery and the need for general anaesthesia, almost completely avoiding the risk of injuring the Achilles tendon.

Within an hour of the treatment, patients return home. Six weeks of wearing a special appliance a few hours each day to relieve stress on tendons and muscles usually leads to a complete recovery. ESWT is neither new nor revolutionary. It has been used for many years to break up kidney stones, and it may also prove valuable in healing small stress fractures and broken bones that refuse to heal. With no general anaesthesia, no specialized nursing, and no hospital bed occupied, ESWT may appear to be precisely the kind of technology the health care system needs to speed up access and reduce costs.

"But they won't fund a penny of it," grumbles Coulter. "So I have to charge my patients for it, and that's not right."[1] *By "they," Coulter refers to the Ontario Hospital Insurance Plan, or OHIP, which refuses to recognize ESWT as a procedure qualifying for government funding when it's used for tennis elbow and Achilles tendinitis. Coulter's fee of $1500 for treatment of Achilles tendinitis is not unreasonable given the relief it can provide, but*

the cost can represent a serious financial blow to retirees and others. Professional athletes can easily afford it, of course, which explains the autographed posters and uniforms adorning the walls in Coulter's office. And from a philosophical standpoint, ESWT undermines the entire debate about two-tiered health services in Canada. If you can afford it, the treatment is available, often within days. If you cannot afford it, you will wait several weeks for risky traditional surgery or depend upon analgesics to control the pain.

AS AN ORTHOPAEDIC SURGEON, Coulter represents a sector of Canada's health professionals squeezed in a vise of increasing demand and reduced access for patients, and controversial fee structures for doctors. He finds a colleague in both his professional training and his frustration in Edward Harvey, who serves as chief of orthopaedic trauma at Montreal's McGill University Health Centre. With fourteen years of postgraduate training, Harvey is contemplating a return to the United States, where he practised for some years before returning to Canada. "When I came back [to Canada], it was a trade-off, sacrificing pay for lifestyle," Dr. Harvey says. "I accepted the trade-off for a while, but it's changed so much," he adds, citing growing difficulties between the province's health ministry and physicians generally.[2]

Canadians have become familiar with grumblings from health care providers, who often sound as vociferous and truculent as their frustrated patients. The concerns expressed by Coulter and Harvey, however, are disturbing because these two doctors represent those health care professionals who may be both the greatest future need and the most difficult to access in coming years. They also hint at distress among the profession, dealing with stress and, in some cases, burnout.

WE ARE LIVING LONGER AND TOO OFTEN ENJOYING IT LESS

We rightly concern ourselves with cancer, heart disease, and stroke, the most feared and fatal ailments we are likely to face. Their prominence and notoriety attract technological solutions and professional practitioners to a degree that reflects their fearful reputation more than their incidence. At any given time, about 3.9 percent of Canadians are being treated for symptoms of heart disease, while 1.5 percent qualify as cancer patients.[3] On a purely statistical basis, this represents a small proportion of the overall population. As we continue to alter our lifestyle through reduced smoking and a growing awareness of dietary effects on both illnesses, their incidence may remain static or even shrink on a per capita basis, extending the life expectancy of Canadians. Perhaps we'll climb higher than our current ninth-place position among the world's industrialized nations.

In 2006 our life expectancy, averaged between males and females, was a month or so short of eighty years, placing us among the longest-lived citizens in the world. Growing older may bring its rewards but it also brings painful challenges. In this case, the pain is measured both fiscally and personally. Among the most painful of these challenges will surely be the substantial number of Canadians suffering from osteoarthritis, an ailment that is likely to grow in lockstep with our aging population while the mortality rates of other diseases level off. The decline of some serious illnesses will result to a large degree from people taking greater personal responsibility for their own health care.* Through 2006, for example, about 4000 fewer Canadian males were diagnosed with lung cancer than thirty years earlier because smoking among men had declined substantially.[4] For the barely 4 percent of Canadians who were dealing with heart disease, the ailment is not nearly as immediately fatal as a generation ago, thanks to major advances in diagnostic and therapeutic procedures. But in the same time period, fully 10 percent of us, across all age levels, were suffering the pain and impediments of arthritis. By age seventy, the incidence of osteoarthritis hits 85 percent. A study by the Canadian Orthopaedic Association predicts that the number of orthopaedic surgical procedures in Canada to correct arthritic problems will more than double between 2005 and 2025.[5]

*Unfortunately, too many of us are shifting the impact away from lung cancer to ailments caused by obesity—one of which is osteoarthritis.

We may prefer to deal with arthritis rather than cancer, which remains a terrifying disease for most people. When assessing a health care system dedicated to providing freedom from pain and discomfort to all citizens according to their need, however, we tend to minimize the effects of arthritis, failing to treat the disease and its symptoms with sufficient respect.

First, consider the scope of the problem, both today and tomorrow. In 1921, only 5 percent of Canadians were over the age of sixty-five. By 1998 over 12 percent of us had passed the traditional retirement age, and estimates suggest that about 16 percent, or 6 million people, will be older than sixty-five in 2016.[6] It's reasonable to assume that at least half of them will suffer from osteoarthritis to a degree that requires medical attention.

Next, assess the human and economic costs. Arthritis is a painful, often agonizing ailment that can immobilize sufferers, confining them to wheelchairs and removing them from both productive and recreational aspects of their lives. The drain on their quality of life is easily matched by a drain on the resources of the health care system through salaries for caregivers, purchases of special equipment and appliances, and expensive medications.

Arthritis medications bring secondary expenses with them. Anti-inflammatories can cause gastrointestinal bleeding and other complications, and patients forced to remain immobile due to arthritis may develop deep vein thrombosis. The most recent study of the total annual cost of osteoarthritis in Canada, including direct therapeutic expenses and lost productivity among workers, measured figures from 1997. The estimate? Almost $18 billion.[7] Ten years later, the figure has surely exceeded $20 billion.

All of this explains why joint replacement surgery is one of the fastest-growing procedures conducted in Canadian hospitals. While the immediate costs of replacing a knee or hip are substantial—between $8000 and $10,000 in most instances—the benefits of greater mobility and reduced expenditures on medications, along with the complex side effects they can produce, make this a rational procedure measured in both economic and human terms. On that basis, Canada should be encouraging an increase in the number of qualified orthopaedic surgeons and paying them reasonable rates for carrying out the operations.

Yet in our two most populous provinces, Ontario and Quebec, orthopaedic surgeons were on the verge of open rebellion in 2006. In Ontario, orthopaedic surgeons grumbled that their fee for hip and knee replacements was the lowest of all the English-speaking provinces, and patient wait times were growing intolerable. Only in Quebec were orthopaedic surgeons even more angry and frustrated, driving some into private practice for motives that extend beyond the opportunity to earn more money.

"I love orthopaedic surgery and I am proud to be an orthopaedic surgeon," Dr. Nicolas Duval, a Montreal surgeon, explained in a letter to the Canadian Orthopaedic Association.[8] "The satisfaction I get from easing people's pain with the work of my own hands is unique." The primary problem, according to Duval, was the limited opportunity for him to provide this relief from pain. "In the public system," he explained, "I had to fight every month to have access to the operating room one day per week. On the other hand, my waiting list for elective cases was well over a year."

Dr. Duval's response to growing demand and limited access was to walk away from the public health system entirely and launch the Duval Orthopaedic Clinic. Patients seeking a knee or hip replacement stay overnight in Duval's surgical facility before being transferred to a convalescent centre for a ten-day recuperation period. The cost: up to $12,000, payable by cash or certified cheque.

"I don't think it's wrong to ask for money from patients if they want their surgery done before others," the surgeon says. "What *is* wrong is to perform *free* surgery for some patients before others because [the patients] are high-level athletes, public artists like actors or singers, politicians, or presidents of companies who are able to give money to the hospital foundation."

DOUBLE YOUR MONEY IN ONE EASY MOVE: GO WEST

Are Quebec doctors more excitable than other Canadian care providers? It's doubtful. Their concerns about the wide discrepancy in salaries are solidly based, as these selected comparisons confirm:

ANNUAL PHYSICIAN INCOMES, 2004–05

SPECIALTY	CANADA	ONTARIO	ALBERTA	QUEBEC
Family Practice	$202,481	$213,088	$232,742	$164,568
Internal Medicine	$301,450	$351,826	$321,970	$219,434
Paediatrics	$210,655	$235,227	$226,115	$169,313
Dermatology	$306,682	$304,680	$578,134	$246,669
General Surgery	$299,819	$335,220	$370,425	$211,730
Cardiovascular Surgery	$406,372	$432,402	$647,370	$297,333
Orthopaedic Surgery	$294,965	$338,152	$347,506	$205,013
Ophthalmology	$455,025	$457,667	$608,308	$313,449

Average gross fee-for-service payment per physician who received at least $60,000 in payments, 2004–05. Alternative forms of reimbursement, such as salary and sessional, are not included.

SOURCE: "AVERAGE PAYMENT PER PHYSICAN REPORT, FEE-FOR-SERVICE PHYSICANS IN CANADA, 2004–2005," CIHI

How much is it worth for physicians to relocate their practice in Canada? If you are a dermatologist in Quebec, you can more than double your gross annual income by moving to Alberta. In every area of practice, incomes are at least 25 percent higher elsewhere in Canada than in La Belle Province, one discrepancy that contradicts the concept of a uniform structure. Like other inconsistencies we will encounter, this is a direct reflection of the fact that Canadians enjoy not one national program but thirteen provincial and territorial programs, all shaped and managed according to the goals and whims of their government-of-the-day.

Canada's health care system is federal in funding only. Ottawa provides much of the cash and a few of the guidelines; the provinces and territories provide more cash plus structure and implementation. Moving from one province to another means dealing with a health care delivery system that differs not only in name but also in design and operation. This is where the opportunity and, some would suggest, the danger lie.

In 2006 almost one out of four physicians and surgeons in Quebec who responded to a survey conducted by Leger Marketing said they were considering leaving the province within five years.[9] Many were plastic surgeons, performing cosmetic procedures that the public system did not cover, but a growing number were orthopaedic surgeons, ER specialists, ophthalmologists, and GPs. In 2005, Quebec also boasted 60 percent of all the MRI scanners in the country and almost half of the CT scanners in Canada. Many were installed in private medical-imaging clinics attracting patients from Ontario (where private radiology clinics are outlawed), who paid $800 for the privilege.[10] And the country's first private emergency clinic was founded in Montreal; in its initial six months of operation, the MD Plus Medical Clinic welcomed over 500 patient-customers who paid for assessment and treatment of ailments ranging from simple chest pains to an attack of flesh-eating disease.[11]

Health care in Quebec may be the harbinger of change in this country's health care system. This change will be driven either by economic pressures that can no longer be ignored, or by a long-standing political reality that defines Canada while representing the country's major constitutional weakness: the federal government's relationship with Quebec.

GUESS WHO IS THE STRONGEST SUPPORTER OF B.C.'S MOST SUCCESSFUL PRIVATE CLINIC?

Examine evidence to either support or decry a two-tier health system in Canada and attention inevitably falls on Alberta and British Columbia, two hotbeds of encroaching private health care. Every whispered aside in support of the private sector in Edmonton or Victoria is presented by Ottawa as another step toward the slippery slope of privatization. This is an error. No province affords more opportunities for its residents to patronize private health care than Quebec.

Consider: During 2006 only one private surgical facility operated in Alberta under the guidelines established by Bill 11, the legislation Premier Ralph Klein created, it was said, to wrench his province out of the national system. But the surgeons at this private Calgary clinic continue to bill the publicly funded provincial system, not the patients directly. Is this really "two-tier"?

Similarly, Vancouver's privately owned and managed Cambie Surgery Clinic provides facilities for over ninety surgeons, including eighteen orthopaedic specialists, all of whom bill B.C.'s health care system. With six operating theatres, two of them digital, Cambie claims to have more operating capacities and greater technological advances than publicly owned provincial hospitals.

Cambie was founded by Dr. Brian Day, who leapt into national prominence in 2006 when he was elected president of the Canadian Medical Association. The idea of a CMA president who supported private health care not only in principle but also in practice sent many observers at the federal level into a state of near-panic. Members of the B.C. legislature familiar with at least one aspect of Cambie's operations, however, were more sanguine. In fact, they had reason to be downright grateful.

Despite claims by B.C.'s unionized health care workers that Cambie represented the leading edge of a two-tier health system promoted by corporate Canada to reduce taxes on the country's upper middle class, fewer than 5 percent of Cambie's patients are drawn from top-level income earners. According to Day, the vast majority are middle-class people suffering work-related injuries. They do not choose Cambie over a publicly managed facility; they are directed to it by the province's own Workers' Compensation Board (WCB) and the Insurance Corporation of British Columbia, the Crown corporation providing universal insurance coverage for B.C. drivers.

Why would provincial government offices, supposedly staunch supporters of universal publicly funded health care, shunt citizens to a private health care facility? Because, according to Day, it makes good economic sense. Each B.C. resident who is unable to return to his or her job due to work-related injuries represents a drain on the WCB's finances. Cambie, and a few others functioning as private alternatives to the public system, provide treatment facilities to WCB claimants within weeks or even days instead of delays of several months, common among publicly funded hospitals and clinics. Workers return to their jobs sooner, stemming the flow of cash out of WCB coffers. Day claims that private clinics save the WCB about $100 million annually in wage-loss benefits. "These patients," he notes, "would have otherwise been waiting to get into hospitals."[12] And with some irony, Day is aware that many of these WCB patients are drawn from the province's Health Employees' Union, the group that is most vociferous in criticizing Cambie and other private sector initiatives.

Left-wing critics of Cambie and other private clinics rarely address the hypocrisy of government support for them because the economics are so convincing, and because the physicians and surgeons remain within the public system to collect remuneration for their services. In that sense, Cambie is not a purely for-profit operation because its heaviest financial load—the salaries of medical professionals delivering care to its patients—is borne by the tax-paying public and the fees are fixed.

Elsewhere, things grow more complex. In Quebec, physicians are permitted to opt out of the public system, a move prohibited in next-door Ontario. Quebec was also the first province to permit private radiology clinics, an option not available in Ontario and other provinces. Yet cries of alarm about the supposed dangers of a two-tier system are directed almost exclusively, it seems, toward the two western provinces. Is Quebec being given something of a free ride on this subject?

The answer is clearly yes.

POLITICAL REALITIES: REASONS TO LOOK IN ANOTHER DIRECTION

Until the arrival of the Harper Conservative government in Ottawa, Alberta premier Ralph Klein had few friends at the federal level, a situation he employed as a tool to manipulate public opinion in his favour. His threat to pull his province out of the Canada Health Act and his threats to delist some medical services sparked sharp criticism from Ottawa while the Liberals were in power, endearing him to the hearts of his right-wing supporters.

As a result, Klein and his followers were portrayed to the Canadian public as barbarians at the gate, a snarling vanguard of encroaching private, for-profit health care advocates. Yet since 2000 the most successful infiltration of private health care in Canada has occurred not in the shadow of the Rockies but along the shores of the St. Lawrence.

The federal government featherbedded Quebec's drift toward privatization in recognition of the province's efforts to do too much work with too little money. Quebec's elaborate social infrastructure extends well beyond universal health care to include public drug insurance, cheap daycare fees, and the lowest university tuition fees in Canada. Paying for these services involves, among other things, setting higher rates of personal income taxes for Quebec residents and lowering income ceilings on the salaries of Quebec physicians and surgeons. As we have seen, some medical specialists in other provinces had more than double the annual incomes of those performing the same services in Quebec.[13] While this permitted the province to spend hundreds of dollars less per capita on health care than the national average, it also drove badly needed physicians and specialists out of Quebec and served as a deterrent for surgeons from other regions to arrive and fill the gap. The shortage in orthopaedic specialists produced wait times for hip and knee replacements several times longer than those available in other provinces, a situation that finally pressured Quebec to remove the cap on income in December 2006 and loosen restrictions on private health care generally. If private clinics represent a means of slashing wait times for surgery, the reasoning went, they should be tolerated. And they are, by both federal and provincial representatives.

The tolerance ends at Quebec's border. In 2004, British Columbia was penalized $126,000 by Ottawa for permitting user charges in violation of the Canada Health Act. Yet the launch that year of the Institut de Polychirurgie de Montreal, a private clinic imposing user charges on its patients, prompted no similar response.

Culture may also influence Quebec's embrace of a two-tier system. It is, after all, our most European province, more attuned to practices on that continent than in other regions. Europeans, for the most part, accept and favour a combination of public and private health care, an approach that Quebec tolerates with greater equanimity than provinces elsewhere in Canada.

Finally, political realities in Canada cannot be ignored, especially by Brian Day, the Cambie founder. Quebec is cut more slack by Ottawa, he suggests, for reasons that have nothing to do with health care and privatization, and everything to do with the need for Ottawa to face the French fact. "No federal government is going to risk losing votes in Quebec," Day says. "An attack on the autonomy of Quebec would hurt them in an election."

All the points are valid. And all suggest that, despite the federal government's traditional opposition to a role for privatization in the health care system, a move in that direction is virtually inevitable, heralded by the bombshell Supreme Court verdict of June 2005. The verdict was handed down in response to a challenge posed by Dr. Jacques Chaoulli, who argued that the Canada Health Act violated the country's Charter of Rights and Freedoms, specifically its guarantee to "life, liberty and security of the person." He pursued his claim all the way to the country's highest court on behalf of a patient forced to wait almost a full year before receiving an artificial hip.

Chaoulli, an eccentric Montreal physician who once challenged Premier Jean Charest for leadership of the Quebec Liberal Party and pitched a tent in the city's Jacques Cartier Square to protest restrictions on making house calls, could restrain neither his elation nor his use of hyperbole when celebrating the victory. Comparing himself with Gandhi, Chaoulli declared, "The British Empire made people die with guns. In Canada, the state's monopoly makes people die on waiting lists, in total silence." Then, bringing his triumph into the national political arena, he predicted the ruling would be felt nationally. "How could you imagine that Quebecers may live and the English Canadian has to die?" he asked. "That would give new meaning to Quebec being recognized as a 'distinct society.'"[14]

A MATTER OF STRESS ON PROVIDERS AND PATIENTS ALIKE

Canadian doctors are expressing concerns that extend well beyond familiar problems like extended wait times, high patient loads, restrictive income limits, and difficult working conditions. They are also, according to various sources, upset about the effects of these conditions—effects that include excessive stress, depression, and thoughts of suicide.

A column penned by a Toronto neurosurgeon in a 2003 edition of the prestigious *Canadian Medical Association Journal* generated concern among observers both within and outside of the profession who saw it as yet another condemnation of our health care system. The text, which although written in the third person clearly reflects the writer's own opinions and experiences, describes a life that many people were surprised a neurosurgeon would endure, and that no one would wish to emulate:

> He wakes up soaked in sweat at 3:30 A.M., rescued by consciousness from a string of nightmares.... He rolls out of bed, panting with panic. There is no point in trying to sleep a little longer.... He stumbles downstairs and throws on his coat. The air is frigid; he feels his way in the dark to his car. The engine won't be warm until he pulls into the parking lot at the hospital. For three hours he answers e-mails, dictates discharge summaries....
>
> He goes downstairs to the coffee bar and gets a large regular coffee, his only meal of the day.... At 7:45 A.M. he goes to the

> operating room.... He gets through two tumour surgeries and [a] sweet little lady with a back problem....
>
> He stumbles back to his office at 6:00 P.M. to do paperwork and gets home at 8:30.... He makes a gin and tonic and after gulping it in 20 seconds pours a glass of red wine to lubricate the rapid downing of his first meal in 24 hours....

The most telling, poignant scene the author saves for last:

> The next evening he gets a phone call from one of his daughters, who is out on the town with friends. She sounds so grown-up, yet so dear and tender.... Before he hangs up he tells her how much he loves her. Then he sits on the side of the bed and sobs like a baby.[15]

The article launched a wave of comments from health care professionals complaining about overwork, stress, burnout, and suicidal thoughts. The fact that this frightening scenario was built around the experience of a neurosurgeon added dramatic and poignant impact. What profession, after all, demands greater coolness under pressure and an ability to separate one's private thoughts and public persona than brain surgery?

We do not expect our physicians to suffer the same torments that we endure; we expect them to *relieve* these torments. One response from two associate deans in the medical education program at Queen's University highlighted a disturbing fact. Doctors, they pointed out, often suffer from the "silent anguish of the healers." They have "difficulty setting limits, chronic doubts about 'doing enough,' profound feelings of guilt, and a resultant inability to enjoy life."[16] Complicating the condition, the authors, noted, was the difficulty physicians have in openly discussing and treating the ailments. "The stigma of mental illness," they pointed out, "and the potential impact on professional status inhibit disclosure."

Understandable, if regrettable. But just how wide is the scope of the problem? The same authors provided some startling statistics, culled from various sources:

1. According to a study reported in the *New England Journal of Medicine*, physicians in distress face emotional exhaustion, cynicism, feelings of ineffectiveness, and depersonalization.[17]
2. Two-thirds of physicians consider their workload too heavy, and more than half say that personal and family lives have suffered due to their career choice. A 2003 CMA survey of 2,251 doctors found 45.7 percent of respondents in an advanced state of burnout.[18]
3. Studies have shown that physicians have an increased risk of mental health problems such as depression, suicide, and substance abuse.[19]

Burnout, overwork, depression, heavy workload? According to these observations, Canada's doctors must barely be able to function not only as care providers but as social beings—and obviously, some critics of the public health care system charged, this is the result of problems created by the system itself.

While people such as the neurosurgeon who sat sobbing on the edge of his bed deserve our sympathy, the problem may not be as wide in scope as it appears … and the public system may not be the cause. The dramatic descriptions of physicians suffering from emotional exhaustion, cynicism, and feelings of ineffectiveness leading to depression, suicide, and substance abuse are tragic and disturbing, but they were pulled from a U.S. study conducted in 1982. This hardly establishes a link between doctor burnout and Canada's public health care system.

The CMA study suggesting that two-thirds of doctors consider their workload too heavy and that almost half of respondents believed they were in "an advanced state of burnout" is both Canadian and recent. Various factors beneath the surface of the study, however, weaken the perception that half our physicians and surgeons are candidates for Prozac and deep mental therapeutics. Note the following:

- Of 55,000 CMA members, only 8000 were selected—presumably at random—to complete and return the survey questionnaire. Of these, 2250, or fewer than 30 percent, responded, which represents only 4 percent of the overall CMA membership—hardly an extensive sample.

- The response to any attitudinal study seeking negative opinions will be skewed toward those harbouring such opinions. As individuals, we are far more likely to respond to opportunities inviting our complaints and concerns, and asking why we feel that way, than to queries asking if we are happy and satisfied. How many of the 5750 physicians who did not respond to the survey felt relatively pleased with their profession and themselves?
- The *National Post*, in its coverage of the CMA results, was astute enough to note that surveys such as this one normally find that 40 percent of respondents identify themselves as "burnt out." In some professions, such as advertising, the burnout rate exceeds 50 percent. Obviously, we should be more concerned about burnout among surgeons than that among copywriters, but how much of our health system is really to blame here?
- Timing is everything, even in attitudinal surveys. This one was conducted between February and June 2003, a period encompassing the disastrous SARS crisis that revealed substantial flaws in the system, especially in Vancouver and Toronto. Health care workers were more than justified in criticizing the system at that time, but how much of this negativity influenced their responses?
- The impact of a medical practice on family life can be distressing, to be sure. Again, where is the distinction between those in the medical profession and those determined to achieve great things in another profession, such as law? How many schoolteachers decry the workload that requires them to devote evening and weekend hours to marking papers and preparing lesson plans? We might expect physicians to feel exceptionally driven to meet the expectations of patients and administrators, because this is often the type of personality that chooses to practise medicine in the first place. Surgeons are especially noted for personality traits that include obsessive approaches to study, competitive nature, and elevated egos—qualities that are commonly associated with higher suicide rates in all walks of life.

- Long hours and intense pressure may serve as both incentive and identity to unmarried twenty-something medical students and interns. As married forty-somethings with children, they find the same working conditions more difficult to endure and accept, raising doubts about the wisdom of their earlier decision to pursue a career in medicine.
- The personal makeup of those who choose to practise medicine often includes the seeds of the despair shown in the CMA survey. Another survey revealed that only 45 percent of Canadian doctors have a personal physician providing regular care, compared with 66 percent of lawyers and 65 percent of pharmacists. The reason for this difference is rooted again in the very qualities that persuade an individual to enter medicine in the first place—a sense of personal ability and independence. Doctors score substantially higher in these areas than people in other endeavours. The same qualities that propel a young man or woman into medicine may generate a belief that being ill is a sign of weakness, and that no physician is as qualified to assess their state of health as they are.[20]

None of this is intended to belittle the problems of medical practitioners such as the tearful neurosurgeon. It suggests only that those critics who were quick to attribute these problems to a publicly funded health care system—and there were several—presented a weak or even non-existent case.

Along with the concerns and complaints of Canadian physicians should be weighed the response to a poll conducted by *Medical Economics Magazine*, a highly regarded publication addressing the fiscal concerns of health professionals in the United States. Conducted in mid-2002, the poll asked GPs, "Are you sorry you went into primary care?" Drawing a bigger response than any other poll in the magazine's history, the survey revealed that 63 percent of those who participated chose "Yes—The compensation doesn't make up for the hours and stress," while another 10 percent checked "Yes—It's not at all what I expected."

Even accounting for the fact, noted earlier, that the disillusioned and dissatisfied are most likely to respond to a poll inviting criticism, this suggests that three out of four GPs in the United States dislike, or are at least disappointed in, their medical careers. One physician in Texas lamented, "Where else but in medicine can you find a job that has no vacation pay, no retirement benefits or health coverage, and no certain pay check? No wonder med school admissions are down. Kids aren't that stupid!"[21]

This doctor's comment about med school enrolment strikes a nerve on both sides of the border. Much has been written about Canada's shortage of doctors, and while it's true that the country could use more doctors, it does not follow that the situation is endemic and hopeless. It may be simply cyclical. And it may not be critical.

THE CHANGING ROLE OF PHYSICIANS AND OTHER HEALTH CARE PROVIDERS

"Our expectations of physicians have changed and keep changing," says Brian Hutchison, newly retired from a career that began in family practice and evolved into extensive research on health services and policies. "The major expansion occurring in Canada's medical schools now will begin paying off with the arrival of more medical school graduates around 2010 and beyond. Some of this expansion will be offset by the retirement of aging physicians, but that in turn may be balanced by the involvement of other professionals in primary health care, including nurse practitioners, social workers, and others."

Dr. Hutchison sees medical practice evolving in a surprising number of directions. "Physicians are encouraging their patients to become much more involved in decisions regarding [their] health care," he explains, "and that's a good thing. Look, you can't know what is best for somebody else. The choice of treatment, or even [whether] to have treatment at all, is dependent as much on the patient's values as on the treatment itself." Most physicians agree that the role of the family doctor is undergoing a major evolution in Canadian society. In our parents' day, family doctors were considered oracles, fonts of wisdom and knowledge capable of assessing, diagnosing, and treating, with the assistance of specialists, all aspects of a patient's health. Patients today are moving toward playing a more active role in the diagnosis and treatment of problems, to the point where physicians will seem less like oracles and more like consultants.

"Future changes will bring more emphasis on a team-based approach to primary care," Brian Hutchison suggests. "This will change relationships, bringing some advantages with it but some concerns as well. The advantage may be more efficient delivery of services. For some procedures, such as blood pressure checks, I may deal only with a nurse practitioner, or I might be directed towards a mental health worker if that appears to be the primary source of my problem." The downside of this team-based approach would be the potential loss of certain positive aspects of the traditional one-on-one relationship, especially to those suffering from chronic ailments. Other patients may welcome a relationship that is not built exclusively on the abilities and personality of a single individual.*

Changing relationship or not, what about the question of excessive patient loads on physicians? It is not uncommon for Canadian doctors in family practice to maintain a roster of 2000 or more patients. Isn't that excessive?

"Not necessarily," Hutchison replies. He explains that the ability of a physician to handle so many patients depends on factors such as the role of nurse practitioners, who can relieve the physician of routine procedures, and the widening ability of technology to provide near-instant access to patient records, among other advances. "It also depends on the location of the physician's practice. Doctors in a prosperous suburban area, for example, can easily handle many more patients than their counterparts in an inner-city neighbourhood. The socio-economic status of

*For a different view of this development, see "Restoring the Benefits of Physician/Patient Relationships," p. 227.

each differs widely. People in a higher socio-economic class tend to look after themselves better. They drink less, smoke less, eat better, and are more likely to take their medication as directed. As a result, they need less attention from their doctor."[22]

The role of nurse practitioners, like that of physicians themselves, continues to evolve and may in time represent part of the solution to providing more health services to meet an aging population. First introduced more than thirty years ago, nurse practitioners continue to seek recognition as meaningful contributors to primary health care in Canada. Qualified and authorized to diagnose common health problems, nurse practitioners may also prescribe medications (from a limited list), order routine tests, and when necessary, refer patients to a physician for more demanding assessment and treatment.

In 2002, however, a line was crossed when the Ontario government approved the appointment of a nurse practitioner to essentially fulfil the role of a physician in the rural community of Havelock. When the town's physician retired and no one could be found to replace him, the 2000 residents of Havelock faced driving forty-five kilometres to the city of Peterborough for medical attention. In response, the local medical officer of health appointed a nurse practitioner to perform primary care duties, a move that sparked criticism from several quarters, including among physicians.

"The government is happy to stick nurse practitioners in to replace family doctors," said one of two doctors assigned to monitor the nurse practitioner's work, "but not to add them into the system to help family doctors. They should be bloody well ashamed. People think if [nurse practitioners] sound like a family doctor, smell like a family doctor and they do [doctor-like tasks], they must be a family doctor. But that is not the case."[23]

The doctor's comments may reveal more about his prejudices than about reality. Nurse practitioners have been providing basic primary care in remote Arctic and sub-Arctic communities on a needs basis for years. The village of Havelock may be substantially closer to

Metropolitan Toronto than it is to Iqaluit, but to bar nurse practitioners from treating middle-class Ontarians while they carry on treating the Inuit hints at a double standard.

According to one study reported in *The Medical Post*,[24] nurse practitioners perform more than four out of five procedures associated with primary health care. In Havelock, the nurse practitioner prescribed antibiotics for simple infections, counselled patients on birth control, conducted breast examinations and Pap smears, administered vaccinations, made specialist referrals, and provided pre- and postnatal care, among other tasks. She maintained dedicated fax and telephone lines to two physicians in Peterborough, who took turns making monthly visits to review her procedures.

Meanwhile, British Columbia was moving to deploy nurse practitioners throughout the province, supported in this case by a prominent physician. “I'm not advocating having nurse practitioners as stand-alone providers,” observed Dr. Peter Newbery, who practises in Hazelton, B.C., and is a past president of the College of Family Physicians of Canada. “I support them working in collaboration with physicians to address the primary care needs for patients who would otherwise be left without care.”

Elsewhere in Canada, even those provinces and regions that had once rejected the notion of nurse practitioners playing a major role in primary health care began changing their minds. For years, the concept of nurse practitioners had been rejected by the Collège des Médecins du Québec, effectively blocking nurses from doing anything beyond providing basic physician support services, regardless of their training and experience. In November 2005, the Quebec government and the college finally agreed that qualified nurse practitioners could conduct diagnostic examinations, use non-invasive diagnostic techniques, and prescribe certain medications.

Prince Edward Island was considered even less progressive on the subject of NPs. One pilot project collapsed when all of the province's physicians refused to deal with or even acknowledge the NPs' presence.

Finally, in September 2006, nurse practitioners began providing services in the communities of Souris and Hunter River, but only after agreeing to work according to guidelines established by local physicians. Patients in those communities can choose between seeing their physician or seeing a nurse practitioner. "If the family physician doesn't have an open appointment for some time," says Sherri McKinnon, the NP in Souris, "and it's something that needs to be addressed sooner, like a sore throat or a urinary tract infection, [the physicians] will offer the services of a nurse practitioner. I generally have a couple of openings, so it's a little bit quicker to get in to see me than some of the physicians."

Then she adds a telling note: "[Patients] are quite comfortable knowing that if something is beyond my scope, I'll consult with the physicians that are here."[25]

As this demonstrates, and as we shall see in other instances, Canadian patients are often more willing to adjust to modifications of the health care system than Canadian providers are.

The largest provincial regulator of doctors in the country, the College of Physicians and Surgeons of Ontario, believes wider use of nurse practitioners is not just good economic sense but a step toward better patient care. "We've been advocating collaborative care practice models for some time," says CPSO president Dr. Dale Mercer. "We strongly believe that nurse practitioners in a collaborative practice model free up physicians to do what physicians are trained to do, which is to provide the patient with quality patient–physician time."

Dr. Mercer's comment speaks to an issue high on the list of Canadians' complaints about the health care system. A patient's opportunity to discuss wider concerns, providing a doctor with insight into conditions other than the one being addressed, has become minimal in recent years. Doctors regret this as much as patients do, not only because reduced face-to-face time with patients is the result of excessive workloads, but because personal contact is valuable in making an accurate diagnosis. Are a patient's chronic headaches indicative of a physical ailment or a state of mind? How many complaints can be traced to the patient's verbal description and how many to her body language and gestures? How has the patient's demeanour changed over the last few visits? These questions are best asked and answered in a relaxed environment, rather than one that appears devoted to either prescribing a treatment or generating referrals to a specialist. They represent the benefits of Dr. Mercer's "quality patient–physician time."

A specialist in chest surgery, Dr. Mercer spins the topic of nurse practitioners toward his own area of expertise. "Why does a patient need me, as a surgeon, to take out her sutures?" he asks. "She needs me to put them in, but she doesn't need me to take them out."[26]

General agreement exists to support the idea that nurse practitioners are most effective, both economically and therapeutically, when working in a partnership arrangement—as part of the team-treatment or collaborative-practice strategy discussed by Brian Hutchison and Dale Mercer. The problem arises when the question of payment is addressed, not only for nurse practitioners but for physicians as well.

HOW MUCH TO PAY PHYSICIANS, AND HOW AND FOR WHAT

From the day in 1962 when Tommy Douglas's goal of public-funded health care in Saskatchewan was made a reality, no single factor has upset Canada's physicians more than the question of payment. And why not? The degree of training and dedication needed to become a physician or surgeon, along with extensive hours spent working under often stressful conditions, qualifies doctors for entry into the highest sectors of net income. Yet on an annual basis, many established physicians take home less money, after paying overhead charges and staff salaries, than an effective used-car or real estate salesperson.

Physicians are not employees. In theory at least, they are independent contractors operating very much like—in a philosophical sense, of course—local tradespeople such as plumbers and electricians who arrive to repair, renovate, or expand certain functions of your house.

Plumbers can pick and choose the projects they work on, and can vary the fees they charge according to market demand and their own work schedule, and this was true pretty much for doctors before the introduction of medicare. When the system of delivering medical care changed, physicians who were enrolled exclusively within the public health care system lost that flexibility.

From the outset, Canada's doctors were paid on a fee-for-service payment schedule, and most continue to earn the majority of their income in this manner. But as more than one observer has noted, fee-for-service payment is essentially piecework. Make ten widgets for a dollar each in a widget factory and you earn ten bucks; deliver ten babies in a hospital ward for $150 each and you earn $1,500.

That's where the parallel ends. Many physicians' responsibilities are more cerebral than procedural. Dr. Michael Rachlis, an epidemiologist who has focused much of his energy and attention on assessing Canada's public health care system, suggests, "Fee for service pays doctors much more to cut and prod than to listen and think."[27] Should a physician counsel a patient on diet, drinking, smoking, and other life habits as part of an overall therapeutic program? Of course. But he or she is not reimbursed for the time taken to do so.

In their effort to replace stark fee-for-service payments, provincial health bodies offer a smorgasbord of alternative payment plans, including block funding, capitation, and various incentives. Block funding pays physicians a fixed amount in return for the care of an identifiable patient group, making it the simplest of all income options to administer. Capitation pays physicians a fixed amount, based on the patient's gender and age, to provide necessary primary care for individual patients, bypassing the fee-for-service schedule. This carries a built-in incentive for physicians to monitor all aspects of a patient's lifestyle because healthy patients see their doctor less often and for shorter visits, leaving physicians with more money in their pocket at the end of the year. That's an incentive to go beyond cutting and prodding. But it's not perfect. If a patient visits a walk-in clinic, for example, the physician may be docked a portion of the capitation payment to cover the charge. Incentives are usually offered as encouragement for physicians to practise in rural areas and in communities lacking sufficient medical professionals.

Perhaps physicians should be salaried—an alternative not widely supported among most doctors, but attractive to provincial health ministries because it would simplify annual budgeting. This is not, however, considered a serious option. Salaries imply employees, which would alter the position of physicians as independent contractors, a role they value highly.

Remuneration options, such as multiple payment agreements combining a base salary for every physician with a lower fee-for-service pay scale and perhaps a modified capitation payment schedule, are proposed from time to time, but are generally not seriously considered.

Since it's your money that is being passed along to physicians, you should know the basic pros and cons for each remuneration option:

REMUNERATION	FUNDER VIEW	PHYSICIAN VIEW
Fee for Service	• Incentive to over-service • Unpredictable budgeting	• Autonomy • Volume driven • Create target income • Patient freedom
Block Payments	• Simplified administration • Possible under-servicing	• Fixed income • Less paperwork
Capitation	• Encourages efficiency • Limits unnecessary services • Predictable budgeting	• Easier administration • Larger patient base • Encourages culture of patient responsibility for self-care
Salary	• Predictable budgeting • No over-servicing incentive • Simple to administer • Rewards seniority & efficiency • Make under-serviced regions more attractive	• Reduced autonomy • Reduced status • No incentive • Net loss of income

All of this supports the premise that, burnout and excessive hours aside, the Canadian public health system is not so much a means of providing medical services to the public as it is a matter of providing payment to the suppliers. In many ways, this represents the heart of the private-versus-public debate on health care in Canada, because physicians in a true private enterprise system are free to set any fees they choose. Supporters of an exclusively public-funded system argue that physicians would abandon it if a private option were available, in pursuit of larger incomes. Yet as we saw with the comparison of annual incomes, this can be achieved for many by relocating their practice. And as we shall see later, the pursuit of more income is not the only motivator driving physicians. In fact, solving the entire private-public alternative involves addressing far more complex problems than income alone.

2

INFORMATION TECHNOLOGY

FIFTY YEARS BEHIND THE TIMES

In the photograph in the Canadian Medical Association Journal, *Claire Lewis appears as the quintessential eleven-year-old, an age when the innocence of childhood shines through a face that already displays some wisdom of life. Her dark-eyed gaze is direct, her smile is natural if perhaps a little embarrassed at the camera's attention, and her hair frames her face before curling inward at her chin. Claire Lewis will always be eleven years old.*

In one of those overwhelming twists of fate that challenges everyone's faith, but especially that of the victim's family, Claire was diagnosed with a benign tumour about the size of a robin's egg on her pituitary gland. It could be treated only with surgery to enter the skull and remove the tumour before it first blinded and then killed her. The procedure was scheduled for October 12, 2001, at Hamilton General Hospital.

The prospect of their child's undergoing such an intrusive procedure was as frightening to Claire's parents as might be expected, although the anxiety was reduced somewhat by her father John's experience as a registered nurse. With an insight into the procedures that Claire would undergo, and a father's determination to attend her recovery as much as possible, John Lewis obtained permission to be with his daughter in the O.R. up to the point she was anaesthetized. John had been a professional guitarist before turning to nursing in order to spend more time with his family, and he and Claire sang the old Carpenters' hit song "Close to You" within the metallic chill of the O.R. until the anaesthesiologist put Claire under and the room went silent. One of the neurosurgeons commented on how smoothly the induction had gone, predicting, "We're going to have a great surgery."

By all accounts they did. Eight and a half hours later, surgeons announced that the operation had gone smoothly and Claire would be transferred across the city to McMaster University Medical Centre (MUMC) to recover in that facility's paediatric ICU. Things looked good. Hamilton General was a first-rate hospital for brain surgery. MUMC was a teaching hospital with a ward set up especially for paediatric care. Claire's parents could relax.

In the paediatric ICU at MUMC, Claire underwent various treatments to stabilize her. Among the conditions the staff feared was Diabetes insipidus (common among patients who undergo procedures similar to Claire's), which causes excessive loss of fluids through the patient's urine. The standard response to Diabetes insipidus is to inject the patient with the drug DDAVP, which helps the body retain fluids; Claire received several injections during her first hours at MUMC.

The order to provide Claire with DDAVP was not accompanied by an instruction for an endocrinologist to monitor her, and no one was in attendance to assess this aspect of Claire's condition.

The next morning, John Lewis was alarmed to find his daughter shaking while in a deep sleep. Claire, he realized, was about to have a seizure, and in fact she did—a violent convulsion lasting three minutes. Drugs were injected to relax her muscles and a brain scan was ordered to ensure there was no bleeding inside her skull. There wasn't. Back in the ICU, nurses adjusted her sodium level to restore a balance and continued to add fluids to treat Diabetes insipidus.

On the third day, Claire appeared to be recovering. She sat up in bed. She talked and laughed with her parents. She began to grow tired, and her parents left as she drifted off to sleep. That evening she died. An autopsy and investigation revealed that Claire had succumbed to pressure on the brain caused by an excess of fluids in her body. Claire had not suffered from Diabetes insipidus at all, thanks to procedures conducted by staff at Hamilton General Hospital, where the initial surgery took place. In fact, the last thing she needed was treatment to retain fluids. The administration of DDAVP and fluids, and the failure of an endocrinologist to monitor her condition, killed a little girl who had survived a dangerous operation to remove a brain tumour.[1]

Professional incompetence? Inadequate hospital procedures? Perhaps, but neither would have been an issue had a single, simple, silly mistake not been made in the eight-kilometre journey between two highly regarded hospitals. Everything Claire needed for her full recovery from the surgery travelled in the ambulance with her ... except her medical records. No one at MUMC knew about the post-operative treatment she had received at Hamilton General Hospital. Without the unnecessary and ultimately fatal treatment for Diabetes insipidus, Claire would probably have recovered completely from the brain surgery. One of the most complicated procedures in medicine was foiled by the simple failure of one group of medical professionals to inform another about the patient's treatment.

WHENEVER EXPERTS ACCESS THE FUTURE of health care in Canada, especially the means to deliver it at acceptable cost whatever the funding source, technology is frequently offered as a potential panacea. MRIs, CT scans, and other devices will provide faster, more accurate diagnoses. Microsurgery and the wider use of computer processors in laboratory applications will reduce time in hospitals. Explorations of the human genome will identify an individual's likelihood of acquiring serious diseases and assist in directing the best possible therapy to correct them.

All true, to a point. New technology frequently motivates both the physician and the patient to collaborate in demanding it be applied, even when existing technology may be far less costly and perhaps more beneficial.

One technological advance, however, wins plaudits from virtually everyone associated with delivering health care to Canadians. While being constantly refined, the technology is proven. In fact, it is used by virtually every Canadian every day, its implementation would save potentially billions of dollars annually in hospital and drug costs, and it almost certainly would have saved the life of Claire Lewis. It is the electronic keeping of records, and the medical profession in Canada is woefully inept in employing it.

Here is a fact you probably never considered before but will almost certainly comprehend: *Health care arguably is the world's most information-intensive industry.* Health care creates a greater volume of data on a wider range of subjects to be comprehended by a more extensive array of disciplines than any other human activity. With that in mind, consider how medical data are recorded, stored, and shared in the majority of instances across the country:

- Prescriptions are written on a piece of paper that you carry to a pharmacist, who interprets the physician's scribbles, then creates another piece of paper to be applied to the medication and a record of the transaction before filing the information in the pharmacy's data bank.
- Similar methods are still used in many areas to order lab tests, X-rays, and other diagnostic procedures. The results are printed on other sheets of paper to be transferred, read, and stored for future reference.
- In many cases, X-rays and other diagnostic records are filed in drawers like precious works of art and exchanged between technicians, physicians, and surgeons in the same manner that public libraries circulate books. (Until recently, one of the most vital jobs in the health care system of Metro Toronto was filled by several dozen couriers who scurried back and forth across the city carrying X-ray film in large brown envelopes.)
- Discussions and exchanges of patient records are conducted via telephones and fax machines. A missed or misunderstood

telephone conversation or a recalcitrant fax machine can delay vital decisions.

- Banks and major financial and investment institutions spend about 12 percent of their annual budget on IT and computer technology; retail operations spend about 6 percent for the same services and facilities. Health care spending for the same purpose is perhaps between 1.5 and 2 percent.[2]

"The health care system in Canada," noted one qualified observer, "runs about the same way our banking system worked in 1970." And this from a major health policy conference: "Building a first-rate health information system may have as great an effect on 21st-century health care as medicare did in the 1960s and 1970s."[3]

The comment is more true than hyperbolic. It has been years since many of us completed a bank deposit slip, had a passbook updated by hand, or used a teller exclusively to conduct routine financial transactions. Banking, once considered among the most obdurate of professions, revolutionized itself in less than a single generation. With the exception of those Canadians to whom chatting with a bank teller represents an important social event, we access information and money via electronic means with nothing more complex than a small piece of plastic.

PHYSICIANS' USE OF ELECTRONIC MEDICAL RECORDS, 2001

Sweden	90%
Netherlands	88%
U.K.	58%
New Zealand (2000)	52%
Germany	48%
Australia (2000)	25%
U.S.A.	17%
Canada	14%
France	6%

SOURCE: 2001 EUROPEAN UNION EUROBAROMETER AND 2000 COMMONWEALTH FUND INTERNATIONAL HEALTH POLICY OF PHYSICIANS (HARRIS INTERACTIVE, 2002)

For the majority of physicians in this country, old and slow computers with little or no imaging capability, connected to dot-matrix printers, are their major concession to electronic technology. Aside from limitations on connectivity and compatibility, these old systems are often more of an impediment than an advantage to doctors because they were designed to generate hard copies on paper forms. "The problem was the old paper-based system interfered with patient care," noted one Ontario physician who spent $30,000 to purchase updated hardware and software for herself and her support staff (the province reimbursed her for 70 percent of the expense). "I was tired of seeing lab tests lost or waiting weeks for results. We were drowning in a sea of paper!"[4] Besides maintaining patient records in digital format, the physician's new computer system connects her with three large laboratory services that deliver X-ray and ultrasound images to her laptop. Software programs handle billing and patient scheduling, and provide prompts for diagnostic and therapeutic actions to be followed according to patient symptoms.

It is not an exaggeration to suggest that the most important single factor in reducing health care costs and maintaining them at an acceptable level may be the country's adoption of electronic records and transfers. Among all the cacophony and finger-pointing over long wait times for diagnosis and treatment, little has been said about the remarkable benefits of moving medicine toward the same kind of electronics data transfer long employed by banks and airlines. The potential savings in costs, suffering, and lives are immense and derived from are many sources. The costs of printing, storing, and retrieving paper records for individual physicians and facilities may appear minuscule compared with capital expenditures on MRIs and CT scanners, but the aggregate sum is substantial. The use of electronic health records (EHR) appears to reduce both the number of expensive lab tests considerably, likely because of easier access to previous test results, and the incidence of adverse medical events resulting from mismanagement of a patient's condition, such as what befell Claire Lewis.

No country in the world stands to benefit more from widespread application of electronic health records than Canada. When we look at per capita expenses for medical care, the country's national average hovered just over $3000, but costs for Yukon Territory exceeded $4500, those in the Northwest Territories were well over $5000, and in Nunavut we spent a towering $7610 per year on each resident. Many reasons exist for this disparity, but the one with the most impact is travel. For years, Canadians living in the Far North have been flown thousands of miles to Yellowknife, Edmonton, Whitehorse, Goose Bay, and other locations to undergo tests that are available within a few blocks of most Canadian residences. The system cannot morally exclude providing the same health care to residents in a far-flung settlement of Nunavut as it provides residents of a suburb of Winnipeg, but neither can it afford to provide these services on a grand scale in more remote parts of the country.

In early 2001, the federal government launched Canada Health Infoway to "accelerate the development and adoption of modern systems of information technology, such as electronic patient records, so as to provide better medical care," priming the new organization's pump with $500 million. Two years later, Ottawa added another $600 million "to accelerate the development of EHRs, common information technology standards across the country, and the further development of telehealth applications."[5]

The wide-ranging benefits of EHR in money, time, and well-being have been dramatically illustrated by the experience of installations such as Ontario's Northern Radiology (NORrad) network, the largest medical-imaging network in North America. Serving residents in an area covering 150,000 square kilometres, NORrad originally encompassed Moose Factory, Hearst, Kapuskasing, Kirkland Lake, Cochrane, and other communities stretching toward the shores of James Bay. Since its introduction, NORrad has expanded to include over two dozen hospitals in Northern and Central Ontario.

Traditionally, two radiologists served the region from a single facility at the Timmins and District Hospital. Patients requiring detailed analysis of X-ray film and other diagnostics were sent there by automobile or air ambulance, a trip that could take several hours each way. With NORrad, established in 2002, images are transmitted from physicians and clinics throughout the northern regions to the Timmins radiology centre over high-speed telecommunications lines, and assessments are returned the same way. This method of exchanging information was nothing new to industry and commerce, but the process dramatically altered both the cost and the level of health care throughout the region.

"This means we're moving the patient's information instead of the patient," commented Dr. Claude Vezina, who directs diagnostic imaging among the nine hospitals making up the network. "In the end, it often means the patient can stay where he or she is. And if something doesn't look right with a patient … three or four physicians can view the images at the same time on computers, all in different places, to determine what's wrong with the patient and decide on the best course of treatment."[6] The system includes a feature that automatically queries a central archive to search and retrieve any previous images associated with the patient. The radiologist can then compare X-rays, ultrasounds, or MRI scans taken in the past. With these references, any change in anatomical structures, such as improper healing or the emergence of tumours, can be instantly identified.

And while travel costs represented the major savings, upgrades and expansion of equipment have generated substantial economies along the way. For example, X-ray film costs the hospital about $2 per sheet, and a digital recording device costs about $2000. But an X-ray sheet holds only one image; the digital recording devices employed by the hospital hold about 20,000 exposures each, reducing this single cost factor from $40,000 to $2000 while providing images sharper than those from film-based technology. Timmins and District Hospital estimates its annual cost of generating and storing radiology images has been reduced from $400,000 to about $6000.[7]

The potential cost savings in electronic-based health care have attracted attention from governments and health care suppliers beyond Canada's borders. One U.S. study estimated a minimum of $162 billion could be saved each year in that country alone from increased efficiencies ($77 billion), reduced prescription errors ($4 billion), and better prevention and disease management ($81 billion). Yet in 2005 barely a quarter of U.S. hospitals, about 20 percent of the country's physicians, and fewer than 13 percent of small medical group practices (five or fewer full-time physicians) had adopted the technology.[8]

Why the reluctance? In the United States, one factor may be initial expense, usually absorbed by the physician or group practice. While future returns appear promising, the doctors may choose to postpone the capital cost as long as possible. In Canada, federal and provincial governments appear to prefer making expenditures in bricks, mortar, and beds rather than electronic advances that won't pay off for years. The health services agenda includes too many competing components for something as ethereal as electronic data exchange to make much of an impact. Widespread use of EHR remains years away; stories about wait times at hospital emergency rooms are in newspapers every day and generate demands for a solution, preferably immediately. The need for better health information fails to rate highly among consumers and providers of medical care in Canada. Nor, for that matter, among politicians who control the purse strings of the system.

Most politicians have difficulty visualizing and implementing ideas whose benefits will not be felt until after the next election. As one proponent of wider information technology applications for the medical field put it, "Spending hundreds of millions of dollars on the infrastructure for EHR is like building a road to nowhere—you look pretty silly until all the houses and businesses start popping up along the highway." The few politicians who have attempted to anticipate future needs in health care have, for the most part, encountered stonewall resistance.

In 2003, federal industry minister Brian Tobin attempted to introduce a budget item covering coast-to-coast broadband services, aimed at creating universal access to medical records and other data via the internet. When Finance Minister Paul Martin deleted this provision without informing Tobin, Tobin resigned from the government and departed the political scene.*

To be fair to cautious politicians, the implementation of universally accessible e-health records is not risk-free. Perfection is unattainable, cost estimates are unstable, failures are inevitable, and the benefits are often indiscernible. But as the tragedy of Claire Lewis proved with devastating heartbreak, the need is beyond doubt. The case of Carson Lambert demonstrates the benefits of e-health records from a different, encouraging angle.

Born in 1996, Carson suffered acute respiratory difficulties that led to a host of related medical crises when he was barely ten months old. Medication to treat the respiratory problem resulted in liver and kidney failure. He also suffered cardiac arrest, leading to an acquired brain injury and feeding problems. For a tiny child yet to celebrate his first birthday, the outlook for survival, let alone a reasonably normal life, appeared remote. Not only has Carson survived but he has become an active, sports-loving boy who enjoys swimming, riding a bike, and playing hockey and basketball—all made possible to a large extent by EHR technology.

It took a team made up of an orthopaedic surgeon, a general surgeon, a gastroenterologist, and a physiotherapist, as well as paediatricians and Carson's own family physician, to achieve this success. While Carson's recovery represents a minor miracle in itself, the most remarkable aspect of the tale concerns the team's location. For much of the diagnosis, therapy, and treatment, these doctors worked at Toronto's Hospital for Sick Children while Carson and his family

*For more details on this event, see Tobin's book *All in Good Time* (Penguin), pp. 248–55.

remained in their hometown of Sault Ste. Marie, about 600 kilometres away. The specialists exchanged test results with Carson's doctors in Sault Ste. Marie and engaged in videoconferences via Ontario Telemedicine Network or OTN.

To businesspeople, teleconferences are about as new and revolutionary as ballpoint pens. The practice of holding discussions with and viewing documents shared by individuals located halfway across the globe has been going on for decades. The relative novelty of this technology as a means of exchanging patient information and physician opinions illustrates how far the health system must travel to keep pace with the rest of the world.

"If you were to measure the progress in the health system's application of information technology as a journey of 100 kilometres," Mike Connolly comments, "we're about five kilometres down the road." Connolly, former CEO of Ontario's Smart Systems for Health Agency (SSHA), is something of an anomaly in the health care sector, where most members, especially those in positions of authority, rise through the medical system. Connolly, while associated with government ministries for some time—his last post before moving to SSHA was with the province's Ministry of Natural Resources—is a self-described "techie" whose primary interest is not in measuring blood pressure or prescribing medication but in creating systems to exchange information.[9]

Various obstacles prevent wider applications of EHR programs, even though their implementation may save lives and money on a grand scale. As addressed earlier, the decision to invest several hundred million dollars in communication services amidst emotional exchanges in newspapers and on talk radio over ER wait times is a difficult one for any politician to make.

Another hurdle facing the medical IT crowd is resistance to the concept from individual physicians and, to some degree, hospitals and medical practice groups. "There are two ways of overcoming this insular view of the profession," Connolly says. "One is the brute force technique used by major hospitals who say to doctors, 'If you want privileges in this place, you will use our IT system and that's that.' The other is to locate a high-profile physician, surgeon, or radiologist, show them what the system can do, and generate enough enthusiasm for the idea that they talk to their colleagues about it and convert them one by one." Connolly sighs. "It can be a long and difficult process." Still, progress is being achieved. "There have been a number of significant wins in this province and across the country," Connolly suggests. "But they are never talked about because they can't compete with the daily horror stories."

Funded by the province's Ministry of Health and Long-Term Care, SSHA has scored a number of significant achievements under Connolly's direction. Some, such as the case of Carson Lambert, are basic extensions of teleconferencing. Others, such as advising a Belleville, Ontario, hospital to save $110,000 annually by using voice-over internet protocol (VoIP), are somewhat more cutting-edge yet hardly revolutionary.

Two developments, however, deserve recognition not only for the manner in which they point the way to future applications, but for their practical life-saving benefits as well.

"Remember the SARS crisis in 2003?" Connolly asks. "Every report issued after the crisis had passed blasted the hell out of us for [Ontario's] information technology and our inability to communicate." Perhaps more than any event in recent memory, the outbreak of severe acute respiratory syndrome that struck Toronto and, to a lesser extent, Vancouver in March 2003 spotlighted weaknesses in IT throughout the country's health care system. Official investigations into the handling of data by the key participants resulted in assessments that were nothing less than devastating. The investigation, headed by Mr. Justice Archie Campbell, pulled no punches in decrying Ontario's woeful lack of communication among its medical professionals. "The lack of a single, effective, accessible information system," the commission's interim report said in unusually scathing language, "combined with a constant, intense demand for information from a number of different people and groups, resulted in chaos.... The proliferation of data systems, and the confusion and burdens it created, was an inevitable consequence of Ontario's lack of preparedness for a major outbreak of infectious diseases."[10]

Adding to its overall caustic tone, the Campbell Commission peppered its criticism with personal observations from several front-line participants in the crisis, such as this:

> Imagine six people chasing the same people looking for information, calling the same people all the time, it drove the health units nuts. It drove us back and then they would say that we faxed it to you earlier in the day, but we did not know what fax it went to ... because they are coming in by the thousands. They would say we sent you an email, but [there were so many] we couldn't open a third of the emails. It was a circus. It was unbelievable.[11]

No government can afford to ignore such criticism, and Ontario responded with both substantial funding and political will. "We put in computer systems to track every communicable disease at its source across every hospital in the province," Connolly says, "supported by quarantine management systems and systems to manage outbreaks anywhere in the province, plus forums to exchange views and events, information on how physicians are to don protective gear.... It is now the largest telehealth network of its kind in the world, but nobody hears about it." Nor will they, Connolly suggests, until another crisis similar to the SARS event occurs.

With good fortune, Ontario may never need to implement its SARS-inspired IT system, but another IT application launched by Ontario is proving its worth well beyond the province's borders. Labelled Telestroke, the program links stroke patients with a distant neurologist specializing in treating these often lethal events. Treatments vary according to the nature of the stroke; the prescribed treatment for one variety could be deadly if applied to another, and only a skilled specialist with access to MRI or CT scan data can determine the treatment needed in each case. Stroke neurologists, as you might expect, are not listed in every community's telephone directory and tend to be found in larger cities with substantial facilities. Telestroke enables a doctor to forward a brain scan via the internet from the patient's location to a specialist who can determine the best treatment according to the patient's condition, the type and extent of stroke suffered, and other factors.

By 2006 at least five other provinces—Alberta, Newfoundland and Labrador, Nova Scotia, P.E.I., and Saskatchewan—had launched similar programs for stroke victims. And by 2009, according to Canada Health Infoway, physicians treating 50 percent of Canadians will have access to electronic records of their patients' X-rays, lab test results, immunizations, allergies, and virtually every other type of data to help them in their diagnosis and treatment.

The extent to which EHRs may alter our lives remains to be seen. The technology is already being applied in borderline medical applications, such as two-way videoconferencing to train chronic pain sufferers in meditation techniques and reduce their dependence on drugs. The use of EHRs in natural disasters is an area to be fully explored as well. Among the few positive aspects of the U.S. government's response to the devastation created by Hurricane Katrina on the country's Gulf Coast in 2005 was the U.S. Department of Health and Human Services' (HHS) use of electronic prescription drug records. This enabled the federal agency to compile and monitor the distribution of prescription drugs to evacuees from the storm site. A wider base of more detailed EHR data might have saved lives through accurate tracking of medical needs, diagnoses, and therapies. Certainly, the promise that EHR will assist in the management of chronic diseases is valid. Moreover, these records can be used for everything from avoiding adverse reactions to medications and better dispensary control to reducing ICU mortality rates, which more than justifies the implementation.[12]

Digital imaging and other aspects of the technology have their critics. For example, although digital X-ray imaging eliminates the cost, storage, and accessibility problems of film-based images, and provides images that can be shared across a computer network within minutes of a procedure, questions have been raised about image validation. Critics of digital imaging claim that altering an original sheet of X-ray film is difficult, but digital images, they say, are notoriously easy to manipulate and modify, which gives doctors the opportunity to conceal a serious error in diagnosis.

Concerns have also been expressed about privacy and confidentiality where EHRs are employed. The province of Alberta, for example, assures all its citizens that they have the right to know who has accessed their EHR. Denmark has provided this opportunity to its citizens for years; violating rules of access to health records is considered a serious offence, and conviction could result in a heavy fine plus the suspension of licensing by the appropriate professional organization.

Many physicians who have witnessed awkward attempts to design and implement EHR systems in the past warn of other risks. Some older systems, especially those created and installed by individual hospitals, have proven so difficult for physicians and their staff to utilize that they have been abandoned as "not worth the trouble." Others, although easy to learn and apply, have proved incompatible with existing systems, requiring a paper bridge between two systems ostensibly designed to save time. Frustration has led to rejection and hostility; it will take special attention to detail to overcome this attitude among some medical professionals. But the need is substantial and the ambition equally so. In late 2006, Canada Health Infoway had \$1.4 billion on hand to assist the national health care system in adopting EHRs; it wants 50 percent national coverage of an interoperable system by 2009. The Health Council of Canada has set a goal of 100 percent compatible coverage by 2010—a target that some observers consider unachievable.

Their skepticism is founded in something that one physician calls "the doctor factor"—an inclination of physicians not to accept change readily. Doctors seek comfort in their usual way of doing things, he suggests, and when necessary will employ excuses such as "I am a slow typist." In some instances, they are either unaware or dismissive of positive experiences with extended EHRs in countries such as the United Kingdom, New Zealand, and Australia.

Yet beyond new therapies, beyond "breakthrough" pharmaceuticals, and perhaps even beyond the secrets of the genome code, universal EHR may prove this generation's biggest advance in health care. Like all revolutions, it will come with a price measured not in the billions of dollars needed for investment, as several employees at hospitals making up Toronto's University Health Network have discovered.

When staff members learned and adjusted to the network's new EHR system, almost everyone praised their new ability to share X-ray films seamlessly between the hospitals from the archived digital viewing system. The only employees not pleased with the technology were those who lost their jobs to it. They were called "runners," and more than twenty-five years after the dawn of the digital revolution they had a job that was mired in the past: to run between hospital floors carrying lab orders and results while physicians, nurses, and patients waited expectantly. Now the results are displayed on screens in ORs and ICUs as soon as they become available.

The loss of their jobs was unfortunate to the runners, but the elimination of errors such as the one that doomed Claire Lewis can only be praised.

3

PHARMACEUTICAL COMPANIES

ANGELS OF MERCY OR 500-KILOGRAM GORILLAS?

Dr. David Healy was a wanted man in mid-2000. The director of the Department of Psychological Medicine at the University of Wales, Healy had published a number of articles relating to neurological medicines and was a minor celebrity in the U.K., where he was frequently called to testify in legal cases involving antidepressant drugs.

When Toronto's Centre for Addiction and Mental Health (CAMH) and the University of Toronto's Department of Psychiatry went looking for someone to fill the position of clinical director of their mood and anxiety disorders program, Dr. Healy emerged as their first choice. Faculty at CAMH and the university courted Healy for more than a year, offering him the position of full professor. The opportunity to join a Canadian university whose medical program was highly regarded throughout the world won the doctor over, and in September 2000 he began arrangements to relocate his family to Canada. The CAMH and the university were pleased; Dr. Healy's association would enhance the status of both organizations.

Marking his move, Dr. Healy agreed to participate in a symposium at the university in November and delivered a lecture he was scheduled to repeat at Cornell University in the United States and the Centre for National Research in Health in Paris, France. According to those attending the U of T event, Dr. Healy's presentation was a resounding success, scoring highest in measured ratings for meeting the needs and objectives of the audience.

The doctor's new employers were not so enamoured of the presentation, however. In fact, they were so troubled over his message that the physician-in-chief at the CAMH informed Dr. Healy that his contract had been cancelled; the highly regarded international expert on psychological medicine was suddenly persona non grata at the university that had pursued him for almost eighteen months.

What happened? Had Dr. Healy attacked the university's qualities, its administration, its reputation? Had he revealed a weakness in his qualifications, a hitherto unknown piece of academic failure? Had he exhibited some degree of moral turpitude? The answer in every case was no.

Dr. Healy disqualified himself by criticizing the pharmaceutical industry. "I happen to believe," he declared during his presentation, "that Prozac and other SSRIs can lead to suicide. These drugs may have been responsible for one death every day that Prozac has been on the market in North America." After questioning why no research has been conducted on this aspect of the drug, Dr. Healy went on to suggest that the pharmaceutical industry would exploit information derived from the human genome project for its exclusive use. "This knowledge," he suggested, "which is so democratically important, will operate against the interests of democracy."[1]*

The criticism was strong, but Dr. Healy was not the first to offer the view. Medical professionals had been making similar observations about Prozac for years. Besides, what had become of academic freedom? Weren't universities expected to be the source of new, provocative, and perhaps disturbing ideas? Only up to a point, apparently, and the point appeared to rest in the laps of pharmaceutical manufacturers. The chair of psychiatry at U of T explained the school's about-face by claiming Dr. Healy's

---

*Selective serotonin-reuptake inhibitors.

views were "based on extraordinary extrapolations and incompatibility with scientific evidence," and although the school had been aware of Dr. Healy's position on the matter, in the view of the psychiatry department chairman his opinions "shocked a large number of future colleagues to the point where they felt he did not have the respect and support of the staff."[2]

The latter statement sounds suspiciously as though the doctor's new colleagues were insisting that he not disturb their entrenched opinions with his own, a strange response for the faculty of a liberal university. The Canadian Association of University Teachers (CAUT) suggested a quite different explanation. Dr. Healy, CAUT surmised, had been rejected because he was too critical of the pharmaceutical industry. The university, after all, was affiliated with various teaching hospitals that were dependent on largesse and support from major pharmaceutical firms, and the risk of alienating the drug companies was not worth the hiring of a single individual, no matter how highly regarded he might be on the international scene.

Returning to his teaching position in Wales, Dr. Healy launched a $9.4-million lawsuit against the CAMH and the University of Toronto. An out-of-court settlement reached in 2002 left many of the terms undisclosed, although both sides agreed that Dr. Healy would be engaged in week-long lectures at the school for several years.[3]

The case continued to resonate among university observers who questioned various tactics employed by pharmaceutical manufacturers. At the mood and anxiety disorders clinic in Vancouver's Children's Hospital, Dr. Jane Garland called it "the Healy effect. If you even raise the same issues he does, you're classified as being with David Healy and that makes people very reluctant to talk."[4]

VISIT A GENERAL PRACTITIONER today to seek relief from a specific ailment and the physician's sole response may be to prescribe a drug that will address the condition. In a variation of the old line "Take two Aspirin and call me in the morning," you may hear, "Take this for a month and let me know how it works."

Does this solution reflect the ability of modern pharmaceuticals to perform medical miracles? Or is scribbling a prescription the best way for harried physicians to deal with patient overload? The latter suggests a depth of cynicism too dangerous to offer as a generalization, but support for the idea that pharmaceutical companies have overtaken doctors as the primary source of medical therapy is easy to find.

At $20 billion annually,[5] spending on prescription drugs represents both the second-largest and the fastest-growing component of health care in Canada. Roughly half of this amount is paid out of public expenditures via federal, provincial and territorial, and social services funding; the balance is covered by insurers and individuals. Measured in another manner, almost two out of every three Canadians fill at least one prescription every year. It's clear that any discussion on the future of our health care system is incomplete without addressing the question of prescription drug costs and their effectiveness.

Is the expenditure worth it? The question must be posed against the acknowledgment that every dollar spent by the system on prescription drugs is a dollar directed away from other programs that improve the health of Canadians. Some of these expenditures are medically related, such as spending on hospital facilities and diagnostic equipment. Others include social and educational programs, whose effects on our general health may be more diffused but are no less important.

Modern pharmaceuticals have played a role in extending our lives and improving the quality of the years we are granted. The treatment of heart attacks and strokes has been substantially improved since our parents' and grandparents' time. The impact on our lives of ailments ranging from glaucoma to cancer has been dramatically reduced in recent years, and the pharmaceutical industry exerts great effort patting itself on the back while associating itself with these advances. Unfortunately, the rhetoric exceeds the reality in most cases.

Developing, testing, and approving pharmaceuticals is a taxing, expensive, and risky process. No one should discount the ingenuity and dedication of researchers, chemists, clinicians, and evaluators in creating, testing, modifying, and improving these products. Every drug, after all, produces more than one reaction in the body, and it is important to balance the desired benefit against possible and unpredictable side effects. Countless millions of people are alive and free of pain today as a result of drugs developed and marketed in their lifetime. This is hardly news, but it masks other, less admirable aspects of the pharmaceutical industry, and of the ever-increasing financial burden that our health care system absorbs each year.

Let's begin with the industry's well-burnished image of itself as a crusader against the ravages of disease through unceasing efforts in laboratories and clinics. That's the industry's view. Here are other views articulated by Marcia Angell, a physician and former editor-in-chief of *The New England Journal of Medicine*, one of the profession's most respected publications:[6]

1. In the most recent industry-derived figures available, U.S.-based drug companies claim to have invested 15 to 17 percent of their revenues in research and development (R&D) during 2004. This figure is disputed by some observers and represents, if true, a substantial increase over R&D investment just five years earlier. In any case, the industry admits to spending an average of 36 percent of revenues on marketing. For every dollar spent finding ways to make people healthy, the industry spends between two and three dollars promoting its products:[7]

INDUSTRY-STATED R&D REVENUES AND EXPENDITURES, 2004

RANK	COMPANY	REVENUES US$ BILLIONS	R&D SPENT US$ BILLIONS/%
1	Pfizer	50.9	7.5 / 14.7%
2	GlaxoSmithKline	32.7	5.2 / 15.9%
3	Sanofi-Aventis	27.1	3.9 / 14.4%
4	Johnson & Johnson	24.6	5.2 / 21.1%

5	Merck	23.9	4.0 / 16.7%
6	Novartis	22.7	3.5 / 15.4%
7	AstraZeneca	21.6	3.8 / 17.6%
8	Hoffmann-La Roche	17.7	5.1 / 28.8%
9	Bristol-Myers Squibb	15.5	2.5 / 16.1%
10	Wyeth	14.2	2.5 / 17.6%

2. No correlation exists between the cost of developing and testing a drug and the price charged to those who may benefit from it. While claiming that his firm invested over US$800 million in development costs for every new drug it introduced, the president of drug manufacturer Merck noted that the price charged to patients "isn't determined by [the drugs'] research costs. Instead, it is determined by their value in preventing and treating disease. Whether Merck spends $500 million or $1 billion developing a medicine, it is the doctor, not the patient, and those paying for our medicines, who will determine its true value."[8] Translation: Charge whatever the market will bear.
3. Advances in the pharamaceutical industry do not compare to advances in diagnostics and therapeutics, such as MRIs, CT scans, and minimal-intrusive and microsurgery. The industry may claim that these are two widely different technologies, but the impact on health care is similar. Here is the difference: An expenditure of $50 million on widespread distribution of a new patented pharmaceutical that is no more effective than an older generic drug costing one-tenth the price diverts $45 million that could be spent on MRI machines.
4. The drug industry has introduced few products that can claim to be major advances in the treatment of serious diseases. Despite the industry's boast of making enormous investments in R&D, nothing akin to insulin, penicillin, or the Salk polio vaccine has been introduced over the past two generations.

5. Most "new" drugs launched by the industry are either variations on older medications, created to extend patent protection and thus maintain high profit margins, or "me too" drugs, created to piggyback on successful products introduced by competitors. Among the few drugs that could truly be described as innovative are statins, formulations to reduce blood cholesterol levels. The first statin arrived on the market in 1987; twenty years later, six formulations were battling for this market, all claiming superiority in at least one narrow sector, and all variations on Mevacor, the original Merck statin.

Not all multinational drug companies play the same hardball games. The German firm Boehringer Ingelheim, with net sales of more that €10 billion annually, traditionally spends about one-fifth of its sales volume on research and development. It is also remarkably generous when granting rights to generic drug manufacturers for many of its patented formulations. The firm's HIV treatment *nevirapine*, for example, is offered royalty-free to suppliers and dispensed without charge to dozens of developing countries as a means of preventing the transmission of HIV from infected mothers to their offspring.

It should be noted that Boehringer Ingelheim is a private family-owned organization; unlike most other drug manufacturers with analysts to impress and shareholders to please, its management can choose to spend corporate assets where its conscience rather than its business advisors dictate.

COLLEAGUES TURN AGAINST A DOCTOR WHO FOLLOWED HER ETHICS

Perhaps the most notorious tale of pharmaceutical influence on medical practitioners in recent years concerned Dr. Nancy Olivieri, Toronto's Hospital for Sick Children, and the drug manufacturer Apotex. Dr. Olivieri, an internationally renowned specialist in hereditary blood diseases, had been contracted by Apotex to conduct tests on a proposed new drug. When she determined that the medication presented serious long-term medical risks, Dr. Olivieri followed directives from the hospital's research ethics board and disclosed her concerns to all participants in the study.

Her action unleashed a maelstrom of attacks against her, first from Apotex, which claimed she had broken a confidentiality agreement, and later from the president of the University of Toronto, who accused her of jeopardizing a $30-million donation from the pharmaceutical company to the university and its affiliated teaching hospitals. The attacks did not end there. A colleague of Dr. Olivieri's was convicted of orchestrating a campaign of hate mail against her and her supporters.[9]

The Olivieri incident has all the elements of a TV drama, including female target, male attackers, poison pen letters, and massive amounts of money, set against the life-and-death backdrop of a major hospital. Indeed, it drew the attention of media around the world, including *The New York Times* and *60 Minutes*, the ultimate investigatory spotlight. This attention may have suggested this was an unusual event concerning one determined physician dealing with a uniquely rapacious drug manufacturer. Unfortunately, the tale was not an exception but representative of a disturbing pattern of behaviour.

As director of the internal medicine residence program at McMaster University Health Centre in 1992, Dr. Gordon Guyatt announced that the facility's residents would no longer be permitted to accept gifts from pharmaceutical manufacturers, a marketing practice employed by drug companies for many years. The reaction of the drug companies was immediate and direct.

"Somebody from the industry came and threatened me with a loss of funding," Dr. Guyatt recalls, "not only for our educational but also for our research practices. The individual made the mistake of putting it on paper." Dr. Guyatt made the threat public, igniting a storm of controversy in professional journals that spilled over into the public press. The industry accused Guyatt of restricting its access to residents and its freedom of expression; the doctor expressed concern over undue influence exerted by drug companies on physicians. In this case, the hospital agreed with the doctor's proposal, and the awarding of gifts to resident physicians from drug companies ended.[10]

Some of Dr. Guyatt's own colleagues questioned whether the guidelines prohibiting gifts would prove effective. In response, the physician-in-chief at Toronto's Mount Sinai Hospital launched a study to measure the opinions of McMaster internal medicine graduates regarding drug company information against those of a control group whose medical school placed no limits on gifts from the firms. The results were dramatic proof that drug manufacturers wage a successful battle influencing physicians: McMaster graduates were less than half as likely as the control group to consider information from drug companies beneficial to their practice, and substantially more skeptical of claims from advertising and marketing material.[11]

Despite his experience, Dr. Guyatt remains relatively sanguine toward the pharmaceutical manufacturers. "They are for-profit businesses, and so they operate that way," he says with a shrug. "It's their job to make their drugs look better than they really are. If their marketing departments weren't making their drugs look better than they are, they wouldn't be doing a good job."[12]

Drug manufacturers have been aiming marketing efforts at physicians, surgeons, nurses, hospital administrators, and others in the industry for years, and except for concerns such as the one expressed by Dr. Guyatt regarding gifts to undergrads, the practice is considered acceptable. The industry's focus of advertising messages on end-users, however, has stirred controversy throughout the system and, according to your point of view, may represent a dangerous threat to the health of citizens and the system itself.

"Pharmaceutical companies are selling drugs the way that automotive companies sell cars," one medical professional observed, "with people dancing on tables and smiling at their perfect partners on perfect days in a perfect world." The unreality of many advertisements for prescription drugs is heightened by the extensive use of television, an advertising medium suited for generating shallow emotional responses rather than detailed, multi-layered information. The marketing strategy behind these media campaigns is to exploit the limited amount of time physicians have to deal with both drug company representatives promoting their products and patients requesting treatment. Consumer advertising generates demand by patients. Hard-pressed physicians, agreeing that a particular drug is designed to treat the patient's complaint and recognizing no contra-indications, may issue a prescription. This occurs even though Canada, like every other industrialized country with the exceptions of the United States and New Zealand, restricts direct-to-consumer advertising for prescription drugs.

In Canada, the effect of "spillover" advertising—messages appearing on U.S. television and directed to that market but viewed by Canadians—is substantial. The drug industry spent an estimated US$4.8 billion on direct-to-consumer advertising in 2005,[13] and much of it reached Canadians who were swayed by its messages every bit as much as its intended U.S. audience. The amount of this expenditure, if not the quality of the content, also swayed CanWest Global Communications Corporation, which demanded that Canada drop its ban on direct-to-consumer advertising, claiming pharmaceutical companies "get a free ride in Canada" as a result of the spillover effect. Disregarding questions of public policy and consumer interest, CanWest noted that "the legislative regime is unfair to Canadian media companies as it denies them a source of revenue that is available to U.S. media companies." In case the company's lust for its portion of the US$4.8 billion spent with American media outlets was not sufficiently convincing, the company invoked its rights to freedom of expression "as guaranteed under the Canadian Charter of Rights and Freedoms."[14]

This is dangerous territory indeed. The wisdom of restricting direct-to-consumer advertising has been confirmed by the actions of almost every other industrialized country, not only because of the manner in which consumer demand complicates the role of physicians, but also because of the way in which many drug companies develop their medications. The majority of new drug formulations fall into one of two categories: treatment for "invented" ailments, and highly specific therapies promoted for broad applications. Both categories are heavily promoted to patients.

Inventing a disease and introducing a cure for it represents a high degree of marketing genius and a nadir in business morality. Women have been enduring menopause for untold generations, but only within the past few years has the condition been promoted as a disease caused by hormonal deficiency to be cured with a prescription drug. A social condition such as being too tired to participate in sex is labelled "female sexual dysfunction," and once-accepted levels of blood pressure and cholesterol, now deemed too high, can be solved, the industry claims, with a remarkable new prescription drug. Do we really need billions of dollars diverted from our health care budgets for these medications?

CHANGING A SINGLE LITTLE MOLECULE TO MAKE HUNDREDS OF MILLIONS IN PROFITS

Your parents recognized heartburn as passing discomfort owing to diet and perhaps obesity. Their response was to lower stomach acid levels safely and easily by consuming a spoonful of baking soda dissolved in a glass of water or, for greater convenience, chewing a couple of Tums or Rolaids. Labelling the general condition "acid reflux syndrome" (the more accurate term is "gastroesophageal reflux disease," in which the liquid contents of the stomach regurgitates), pharmaceutical giant AstraZeneca launched Prilosec in the 1980s and tapped a gold mine. Prilosec was soon generating US$6 billion in annual sales for AstraZeneca, making Prilosec one of the most successful drugs, from a financial standpoint, ever created.

But in 2001, AstraZeneca faced a crisis: the patent protection for its indigestion cash cow was about to expire, meaning generic drug manufacturers would soon begin marketing the same formulation and charging substantially less than Prilosec's hefty price of US$3 per pill. Would AstraZeneca sit back and watch US$6 billion per year vanish from its bottom line? Not a chance.

First, it announced that it would sue any company planning to introduce a generic version of Prilosec. The suit was doomed, but its launch delayed the introduction of a generic version while the arguments wended their way through the justice system. AstraZeneca used the time to alter one molecule of its Prilosec formulation, a change that had no effect on the drug's application or efficacy but qualified it for patent protection. The new/old drug was called Nexium, and just as the generic drug firms were about to launch their bargain-priced version of Prilosec, AstraZeneca introduced it to the world. In one of the biggest drug-marketing programs in history, AstraZeneca spent almost US$500 million introducing "The Little Purple Pill" that could magically address "severe erosions in your esophagus" caused by acid reflux. Purple was also the colour of the original Prilosec, which Nexium essentially copied. The two products had something else in common: Nexium was also priced at US$3 per pill.

The Nexium promotion employed a paid testimonial by Hall of Fame baseball pitcher Jim Palmer, who talked about his ongoing struggle with heartburn and "the importance of recognizing and treating health symptoms in everyday life." Everyday life apparently did not include stirring a teaspoon of baking soda in water or popping a Tums into your mouth.

Cynicism aside, AstraZeneca's strategy was a work of genius. By the time the generic drug companies began marketing their inexpensive version of Prilosec, about 40 percent of the patients using the drug had switched to Nexium.[15]

Acid indigestion is a relatively minor concern on its own, and while the Prilosec/Nexium tale may illustrate the purely profit motive of the big pharmaceutical companies—they are designed to make money as well as drugs, after all—we should not overlook the industry's advances in more serious areas of health care. Or should we?

In the opinion of at least one qualified critic of the drug companies, most new drugs are not breakthroughs but "great leaps sideways."[16] Here is an example: A pharmaceutical company introduces a new drug, widely promoted to both physicians and consumers, claiming that clinical trials prove it reduces heart attacks by 20 percent. That's pretty impressive. If you had suffered such an attack, or were acknowledged to be a candidate for one, wouldn't you ask to be considered for that drug?

A detailed examination, however, may reveal that the drug's effectiveness applies only to a small minority of patients, depending on the nature of their condition. The drug will reduce heart attacks only among a small portion of those with general symptoms, yet it will be mass-marketed with the intention of persuading patients diagnosed as potential victims of heart attacks to request the medication from their physician. Thus the "20 percent reduction" remains a relative figure; in reality, the drug may reduce the incidence of heart attacks among the general population from 1 percent to 0.8 percent. On that basis, your risk has been reduced from ten chances in a thousand to eight chances in a thousand; out of one thousand patients taking the drug each year, two might avoid a heart attack thanks to its effects. This will be good news to the two lucky people whose health has been protected, but what happens when it's weighed against finding more effective ways to spend our limited health care resources?

Where prescription drugs are concerned, new is not necessarily better, but it is almost always more expensive. And its use may introduce risks that are unexpected. Perhaps the most recent dramatic example of the risks of potential side effects from new drugs has been the "breakthrough" drug Vioxx.

WHAT HAPPENS WHEN THE "POTENTIAL SIDE EFFECTS" INCLUDE DEATH?

Vioxx was Merck's response to a perceived demand that could be filled by a new product. The demand was created by the gradually aging population in industrialized societies, a process that has been accompanied by an increase in the number of people suffering from arthritis. This is a serious, debilitating disease, as we have seen. Any medication that effectively controls arthritic pain with minimal side effects should be welcomed, and its developers congratulated and rewarded.

It's important, however, to understand that arthritis has two distinctly different forms. Osteoarthritis is the result of wear and tear on the body's joints, which leaves cartilage unable to cushion bone surfaces and causes excruciating pain, especially in knees and hips. Rheumatoid arthritis, in contrast, can occur at any time in an individual's life, and is caused not by wear and tear but by inflammation of tissues surrounding the joints.

For years, the most commonly prescribed medications to relieve arthritic pain have been non-steroidal anti-inflammatory drugs, or NSAIDs. You have almost certainly taken an NSAID because the most common drug in this category is everyday Aspirin. Even Aspirin—acetylsalicylic acid—produces side effects that can lead to gastrointestinal ulceration and bleeding, kidney failure, and heart disease. With a growing market for medications to relieve the pain of arthritis, drug companies began developing new NSAIDs, promoted as improved formulations and described as COX-2 inhibitors that reduce inflammation while avoiding intestinal problems. Among the first of these drugs, introduced in the late 1990s, were Celebrex and Vioxx. Prestigious medical journals examined the clinical studies and agreed that both products marked an important step forward in relieving arthritic pain. With that endorsement, advertising for Celebrex and Vioxx began flooding television screens and magazine pages, trumpeting the drugs' success at relieving pain while proving safer than old formulations. Sales volumes leaped to Midas heights. Within a short time, Vioxx was generating over US$2.5 billion in sales in the United States alone.[17]

When skeptics, including Dr. James Wright, professor of clinical pharmacology at the University of British Columbia, began looking more closely at the test results, they noted a significant difference between the six-month clinical tests and the twelve-month results conducted on Pfizer's Celebrex. Over the shorter six-month time frame, used by Pfizer as the basis for its claims of product performance, it appeared that Celebrex indeed had a lower incidence of the gastrointestinal problems associated with NSAIDs. After twelve months, however, the number of patients developing ulcers as a result of taking Celebrex was about the same as it was for those taking

Aspirin.[18] What's more, long-term use of Celebrex appeared to raise the possibility of patients developing cardiovascular problems. Despite concerns voiced by Wright and others, Celebrex remained on the market, although the U.S. Food and Drug Administration (FDA) insisted on new warnings regarding possible dangerous side effects.*

Merck quickly declared that its competing product was quite safe, and managed to maintain the multi-billion-dollar sales volume for Vioxx. But in 2004, the company threw in the towel when its own study demonstrated that Vioxx doubled the risk of heart attacks for its users.

Only then did many in the medical community admit that older patients suffering from osteoarthritis should not have been prescribed NSAIDs or any anti-inflammatory drugs because inflammation was not the cause of their suffering. One prominent critic of the pharmaceutical industry stated, with disarming bluntness, "Most people with osteoarthritis could get better relief with fewer side effects if they avoided NSAIDs entirely and simply took acetaminophen [such as Tylenol], saving 97 percent of the costs."[19]

Prescription drugs, as every physician and pharmacist knows, can kill as well as cure. Even when a medicine proves suitable for a patient's needs, it is often prescribed on the basis of marketing effectiveness, rather than value. "You get what you pay for" may apply to some consumer goods, but not necessarily to medications. Thirty-second television commercials delivering a combination of feel-good emotions and "Breakthrough!" revelations encourage patients to choose drugs on the basis of fashion rather than efficacy, making any measure of value irrelevant.

When dealing with chronic pain or terminal disease, value is already irrelevant for most people. How much is another six months of life worth to a cancer sufferer? How much would you pay to be free of chronic pain you had suffered for years? Some new prescription drugs produce these

---

*The Celebrex/Vioxx event generated public hearings conducted by the FDA. At one session, the drugs received perhaps the ultimate endorsement when a member of the U.S. Army Medical Corps, claiming he was supported by the Department of Defense, declared that the drugs "are essential in the global war on terrorism." (*The Truth about the Drug Companies*, p. 275) results, while others only claim to do so. Attempting to measure their worth in dollars and cents is to launch an unwinnable debate.

Yet the debate almost demands to be opened because the potential rewards to patients, and the cost to the health care system, are immense. Consumers Union, the non-profit publisher of the U.S. magazine *Consumer Reports*, has become a leader in assessing prescription drugs based on their effectiveness, safety, and price, with the goal of providing U.S. citizens with information to choose proven and affordable alternatives to highly promoted and substantially more expensive pharmaceuticals. The Consumer Reports Best Buy Drugs (available free at www.CRBestBuyDrugs.org) project recently identified patients who might benefit from each group of medications, noted the side effects of each formulation, compared their effectiveness, and measured the value of each according to the average monthly cost. The comparative effectiveness information in the reports is based on the drug effectiveness review project, which is based at Oregon Health and Science University.

The process may be novel to the health care industry but Consumers Union, the parent organization of *Consumer Reports*, is well experienced in the mechanics of such comparisons and boasts a bulletproof record for impartiality. On that basis, its findings deserve credence, especially when related to the cost-effectiveness of products with equal effectiveness. The following chart includes highest-cost and lowest-cost alternatives for identical therapeutic treatments over one month, with identical dosage levels. The range in cost for essentially equal medications is startling.

SYMPTOM	MEDICATION	BRAND	COST
Menopausal imbalance	Estrogen pills	Generic	$6–$14
		Ortho-est	$27–$69
	Estrogen skin patch	Alora	$31–$53
		Menostar	$62
	Progesterone pills	Generic	$10–$21
		Aygestin	$77
Overactive bladder	Trospium 20 mg	Sanctura	$58
	Solifenacin	Vesicare	$121

Insomnia	Benzodiazepines	Generic	$6*
		Doral	$75*
Elevated cholesterol	Lovastatin 20 mg	Generic	$32
		Mevacor	$81

For cost-comparison use only—not a therapeutic guide.

NOTE: Figures are in U.S. dollars.

These are, admittedly, U.S. prices for U.S. consumers. The comparison is appropriate, however, because the majority of prescription drugs used in Canada are supplied by U.S.-based companies that exert enormous pressure on federal and provincial governments regarding pricing, market access, approvals process, and other actions. What's more, patent drugs occupy a unique position in the complex annals of the North American Free Trade Agreement, negotiated and signed by the Mulroney government in 1989. In order to participate in NAFTA, the government of the day claimed, Canada would have to extend its patent protection agreement for twenty years where prescription drugs were concerned. In addition, the U.S. drug companies were permitted to block the entry of generic products for a further three years with a simple court injunction as soon as another company filed its intent to manufacture the drug, a legal device unavailable in any other form of civil litigation. Like it or not, our consumption of patented drugs is directly linked with activities of the U.S.-based manufacturers, which exert as much pressure on Canadian regulators as they do on their own.

THE KAFKAESQUE WORLD OF DRUG FUNDING

The pharmaceutical giant Bristol-Myers Squibb provided an example of strong-arm tactics in June 2006 when it announced its intention to

*Based on fifteen doses.

withhold Erbitux, a drug created to battle colorectal cancer, because it disagreed with the price set by this country's Patent Medicine Prices Review Board (PMPRB). Government price-setting tends to be a distasteful action, even among those who support it as a means of managing universal health care. The PMPRB's approach is reasonably equitable, however, given the fact that it is dealing with a product designed to save lives, or at least lengthen them.

When a new drug is submitted for sale in Canada, the PMPRB examines the price set and approved in seven other countries: Germany, France, Italy, Sweden, Switzerland, the United Kingdom, and the United States. The Canadian price cannot be the highest of this group, and in fact, it is usually set at the median point, effectively ensuring that the drug is selling at a lower price somewhere in the world other than in Canada.

The methodology may be open to criticism, but the goal is virtually universal because every country on the list, with the exception of the United States, regulates the price of its drugs in a similar manner. Even in the United States, where political leaders ranging from the speaker of the House of Representatives to the mayor of New York City have fiercely criticized Canada's drug-pricing policy, comparable rules are applied whenever the federal government funds the purchase of prescription drugs. Drugs consumed by U.S. war veterans and their families, along with government-insured consumers, are priced at levels fixed by the government according to the Federal Supply Schedule (FSS). (This point should perhaps be communicated to New York City mayor Michael Bloomberg, who angrily declared that American pharmaceutical companies should "refuse to sell drugs in Canada until they get rid of price controls!") It also should be noted that the highest drug prices in the United States are paid by uninsured consumers who can least afford them.

A detailed study conducted by a University of Calgary economist examined sixteen of the most prescribed patented drugs in Canada and the United States, comparing the Ontario and U.S. government prices in current Canadian dollars, and measuring the expenditures in

Canada from January to June 2003.[20] Most drugs in the study included brand names familiar to anyone who watches more than a few hours of prime-time television each week—Lipitor, Celebrex, Vioxx, Celexa, Fosamax, and others. Prices varied by prescription, with some dramatically higher in one country than another, but in sum the U.S. cost was within 2.5 percent of the amount spent in Canada: $1,489,131,000 in Canada, $1,526,605,000 in the United States.

Western countries regulate the price of drugs, with the exception of those sold on the free market in the United States. France is among the most stringent in forcing pharmaceutical companies to reduce their prices, and as a result, it boasts the lowest average drug cost of the seven countries used by the PMPRB in determining fair prices for Canadians. Do the drug companies complain about it? They certainly do, but their pharmaceuticals continue to be available in France and elsewhere, and the drug companies continue to reap enormous profits. With the exception of sectors where the federal government exercises its right to lower prices, the U.S. market remains the only one wide open to price-setting by pharmaceutical firms; critics of drug manufacturers hasten to point out that the U.S. also spends far more per capita on health care costs than comparable countries, yet leaves 45 million of its citizens without health care coverage.

All of which might seem to weaken Bristol-Myers Squibb Canada's refusal to adhere to an agreement it signed with the federal government in 1987. Under its terms, BMS and its competitors agreed to abide by price rulings from the PMPRB, as described above. The agreement also called for BMS and other firms to increase their investment in research and development in Canada to a level equal to 10 percent of revenues. As part of its bargain, the federal government agreed to restrict a law permitting generic drug companies to produce a drug under patent protection by another company at a lower price than the patent holder. The law remains on the books, but Canada has not implemented it since 1992.

While the Canadian government appears to have kept its end of the bargain, the industry's promise to meet the R&D 10 percent target has not been met. In 2005 its R&D spending as a percentage of sales in Canada registered 8.3 percent, virtually identical to the 1989 level. In fact, the industry's promise of maintaining R&D levels at 10 percent of sales has not been achieved since 2000.[21] Moreover, most R&D expenditures by drug manufacturers in Canada are restricted to clinical tests; instead of employing Canadians as researchers in their laboratories, they use them as guinea pigs in hospitals and clinics.[22]

(To some observers, any discussion about R&D expenditures by the major pharmaceutical companies is as relevant as debates about medieval theology, at least where serious advances are concerned. The drug companies may delight in trumpeting their success at reducing the effects of acid indigestion or toenail fungus, but when it comes to more serious afflictions, they depend on other sources. Example: Of the seventy-seven leading anti-cancer drugs approved for use in the United States, fifty were developed as a direct result of support from that country's National Cancer Institute. And fifteen of the twenty-one drugs considered to have made the most impact between 1965 and 1992 relied for the most part on public funding.)[23]

The confrontation between BMS and the PMPRB over Erbitux provided a dramatic example not only of a drug company's determination to use its muscle as a means of generating more profit, but of our health system's multi-layered complexity and the mind-boggling bureaucratic labyrinth it often produces. At once fascinating and depressing, the BMS Erbitux tempest in a test tube is more illustrative than instructive.

Erbitux was developed to treat advanced colorectal cancer, a disease that kills about 8500 Canadians each year. This is not a universally applicable drug, nor has it been proven, on its own, to lengthen the lives of patients suffering from this form of cancer. It appears to be effective at shrinking the size of tumours and delaying their growth when used in combination with other drugs. It is also considered an alternative to Avastin, a drug more commonly used in colorectal cancer cases.

The refusal of BMS to sell Erbitux in Canada unless the government raised the price tripped a response from various provincial governments, and the tale spins out with all the elements of a surreal farce. In Ontario, the provincial health ministry approved thirty-four of thirty-eight submissions made on behalf of colorectal cancer patients to receive Erbitux-based therapy during the 2005–06 fiscal year and set aside $3.6 million to cover the cost. This, of course, presented the ministry with something of a quandary, since Ottawa and BMS were squabbling over the price, and BMS refused to allow the drug into Canada until the negotiations were completed. Meanwhile, Ontario residents suffering from the disease, and for whom other therapies were proving ineffective, were expected to sit around and listen to their tumours grow.

This was outrageous, and at least one patient decided that if the government body responsible for providing health care for her and others refused to be proactive, she would take the initiative. Suzanne Aucoin, a thirty-five-year-old resident of St. Catharines, Ontario, had been undergoing chemotherapy for two years when her oncologist determined that traditional medications were no longer proving effective and prescribed Avastin and Erbitux. When it became clear to Aucoin and her doctors that the battle between Ottawa and BMS could drag on indefinitely, she travelled to a private clinic in nearby Buffalo, New York, to receive treatment with Erbitux. Payment for the drugs came out of Suzanne's pocket, and when her financial resources were drained, she began fundraising through a website and various media appeals.

"Press conferences, interviews, and becoming a public figure in the fight for drugs was not something I had envisioned," she commented. "This aspect of the overall fight with cancer was very draining and frustrating to me. Working with the health care and political systems is ridiculously exhausting.... There are no straight answers, only inconsistent policies, ignorance, and injustice."[24]

In the summer of 2006, it appeared as though the Ontario health ministry had relented when it announced that the Ontario Health Insurance Plan (OHIP) would pay the required $24,000 each month for Suzanne Aucoin to receive treatment with Avastin and Erbitux at the

U.S. clinic. By this time she had spent more than $50,000 of her own money on treatment at the U.S. clinic and through a special arrangement with the cancer facilities at Hamilton General Hospital. When she asked OHIP to reimburse her for $31,000 spent in the U.S. clinic and $21,000 at the Hamilton facility, both her original request and a later appeal were rejected. In its sixteen-page rejection notice, OHIP revealed the inner workings of government bureaucratic machinery.

The government agency could not use its out-of-country fund to cover Aucoin's payments to the U.S. clinic because the clinic was not, by OHIP's measure, a licensed health facility. Nor could it draw from the fund to cover the treatment she had paid for in Hamilton because, of course, the Hamilton clinic was not located out of the country, which was the point of the original request. Her lawyer argued that the physician who tended Aucoin at the U.S. clinic was indeed properly licensed to practise medicine. Ah, OHIP replied, but the clinic was not licensed. Nor could it obtain a licence, as a U.S. facility, that would satisfy OHIP requirements.

The decision did not come as a surprise to Aucoin. "I was kind of half-expecting it," she said. "I'm tired of being sad and I'm tired of being upset, so I'm not going to give it any energy." She had little energy to devote to it; the same day that OHIP handed down its decision she learned that planned surgery to remove tumours from her liver and lungs had been cancelled because cancerous cells had been found on her lymph nodes.[25]

THE WISDOM AND RISK OF ABANDONING PRICE CONTROLS ON DRUGS

Some observers note, with justification in the case of Suzanne Aucoin, that such bureaucratic ineptness leads to tragic consequences for Canadians and reduces the availability in this country of life-saving medications for appropriate applications. On the same topic, Brett Skinner, director of the Departments of Health and Pharmaceutical

Policy Research and Insurance Policy Research for the Fraser Institute, conducted a detailed study that concluded Canada's imposition of price controls on patented drugs was ultimately unproductive and "at best unnecessary."[26] According to Skinner, thirty of the top 100 brand-name drugs sold in Canada in 2003 were non-patented and thus not subject to price controls. Their cost to consumers was influenced only by the supply and demand of the free market. Yet their prices, based on Skinner's calculations, were on average 42 percent lower in Canada than in the United States, or about the same price relative to the U.S. as the other seventy patented drugs in the study that were subject to price controls. "This suggests," Skinner proposes, "if price controls on patented drugs were repealed, the price of patented drugs would not likely rise much higher than current levels. This analysis demonstrates that government justifications for intervening in pharmaceutical markets through price controls based on the belief that market prices would be too high for people to afford are wrong."[27]

What market factor would ensure a Canadian price that was more than 40 percent less, in comparable dollars, than the U.S. price in the absence of price controls? Skinner submits a classic free-market explanation: "[T]he Canadian prices for branded drugs are likely to remain dramatically lower than U.S. prices because of lower average Canadian incomes." Skinner suggests they will remain that way "as long as millions of Americans don't bid up the prices by crossing the border to buy Canadian drugs at retail."

Can we trust the free market to ensure that drug prices in Canada will be almost 40 percent lower than those in the United States based solely on average household incomes, which do not vary nearly that much? Skinner proposes that we can, before claiming that Canadians are also paying more for generic drugs as a result of price controls on patented medications because "the American market is far more competitive." According to Skinner, Canadian policies give established generic producers advantages that they have exploited to establish individual product monopolies on pharmacy shelves through exclusive distribution agreements with retailers. These monopolies, he submits, produce higher prices.

Skinner notes that five companies accounted for 95 percent of all prescriptions of the 100 top-selling generics in Canada in 2003, adding, "If Canada's market were as competitive as the U.S., huge savings would be generated from price savings on generics, which are 78 percent higher in Canada than in the U.S., even after we make adjustments for currency. By contrast, the U.S. market is characterized by a large number of companies and healthy competition or sales of generic drugs, which leads to lower prices and higher voluntary rates of generic drug use in the United States. *If our market were as competitive as that of the United States, we could expect our prices for generic drugs to fall to U.S. levels and our rates of using generic drugs to increase to U.S. levels*" (Skinner's italics).[28]

Ergo, Skinner argues, eliminating price controls on patented branded drugs would not produce a rise in Canadian prices, compared with U.S. prices, and an across-the-board elimination of controls would reduce the price of generic drugs, which would then become more widely prescribed.

Not everyone is buying the idea. For one thing, Skinner is highly selective in his use of U.S. figures. When factoring in Canada's health care costs and efficiency, he chooses not to compare this country with the United States on the basis that the health care systems are so dissimilar, despite the fact that the two countries are socially and economically similar beyond their approach to health care. Comparative figures on expenditures and coverage clearly indicate that the United States spends about 50 percent per capita more on health care than Canada yet leaves 45 million of its citizens with no coverage at all, as we have seen. His argument that eliminating price controls will drop the price of generic drugs in Canada was greeted with some degree of scorn by people such as Dr. Joel Lexchin, associate chair in the School of Health Policy and Management at York University. "You have to look at the methodology that they used to compare Canadian and American generic drug prices," Dr. Lexchin noted. "Even if you cut [the generic drug] prices in half, a minor amount would be saved, relative to the total drug bill." Lexchin pointed out that Canadian sales of patented medicines were $10.1 billion in 2003, and sales of generic products were $3.2 billion.

The veracity of Skinner's proposal remains to be seen, although many people will simply refuse to accept the risk of eliminating a device that appears to work with a reasonable degree of success. Instead of seeking to reduce drug prices to lower the drain on health care funding, we may be more successful by reducing our consumption of prescription drugs generally. This will require will and commitment from government, patients, and physicians, but the benefits, measured both in dollars and years of good health, could prove significant.

Though it sounds brutal, the value of investing in expensive treatments, especially those associated with terminal cancer patients, requires continued assessment, and a fixed policy must be applied consistently across the country. Dr. Adam Hoffman, a member of the Department of Internal Medicine at McGill University's medical school, cares for cancer patients and is as aware of the manifestations of these hard decisions as anyone. Noting that media reports frequently sway government policy-makers on issues of cancer therapy and their cost, he adds that a single course of treatment with the drug Avastin costs $36,000 and may extend the life of advanced-cancer patients. "I am also aware," he adds, "that proper access to family doctors and colonoscopy screening can potentially save lives by preventing the occurrence of cancer in the first place. If I were a government policy-maker, I might be inclined to take the money saved on Avastin and put it into improved access to family physicians for the populace." Access to Avastin, he concludes, is not a fundamental right of Canadian citizenship, but access to a physician should be.[29]

The question of spending public funds on expensive drugs and procedures that may extend the life of a terminally ill patient but not cure the underlying ailment neatly cleaves a gap between the responsibilities of public and private health care funding. If a citizen and his or her physician identifies a procedure anywhere in the world that holds promise to delay death, how can a publicly funded system refuse to permit it, even if the provider is a private for-profit operation? Can a universally available health care system legally limit coverage for the citizens who fund it?

The painful but necessary answer is that public health care not only *can* restrict payment—it *must.* As Canadians, we have a right to claim fair and free access to health care, but the right does not and cannot come without limits, especially given the accelerated developments in technology and medications. Should every new drug or medical device qualify for support from the public purse? Who determines their value and efficacy? Governments are obligated to provide medical care, but they are also obligated to act in a fiscally responsible manner, and this entails using discretion where funding is concerned.

Consider the actions of private medical insurers in the United States, who neatly sidestep responsibility for providing treatment for pre-existing conditions. Contract cancer after signing on for medical coverage and you'll receive treatment for the ailment, although the annual cost to the insurer will likely be limited. Try to buy insurance coverage after being diagnosed with cancer and you will, in effect, be shown the door. Publicly funded health care does not carry restrictions on pre-existing conditions; it is unfair to expect that it will also place no limits on the money it will pay for unapproved treatment.

A more economically effective (and, it may be argued, substantially more considerate) attitude would present itself were patients more willing to forgo drug therapy and assume greater responsibility for the general state of their health and their participation in therapy. Research conducted by the Ontario Cardiac Care Network revealed that only 10 percent of survivors of mild heart attacks participated in rehabilitation programs, most of them linked to exercise and diet, designed to prevent a recurrence.[30] We can assume that the remaining 90 percent relied exclusively on pharmaceuticals and luck.

A GREATER ROLE FOR PHARMACISTS?

Aid may arrive from a logical yet overlooked source: pharmacists. While members of the profession express no interest in prescribing drugs, except in exceptional instances (such as the "morning after" birth control pill, which must be ingested within twenty-four hours of intercourse), most are eager to play a wider role in patient care and monitoring. As one Alberta physician noted in supporting the move to more closely involve pharmacists in health care, "Patients see their pharmacists up to eight times more frequently than [they do] their physicians."[31]

At the outset, the expanded role of retail pharmacists may appear limited. For example, the comment from the Alberta physician was made in reference to a study by that province of the use of Taro-Warfarin, a commonly prescribed blood thinner. If the second half of the drug's name sounds familiar, it's because the formulation is virtually identical to a long-employed rat poison. Too much Taro-Warfarin and the drug works in the same manner that it kills rats, by causing fatal internal bleeding. Too little, and the patient may suffer a stroke. Pharmacists who underwent a special training procedure were assigned to monitor the blood thickness in patients receiving Taro-Warfarin and adjust the dosage to achieve the optimal level.

Is this a dangerous move away from traditional physician responsibilities, leaving patients to receive inadequate or unqualified medical care? Probably no more so than the wider use of nurse practitioners to achieve the same goal. In fact, when it comes to identifying and avoiding dangerous drug interactions, pharmacists are at least as aware of these risks as physicians.

In response, pharmacy schools have altered their programs in an effort to ensure that their graduates are more patient-oriented. Tom

Brown, director of the pharmacy program at the University of Toronto's Faculty of Pharmacy, notes that "health care really is physician centred, [in] that legislation restricts what pharmacists are able to do, and reimbursement ties pharmacists to a product rather than to their cognitive ability."[32] The implication is clear, if somewhat brutal: since pharmacists' incomes are directly linked to sales of the products they dispense, their actions may be influenced more by sales volumes and profit margins than by patient health.

We may think of the pharmacist's role occurring exclusively at the retail dispensing level, and this indeed may be where the greatest potential for saving exists. But studies have indicated that almost any greater integration of pharmacists into the health care system produces benefits. In one case, the simple act of having hospital pharmacists accompany physicians on their morning rounds yielded a 66 percent reduction in adverse drug effects.[33] Applied universally, the savings in costs for Canada's health care system would be immense.

The function of pharmaceuticals mirrors that of other components of the health care system. We may be impressed and inspired by their life-enhancing potential on a wide scale, but their true value can be measured only patient by patient. Our chosen physician and neighbourhood pharmacist are more closely related to the state of our health than any multinational drug company. This is a point worth recalling each time we are exposed to another TV commercial or magazine advertisement portraying happy and healthy people who apparently owe their giddy disposition to the munificence of a pharmaceutical manufacturer that tallies its profits in billions of dollars.

After all, in Canada we are both patients and, ultimately, providers.

4

PAYING THE PIPERS
EFFICIENCY EXPERTS IN THE MEDICAL ARENA

By all accounts, Dr. Anthony Hsu was both an outstanding physician and an admirable human being. As a paediatrician in the industrial city of Welland, Ontario, Dr. Hsu provided primary health care for children in a region chronically underserviced by medical providers. In fact, in an area of 100,000 potential patients, Dr. Hsu was one of only two paediatricians, and in 2003 his office files held records on 7000 patients.

Even this fails to measure the scope of the physician's work, for he was on call for emergencies every second night and provided free service to the local Children's Aid Society. By all accounts, the doctor was working seventy hours each week to fulfil his responsibilities.

At age fifty-seven, Dr. Hsu might have been giving some thought to retiring. Any such thoughts were banished from his mind in 2002, when the Ontario Health Insurance Plan ordered an audit of his billings, to be carried out by the Ontario College of Physicians and Surgeons. The only apparent prompt for this audit was a computer alert that the paediatrician's billings' record did not match a profile in the provincial medicare's computer system.

With that revelation, the college's medical review committee (MRC) began investigating Dr. Hsu's records and discovered that he had failed to complete all the paperwork associated with the treatments he had been providing patients. It wasn't a matter of inflating the number of patients he had seen or claiming to have provided non-existent care. It was a matter of degree, of detail, an understandable oversight given the demands on Dr. Hsu's time.

Within days, Dr. Hsu was informed that the MRC was denying half of all the income he had received over the previous year, or about $80,000, and charging him $20,119 in interest and $8100 to cover the cost of the audit—over $108,000 in total. He was ordered to repay the amount immediately. Failing to do so would cause OHIP to withhold all payments to him until the amount had been collected, with interest.

Dr. Hsu was devastated not just by the amount but by the fact that the MRC's decision impugned his reputation. "In my office, when I am under pressure," Dr. Hsu explained, "I often write notes down on a different page. But patients ask many questions. I talk to them. I take the notes that are necessary." Then he added: "It is very shameful for me, accusing me of stealing from the public purse. I did not. I did everything I am supposed to do, and more."[1] Without exception, every colleague and every patient praised Dr. Hsu for his professionalism, his dedication, his generosity, and his honesty. "He never turned down any sick child," his wife, Irene Hsu, pointed out. "He [just] did not have time to write down all the negative comments."[2] None of this made an impact on the MRC; its ruling stood.

Under the MRC's terms, Dr. Hsu could appeal its decision but only while following the committee's own guilty-until-proven-innocent terms. These included the following:

- *A fee of $1000 per day for each committee member considering the matter as an audit board. Since each audit board consisted of five members, this represented an expense of $5000 per day to be paid by the physician whose records were being reviewed.*
- *The $5000-per-day payment would be applied even if the resulting audit discovered an overpayment to the physician as small as one dollar.*

- *Interest would be retroactively applied to any resulting claim from the fifteenth of the month following the last date of a review period. Typically, this was a minimum of three years before the physician was advised of receiving any overpayment. Should the physician repay 100 percent of any overpayment upon being informed of the matter, he or she would still be responsible for at least three years' interest on the claimed amount.*
- *Should the physician be totally exonerated of all charges brought by the MRC, neither it nor OHIP was under any obligation to repay the physician's costs.*

With those rules in place, Dr. Hsu had little choice except to pay OHIP the $108,000 it demanded through the MRC and the Ontario College of Physicians and Surgeons, which enforced the ruling. Not having that much cash on hand, he withdrew it from his RRSP account, virtually wiping out the retirement savings he had accrued through his professional career. The money ended the MRC's claim against him, but it failed to end the torment Dr. Hsu endured. His reputation in his community and his profession, he believed, had been tarnished beyond repair.

*At no point was Dr. Hsu accused of overbilling OHIP. In fact, his billings for consultation were only one-third the provincial average. His only crime was a failure to follow a complicated system of billing codes, many of them out of date. Too distressed by his experience to even involve himself in a growing wave of protest among Ontario doctors over the draconian power of the MRC, Dr. Hsu kept his feelings to himself until, on a cold spring day in April 2003, his body was discovered in Lake Ontario, an apparent suicide.**

IT IS ALL ABOUT STREAMLINING and cost control.

Private health care systems rest on a fairly steady three-legged base comprising the service provider (the physician, surgeon, dentist);

*Provincial health ministry officials rejected the suggestion of a direct link between the audit and Dr. Hsu's death.

the service receiver (the patient); and the funding source (the private insurer).

In most cases, the patient either pays the doctor directly and submits a receipt for reimbursement from the funding source, or forwards an invoice to his or her insurance company. This makes it difficult, but not impossible, for the provider to file a claim for unperformed service. It also reduces administration expenses for the insurer, who can assume that few patients will engage in fraud by claiming to have received treatment for which the provider is paid.

Our public health system, like those in most other countries, also employs a three-legged base, although it sidesteps asking patients to confirm they received the treatment for which the physician is paid. In this case, the third leg is trust. By assuming that physicians will not ask to be paid for unperformed services, public health systems avoid the enormous quantity of paperwork inevitably associated with receiving, recording, confirming, and paying claims.

The assumption has been proven faulty from time to time, and at least one of these instances, according to various sources, may have inspired changes to the province's health insurance act, leading to the harsh rules applied to Dr. Hsu and others.

This event in the late 1990s involved an unnamed forty-five-year-old GP who claimed to be seeing between 150 and 300 patients per day, launching an audit to investigate how one doctor could treat an average of sixteen patients per hour. After winning a legal challenge launched by the physician to block the audit, the MRC reviewed several hundred chart entries and interviewed many of the patients. Most of the chart entries, the doctor's assessment of each patient's condition, consisted of one word—"better"—and over half the patients interviewed challenged the number of times that the doctor claimed they had consulted him. Psychotherapy sessions with many patients had also been billed to OHIP; the doctor had no records of these session and claimed he had destroyed them without providing an explanation for this action.[3]

OHIP managed to recover more than $1 million from the GP, and Ontario soon revised its health act to introduce the stern rules applied to Dr. Hsu and others.

Although OHIP is reluctant to openly discuss enforcement of its rules regarding billing and payments,[4] it appears that a computer located in Kingston, Ontario, monitors physician billings and, applying undisclosed features of its program, "red-flags" entries that conflict with certain undefined standards. With an estimated 20,000 physicians filing claims with OHIP, the government plan states that it conducts only about 100 audits each year. Considering that the system is responsible for over $5 billion paid annually to doctors in response to 150 million claims, Canadians may feel that this is a minimal standard to prevent fraud—and it is.

The difficulty arises with those harsh standards installed after the case of the sixteen-patients-per-hour GP—the ones that devastated not only Dr. Hsu but several other physicians as well. Whenever an OHIP audit appeared to reflect bureaucratic obtuseness, the tale was traded among doctors as an example of a potentially hostile system that could easily envelop any medical professional within its tentacles. Among the examples that made the rounds of physicians as proof of government bureaucracy gone mad were the following:[5]

- A neurologist was forced to pay back $40,000 in OHIP fees for failing to perform rectal and breast examinations on patients suffering from Lou Gehrig's disease.
- A specialist in diabetes treatment was penalized $100,000 because she saw her patients every three months, a schedule recommended by the Canadian Diabetes Association but deemed too frequent by OHIP.
- When performing annual physical examinations during October and November, many family physicians provided patients with flu shots, saving them an extra trip to receive this government-encouraged treatment. Through 2003, however, dispensing a flu shot at the same

time as performing a physical examination negated payment for the examination. OHIP fees for a physical were $50; for a flu shot, $8. Combining them did not earn the physician $58 but only $8 for the flu shot alone.

- Toronto neuro-ophthalmologist Dr. Irene Vanek specialized in treating eye tumours, and her skills and experience generated patients throughout the province, sent by doctors who wanted them to be in the best possible hands. But the number of complex eye examinations she recorded triggered an alert in OHIP's computer, and Dr. Vanek was ordered to repay over $100,000 simply because her practice exceeded the norm for eye specialists. "What is too many?" Dr. Vanek asked when informed of the ruling. "I do this for a living.... All of a sudden I'm supposed to pay a tremendous amount of money for work I have already done? ... I really honestly cannot do this anymore. But I love the work. So my [choice is] that I go to the States."[6]
- In one of the more widely covered and ridiculed cases launched by the MRC, a paediatric respirologist was ordered to pay back almost half of all OHIP fees collected over several years. The physician, Dr. Brian Lyttle, was a highly regarded practitioner in that particular specialty, acclaimed for his treatment of asthmatic children. Regardless of his vaunted reputation, he found that 85 percent of the fees he collected for General Assessment of patients, a procedure for which OHIP paid $53.60, were downgraded to Intermediate Assessment, a procedure worth, on OHIP's fee schedule, only $24.80. The difference, amounting to perhaps $100,000 over the period in question, was to be paid by Dr. Lyttle immediately. Why the reassessment? Because Dr. Lyttle, in his diagnosis and treatment of asthma in his patients, failed to conduct rectal and gynaecological examinations. Despite rules clearly intended to derail any such action, Dr. Lyttle appealed and won.

Lest it appear that Ontario is alone in shattering a good deal of trust among doctors through its system of remuneration, other provinces have their share of tales as well. The impact of each reverberates among the health profession with the refrain "It could be me."

In the B.C. town of Ladysmith, on Vancouver Island, Dr. Julian Lisinski successfully appealed an order to return almost $500,000 in fees paid to him by the province's public health care system after he moved to the community and replaced a retiring physician with a substantial practice. "In spring 2000, I heard I was to be audited because I was 'seeing too many patients,'" Dr. Lisinski recalls. "I had inherited a lot of chronic patients in my practice. The auditors arrived and took 80 charts, interrogated my staff, and refused to check for more information. When I protested my innocence, I was told to keep quiet. It seemed everybody thought me guilty. A hearing was scheduled, and it took me more than 200 hours to prepare my defence. After [my] report was sent in, the audit process was abandoned without explanation."[7]

Like Ontario's, British Columbia's system depends on statistical profiles to identify potential abusers, although it has begun moving away from heavy reliance on these alone. The complexity of a physician's practice is considered before an audit is launched, and the province randomly surveys about 75,000 residents each year to confirm that they received the services and treatment claimed by their physicians.

Representatives of the provincial health care systems will argue that many audits do not lead to charges or levies against the physician's income. In a culture of professionals who value their independence, however, tales such as those related above are sparks among dry timber, and many doctors both fear and fume at government bureaucratic actions. The concern of Ontario physicians has been fuelled by an extensive report on medical audit practices in Ontario. When stories of Dr. Hsu's experience with Ontario's MRC generated outrage among physicians and the public, Ontario premier Dalton McGuinty froze the audit procedure in September 2004 and ordered that a report on the system's faults be prepared, along with proposals to correct them.

The report, submitted by the Honourable Peter de C. Cory, arrived on the desk of Ontario's minister of health and long-term care in April 2005. Its executive summary was about as critical of the auditing procedure as might be expected from a government bureaucrat:

> The medical audit system in Ontario has had a debilitating—and in some cases devastating—effect on the physicians of Ontario and their families. In turn, it has had a negative impact on the delivery of health services in the province. It has undermined Ontario's attractiveness as a place to practice medicine and has led some physicians to curtail their practices so as to stay within average billing patterns.[8]

Among the 118 recommendations proposed by Justice Cory were these:

- The creation of a new and independent board composed of ten members of the public and thirty practising physicians.
- New record-keeping requirements that "take account of the realities of medical practice," incorporating templates to assist physicians.
- The elimination in most cases of direct recovery of fee payments, which had permitted OHIP to withhold new claims filed by the physician even while the physician was appealing the audit committee's decision.
- The right of a physician to be represented by a lawyer or agent.
- The right of appeal first to an appeal and review board and, failing that, to the divisional court.
- Flexibility in determining appropriate remedies.

The College of Physicians and Surgeons in Ontario hailed the Cory report as "a civil rights proposal for Ontario doctors," noting that it reflected all of the concerns expressed by the college on behalf of doctors. Ontario health minister George Smitherman promised swift implementation of the report's recommendations. Justice Cory, in turn, observed that every individual physician and every medical association making submissions agreed that some form of auditing was necessary in the fee-for-service honour system. Observers fully expected the medical profession to break into choruses of "Ding dong! The witch is dead!"

Over the next two years, the euphoria began to fade when no action was taken by the Ontario government to implement Justice Cory's proposals. Several explanations were proffered: the changes required new legislation, no timeline had been prepared to launch the new system, the legislature was backed up with other business.

Meanwhile, the Ontario Medical Association named Dr. Anthony Hsu the winner of its Glenn Sawyer Service Award, bestowed on recipients to recognize their significant service to the OMA, the medical profession, and the general public. Posthumously, of course.

THE PROSPECTS OF PREMIUM PAY FOR PREMIUM PERFORMANCE

Any remuneration system that adds a layer or two between the vendor and the buyer inevitably generates friction from time to time. Ideally, buyers of health care services would pay the providers directly, much as consumers purchased eggs from a poultry farmer two or three generations ago. Whether the new layers involve government fee-for-service systems, private health care insurers, or some other arrangement, one side or the other will express concern and dissatisfaction. In Canada, the dissatisfaction about remuneration is generally voiced by physicians and surgeons seeking a greater role for the private sector. Would introducing the private sector eliminate friction? The U.S. experience offers a clue.

In the United States, most dissatisfaction flows in an opposite direction, with private health insurance providers expressing concern about the quality of service being delivered by physicians. The insurers' concern has stimulated a remuneration system that threatens to spill across the border into Canada. Known as Pay for Performance, or

P4P, the concept extends the "piecework" nature of fee-for-service to a new level.

P4P programs provide extra financial rewards to doctors whose care meets certain standards or "measures" intended to gauge quality and cost-effectiveness. The theory is that physicians will save the insurers more through these efficiencies than they will earn from P4P bonuses, creating a net gain to the insurance providers. One estimate claims 30 million Americans are enrolled in private health plans with P4P programs, many in health maintenance organizations (HMOs) and preferred provider organizations (PPOs).* A typical P4P program offers incentive bonuses of up to 10 percent according to a published schedule.

Advocates of P4P programs will object to this comparison, but the strategy is directly related to incentives commonly offered to salespeople as a means of building profits for the employer. The motives are similar: sell more widgets and earn an end-of-year bonus; save the insurer money and earn a performance dividend. Professional athletes, stockbrokers, automobile salespeople, and others are motivated to earn more money for better performance—why not physicians and surgeons?

"Pay for performance assumes that we won't deliver services if we're not being paid enough for it," one Canadian physician commented. "It attacks the concept of self-governance and dedication associated with professionals in every field, especially medicine."

Remarkably, some opponents of P4P in the United States saw this private-sector initiative as a camel's-nose-in-the-tent shift toward a dreaded national health plan. One foe of P4P revealed more about his paranoia regarding publicly funded health care than his concern about a P4P system when he commented, "[O]nce the basic idea of P4P is

*HMOs are multiple-practice clinics, similar to many in Canada, to which insured patients must go for treatment; PPOs are lists of physicians and health providers from which patients may choose for insured treatment.

accepted, a great many doctors will expect more money and practice as they always have, to the best of their ability. Then they will be paid less, or have to justify being paid correctly via more audits, forms and other onerous efforts (extra work for which they will NOT be paid). The budget will continue to explode under the compassions of government-supplied care. More doctors will face charges of fraud, fewer will take Medicare/Medicaid, and the whole wreck will wheeze closer and closer to full nationalization. Then America's patients will really get to see what performance based on pay feels like."[9]

The P4P concept has drifted on the wind into Canada, where some in the medical community are giving it serious consideration. Not surprisingly, the response has been more negative here than in the United States.

"It's like being handed a tip for good service," said one Canadian physician, requesting anonymity. "I'm not a busboy or a cab driver. If I'm dealing with a patient's health and comfort, I'm doing the very best I can and I want everyone to assume that. Paying me more won't make me work better."

Dr. Gordon Guyatt has another take on the idea of P4P and the bonuses offered to exceptional physicians. "The danger is," Dr. Guyatt comments in his office at McMaster University Medical Centre, where he teaches internal medicine, "if I want my patients to have good outcomes, I'll choose to treat people who aren't sick. For example, if I want to control glucose levels in diabetic patients, this will be easier to do with people in high socio-economic levels than those with a low socio-economic status." People in higher social and economic categories, Dr. Guyatt explains, will tend to get more exercise, maintain healthier diets, and refrain from smoking and drinking excessively. "So if I am interested in maximizing my income based on performance levels, I'll choose to treat as many wealthy people as possible."

On that basis, he suggests, P4P programs would have to be developed with great care to ensure that the system wasn't being exploited—something that would be difficult to implement and manage. "It's one way the U.S. private health care system can claim it is more efficient than Canada's public system," he explains. "It chooses to treat healthy rich people, leaving the lower socio-economic groups to seek care from public hospitals."[10]

Private insurers south of the border counter that doctors misrepresent the goals and potential benefits of P4P. Although the United States is facing an estimated 8.2 percent annual increase in health care costs over the next decade, "evidence shows that quality of care has not been improving," claims Jon Conklin, vice-president of performance measurement at Thomson Medstat, a health care information company. In Conklin's opinion, P4P should not be viewed as a means of pressuring physicians to benefit the insurers. "It's basically a best-practices model. It tries to pinpoint those physicians who consistently provide the best-quality care in the most cost-effective manner, then sets the bar for other physicians to reach."[11]

Representing the views of many in the private insurance industry, Conklin trots out a stable of rationales to justify P4P: bonuses would be paid according to "a set of sound, well-established and well-defined measures that are agreed upon by physicians"; the concept makes good business sense "because it results in better care, which improves patients' health care outcomes, leading to improved on-the-job productivity and lower health care costs"; and "by demonstrating a commitment to quality, P4P programs can also improve public relations for health plans and employers."

The programs cover a range of performance measurements. According to one source,[12] in determining exceptional performance qualifying for a bonus, 50 percent of P4P systems measure in-patient admissions and the frequency with which a physician chooses to prescribe generic drugs over more expensive brand-name alternatives. The use of electronic information technology to record and exchange patient records earns another benefit in many programs, along with a dozen or more other parameters. The weight assigned to each varies widely—one program may determine that 50 percent of a bonus rating is based on clinical performance, 40 percent on efficiency measures, and 10 percent on the use of information technology, while another may juggle the proportions and add new references to the use of specialists, generic drug scripts, hospital admissions, and other elements.

To the surprise of U.S. physicians who reacted to P4P like tomcats confronting a Rottweiler, the American Academy of Family Physicians (AAFP) endorsed the idea, proposing that a nation-wide P4P program adhere to seven principles:

1. It focuses on improved quality of care.
2. It supports the physician–patient relationship.
3. It utilizes evidence-based clinical guidelines.
4. It involves practising physicians in the program design.
5. It employs reliable, accurate, and scientifically valid data.
6. It provides positive physician incentives.
7. It offers voluntary physician participation.[13]

All well and good. But none of this is directly linked to the private insurance providers' basic motive for proposing P4P: *To cut the costs of remuneration to physicians and surgeons.* No matter how you dissect that fact, P4P remains a zero-sum goal, and if payments to successful "best practices" doctors are increased, the potential earnings of those who fail to qualify must be reduced for maximum savings to be realized. The costs of managing a system that tracks every prescription written by a physician and every admission and referral she provides to her patients can be picked from only one pocket: the physician's.

Still, the debate continues. Proponents of P4P point to a U.K. example more in line with Canada's health care system, and one that appears to deliver the benefits expected from an incentive program.

A PERFORMANCE-BASED SYSTEM THAT APPEARS TO WORK

Britain's National Health Service (NHS) has for many years employed a modified P4P system, tied in with a complex remuneration program. In the traditional contract, dating back to the inception of the program in 1948, British GPs enrolled in the NHS earned their income according to four different measures: fee for service (15 percent of total income); capitation (40 percent); salary (30 percent); and capital and information technology (15 percent).[14] In 2004, it was generally agreed that the capitation portion of the formula represented the least satisfying option because it failed to adequately account for patient age, lifestyle, and socio-economic status, which in theory might discourage doctors from assuming the care of high-risk (and thus high-maintenance) patients. To correct this weakness in the system, the NHS offered personal medical services (PMS) contracts in place of the traditional agreements. In place of fee-for-service, PMS contracts set a base salary that varies according to local circumstances, and offered incentive payments to physicians who demonstrated high-quality levels in access and prescribing medicines.

Building on this history of multiple income categories and potential incentives, the NHS tested a primary-care incentive program in East Kent over two years, beginning in 1998. Almost four out of five doctors in the region agreed to participate in the test, which focused on meeting targets related to the control and treatment of thirteen conditions, including angina, heart failure, and epilepsy. The standards were easily quantified. For example, among the measured conditions, physicians were required to keep recorded blood-pressure ratings below 160/90 for at least 85 percent of patients, unless a validated reason was documented. Participating physicians received a lump-sum payment of £3000 (approximately Cdn$6500) per year, or about 5 percent of earnings, to be repaid if the performance standards were not achieved.

The test appeared to have achieved success on many fronts. Notable improvements in the management of chronic disease were ascribed to the program's multi-faceted structure, and most physicians supported the concept enthusiastically. According to at least one review of the program, the incentive to participate and meet established standards was not entirely monetary. Many doctors said they were motivated by a sense of professional autonomy and ownership, and they used the results of their assessment as an incentive to improve their performance.

The East Kent example proved so encouraging that it formed the basis for an entirely new contract between the NHS and physicians, launched in April 2004. Under the revised arrangement, remuneration rules were simplified, the capitation formula was more fairly assessed, and an incentive scheme measuring 146 indicators across seven areas of practice was introduced. About half of the incentive payments are linked to clinic assessments of patients; the remainder reflect performance in practice organization and patient experience. Of ten clinical indicators, three—coronary heart disease, hypertension, and diabetes—are the most heavily weighted.

The program appears to be well received and widely supported in the medical community, although critics point out that the system was accompanied by a substantial injection of new funding, which helped avoid the pitfall of robbing average performers to reward above-average participants. It also raised the spectre that some practice areas may suffer when physicians focus more intently on those tied to performance incentives. Mental health, for example, may become less of an issue than heart disease because the performance points assigned to diagnosing, referring, and monitoring that condition are not nearly as high. Similarly, "cream-skimming" may occur, leading physicians to favour healthy, low-maintenance patients and avoid practising among disadvantaged members of the population.

The British experience suggests a potential benefit for Canadians, whose health care system is aligned more closely with that of the United Kingdom than that of the United States. It should be noted, however, that the U.K. system permits much wider participation of the private sector than Canada's, which may or may not be an obstacle to its replication here. Nor should the substantial injection by the NHS of new funds, in conjunction with the new contract, be ignored.

Will physicians and surgeons on either side of the Canada–U.S. border be satisfied with any remuneration system other than direct patient-to-doctor arrangements? Probably not. Yet observers agree that some control must be exercised over rising health care costs, and a modified version of Britain's NHS contract may hold the solution.

5

WORDS FROM THE RIGHT
THE PRIVATE-ENTERPRISE OPTION

"We've been in the forefront of the voices warning about waiting times," says Brett Skinner of the Fraser Institute. "In the beginning we were called right-wing whackos for measuring it. Some claimed it wasn't true and now every politician in the country campaigns on the basis of reducing waiting times."[1]

Skinner smiles wryly at the fact. He represents the rallying point for those Canadians who are convinced that their health care system can be saved only with the infusion of services from the private sector.

"Right-wing whacko" is hardly the description to be hung on Skinner. Highly educated, articulate, and low-key, he speaks with quiet authority in his cramped office above Yonge Street in Toronto, his initial wariness dissolving with each opportunity to explain his organization's position.

As the country's most prominent and most vocal proponent of right-wing policies, the Fraser Institute comments on a wide range of issues, ranging from taxes and school report cards to social affairs and globalization. In recent years, it has become best known for its often strident support of introducing the private sector into Canada's health care system. Since many of its economic and political stances often mirror those of other free-enterprise advocates, most of them in the United States, some Canadians suspect that Fraser proposes a health care system similar to the American one, a concept Skinner is quick to dismiss. "That idea is completely designed to distract from what we're actually saying," Skinner responds. "The U.S. government interferes in health care just as much as Canada. They just make different mistakes."

The Fraser Institute makes a clear distinction between the two countries when evaluating the topic. "When we compare Canada's health care system to other countries, we purposely exclude the United States and Mexico because they do not have universal health insurance coverage as a social goal. We only compare Canada with other countries that have the same goal."

When the institute examines Canada's performance against other industrialized countries, excluding the United States, we appear woefully inadequate in various ways, especially the wait times required for many specific procedures and the economic impossibility of sustaining the steady annual increase in health care costs that have been recorded since the advent of publicly funded health care in this country. Cynics may point out that per capita expenditures on health care coverage in the United States have been growing at an even faster clip than they have in Canada, but since the institute clearly states that it ignores statistics from that country, Skinner prefers to compare us with Switzerland, which has, like Canada, the goal of universal health insurance coverage.

"Switzerland has a totally privately delivered health insurance system," Skinner points out, comparing health care for the Swiss with private automobile insurance in Canada. "In this country, you cannot drive a car without being insured. Switzerland says, If you want to live in Switzerland you have to have health insurance. If you don't have the money to afford it, we'll give you a low-income subsidy so you can buy it."

This combination of a purchase mandate, tight government controls, and a low-income subsidy enables the Swiss to meet the same goals as Canada with substantially more sustainability because the bulk of the funding comes from private sources. In many ways, the Swiss government's primary activity is monitoring the competitive sector to ensure high levels of quality and value for consumers.

The experience of the clever Swiss, Skinner hastens to add, exposes the goal of those who are critics of adding a role for the private sector. "Their real interest is egalitarianism," he says with an air of finality. "They don't want some people getting quicker access to health care than other people. That's why they insist on a public monopoly."

Skinner argues that universal health insurance coverage was the real consensus that medicare was built on in the beginning. Canadians, he acknowledges, wanted to make sure that poor people could access medical care without financial barriers. "But you can do that without a public health insurance monopoly," he points out. "You can do this with both a public insurance system and a private insurance system operating in tandem, and make absolute gains for everybody." Then, tossing in a Winston Churchill quote on the evils of socialism, he smiles and adds: "With the current way of doing things, we're making everybody equally miserable."

SKINNER'S POSITION REFLECTS the Fraser Institute's basic philosophy, which can be summed up in the observation that the private sector can do anything the public sector can do and do it faster, easier, and cheaper. As U.S. president Ronald Reagan liked to put it, "Government isn't the solution to your problem; government *is* the problem!" That single phrase helped launch the neo-con movement that dominated U.S. politics for a quarter of a century, with predictable spillover to Canada. Unfortunately, like all simplified generalizations, it manages to conceal reality beneath a few memorable words.

For example, Fraser and its supporters report that Canada is one of a handful of countries providing universal health care for its citizens with no official provision for private enterprise. The rest of the group, they delight in pointing out, is made up of Cuba, North Korea, and China. Countering that position, groups such as the Council of Canadians note that only two industrialized countries reject the notion of government-supported universal health care: South Africa and the United States.

The core of the institute's argument is firmly rooted in the unassailable notion that we cannot continue to absorb constant annual increases in health care costs that exceed both the inflation rate and GDP growth. In a lengthy, widely distributed study co-authored by Skinner,[2] the Fraser Institute predicted that most Canadian provinces would be spending 50 percent of their entire revenue on health care by 2020, with Saskatchewan and Manitoba achieving the mark in 2015.

Straight-line projections of any statistic, whether it is government funding of medicare or global-warming trends, are both the simplest and the most dangerous means of assessing future risks. Take a straight-line projection of Canada's spending on rising health care costs far enough, for example, and it becomes evident that, at some point, it will represent 100 percent of the country's GDP, obviously a specious argument.

Still, how concerned should we become when a provincial health minister announces, with great fanfare, the injection of $120 million of taxpayers' money into the public health care system to upgrade high-tech imaging equipment, as Ontario health minister George Smitherman did in February 2005? The amount was one of many new expenditures announced by the Ontario government that year; together, they helped to boost the province's health care expense account to its highest level. Right-wing critics of the public system saw this expenditure as unnecessary. Private clinics, they pointed out, would make a similar investment in the equipment, if they were permitted to do so, without draining the public purse. What's more, the private operators would almost certainly operate the clinics with greater efficiency.

Supporters from the other side stated their case in different terms. What if the province, they suggested, had produced 5000 more motor vehicles than the year before, all of them purchased by its citizens, for $120 million in sales? Business observers would quite rightly celebrate the burgeoning health of the economy. But if 5000 citizens received hip replacements to relieve agonizing pain and assist them in becoming healthy, productive citizens, the right wing would consider the expense a drain on the economy and evidence of unsustainable growth in health care spending. Yet what does Canada need most—another 5000 vehicles on the road or 5000 citizens free of crippling pain?[3]

Before plunging further into the debate about the role of private enterprise in the country's health care system, let's acknowledge a fact that Skinner and his Fraser cohorts manage to sidestep: *Health care in Canada is government-funded but almost exclusively privately provided.* Physicians and surgeons are essentially private contractors, choosing where to practise and which specialty, if any, to pursue. They are regulated not by government agencies directly but by professional associations that grant and restrict, if necessary, privileges. They hire and fire staff, invest in their own facilities and instruments, and are responsible for their own retirement savings and other concerns shared by every citizen.

True, compensation arrives via an arm of a provincial government, as opposed to a private insurance provider, or out of the pockets of patients. And it is also true, as we have seen, that governments from time to time have demonstrated excessive zeal to the point of harassment with some physicians, a situation that deserves addressing and correction. But to presume that every medical professional in the country labours white-coated in some bureaucratic gulag is simply not true. And to suggest that private industry represents lily-white redemption from the evils of government control is simply specious.

Those who champion free-market philosophy take heart from commentaries such as the one offered by Larry MacDonald, sometime columnist for *Canadian Business* magazine. Decrying the fact that a friend was able to jump a queue for cancer treatment thanks to the intervention of a neighbour who worked in the medical profession, the author referenced the Adscam scandal that brought down the federal Liberal party in 2006. "The bigger government gets," MacDonald intoned, "the more the opportunities for corruption, favouritism, embezzlement and all those other agency problems economists theorize about."[4]

In another anti-government-funded health care polemic, medical student and columnist David Gratzer stated that problems in Canada's medicare system "all stem from the same source—health care is run by the government. In their zeal to control costs, bureaucrats have worked tirelessly to create regulations, policies and guidelines. As a result the health care sector sees as much innovation and creative thinking as Soviet agriculture in the 1950s."[5] Gratzer, who wrote a book proposing medical savings accounts, or MSAs, as an alternative to direct government funding,* and MacDonald appear to be fighting the same foe from opposite sides of the battlefield, with Gratzer suggesting that government is a skinflint when it comes to funding the service, and MacDonald charging government is too profligate. Of the two, Gratzer's promotion of MSAs appears the most provocative and promising.

Arguing that "the fundamental flaw of the medicare system is that patients bear no direct costs for medical services they receive,"[6] Gratzer promotes the purity of the free market as a means of reducing waste and costs. The problem with a universal health system, according to Gratzer, is "perverse incentives." The system is vulnerable to patients who overuse it because they are not directly responsible for the cost, physicians who maximize profit on a fee-for-service basis, and health care administrators who enhance their budgets by dipping deeper into the publicly funded pot of money.

From that argument, Gratzer moves to decry the current system because it fails to deliver five basic elements needed for good health care:

1. Quality—the latest technology, modern facilities, well-trained professionals
2. Timeliness—quick diagnosis and treatment of illnesses
3. Cost-effectiveness—value for money spent

**Code Blue: Reviving Canada's Healthcare System* (Toronto: ECW Press, 1999).

4. Patient Orientation—serving patients, not providers, free of bureaucratic dominance
5. Accessibility—medical care for all who require it

No matter what their political stripe, few Canadians could argue with those five measures of performance. Gratzer, however, adamantly disagrees that universal health care funded exclusively through taxes can achieve its goals because at least four of them require private enterprise to work most effectively. Accessibility, the fifth horseman, can be assured through MSAs.

The concept of medical savings accounts sprang from the imagination of J. Patrick Rooney, chairman emeritus of the Indiana-based Golden Rule Insurance Company. Watching his firm's income dissipate because skyrocketing health insurance premiums were causing an alarming increase in cancelled policies, Rooney proposed that companies and individuals increase the annual deductible for each policy from $250 to $2000 per individual and $3000 per family, slashing the premium payments. Policyholders balked at the idea, assessing the concept not as insurance but as anti-insurance. Except for catastrophic coverage, most annual insurance payments were under $2000 per individual anyway; why should policyholders accept responsibility for most anticipated medical expenses and pay Golden Rule as well?

Rooney found more enthusiastic support from congressional representative Newt Gingrich, who was promising to slash the U.S. government's Medicare spending by $270 billion over the next seven years. Even Gingrich knew this was not possible without dangling a respectable alternative in front of voters. Then Rooney, who was well connected with Republicans at the federal level, strode into the congressman's office bearing a silver platter. On it was this idea: Offer taxpayers an MSA into which they or their employers can deposit $1500 annually, tax-free. Money in the MSA would cover the high deductible amounts on the private insurance policies that Rooney's company and others would market. Payments made from the MSA for health care would not be taxable. At the end of each calendar year, MSA holders could withdraw the balance as taxable income or leave it within the account to accrue over years in the future.

Gingrich loved the idea. In fact, he loved it so much that he proposed shifting funds out of the country's Medicare program into MSAs for seniors who could use the diverted dollars to pay premiums to companies like Golden Rule for catastrophic insurance coverage. It was a socialist-capitalist dream formula: The federal government pays billions each year to private enterprise, which will provide health care coverage for senior citizens and thus fulfil its obligations to them. There could be collateral damage, however. Seniors with MSAs, knowing they could keep any balance remaining in their accounts at year's end, would become judicious in their spending on health care, perhaps preferring to buy television sets, window blinds, or golf clubs and shifting all that spending into the consumer goods sector. Critics pointed out that removing those billions of seniors' dollars from Medicare would effectively doom the program. Gingrich smiled.[7]

Even Gingrich's own Republican Congressional Budget Office suggested that MSAs would likely cost Medicare, while it still breathed, billions of dollars extra. This was countered by the National Center for Policy Analysis (NCPA), whose actuary declared that MSAs would save the government as much as $195 billion. This seemed impressive, until it was noted that the NCPA was a right-wing think-tank funded by the erudite J. Patrick Rooney.

Still, some aspects of MSAs initially were appealing to American corporations and, surprisingly, to foreign governments. When chemical giant Dupont offered MSAs to its employees, however, fewer than 4 percent chose the option. Almost all of them were young and single with no history of health problems, attracted by the prospect of a thousand or so extra dollars in their pockets at year's end. Dupont quickly withdrew the deal, recognizing that providing MSAs to those who rarely used the coverage would drive up costs of providing coverage for those needing it. Beyond the borders of the United States, the MSA concept has been adopted only by the city state of Singapore, where it accounts for just 10 percent of all health expenditures.

Gratzer's promotion of MSAs as an answer to Canada's health care woes drew fawning approval from both the Fraser Institute and the Montreal Economic Institute (MEI). The MEI, which identifies its mission as proposing "original and innovative solutions for the crafting of efficient public policies, using successful reforms applied elsewhere as models,"[8] takes special delight in offering the U.S. health system as a model of successful reform.

While agreeing that 45 million U.S. citizens lack health insurance coverage, the MEI suggests that this is not an insurance problem but "largely a job problem" because 57 percent of uninsured Americans under 65 had no full-time job or lived in a household in which no one else held a full-time job. One interpretation: the unemployed either do not need or do not deserve health services. Spending on health care in the United States is substantially higher than elsewhere, the MEI agrees—14.7 percent of GDP versus 8.4 percent for other OECD countries—but this is necessary to provide Americans with "access to the latest medical technologies and the most effective treatments, with short waiting times, despite the gaps in their healthcare system."[9] Unfortunately, the organization fails to relate this highly excessive GDP investment by the United States to its lacklustre comparison with OECD countries on average lifespan and infant mortality.

POLITICAL PHILOSOPHY has no bearing on the question of reducing wait times, of course. But the assumption that a direct connection exists between this systemic weakness and federal funding is too simple by half. And alleging that only government-funded activities are subject to corruption, favouritism, and embezzlement, as MacDonald did in his *Canadian Business* column, is nothing less than outrageous.

As we have seen, the Fraser Institute does not include the United States in its assessment of Canada's health care system because it does not offer universal government-funded medicare and thus, the institute believes, its record on the matter is immaterial. This is a curious stance for an organization that proposes minimum public-sector involvement and maximum private-enterprise participation in virtually every other function remotely associated with government. Fraser people would claim it is a matter of comparing apples to apples, but if your overall philosophy is based on promoting the status of oranges, wouldn't you want to include the tropical fruit somewhere in the assessment?

If so, the institute would have to deal with certain realities that weaken some of the harsher attacks made by its supporters against public funding where medical coverage is concerned. Larry MacDonald's argument, in his *Canadian Business* column, that government funding inevitably leads to corruption and embezzlement, and the suggestion that private enterprise acts with greater discretion, is simply misleading. In December 2000 HCA, the largest for-profit hospital chain in the United States, agreed that it had fraudulently charged the federal government for services it had never provided. The agreement came with a $1-billion payment in criminal fines, civil damages, and penalties, the largest fraud settlement ever reached by the justice department.[10] The company had quickly changed its name from Columbia Healthcare Corp., as soon as it became apparent that the federal government's charges were basically indefensible, in an attempt to disassociate itself from the bad publicity.

Were HCA's shenanigans out of character for such firms? Supporters of the private-sector option may claim they were. If so, then the actions of two other major private-sector providers convicted of similar charges, Tenet Healthcare Corporation and HealthSouth, must also be "out of character." Yet they are completely *in* character with similar goings-on documented in infamous cases involving Enron, Worldcom, and several others.

Even if we assume that every other for-profit hospital operation in the United States operated with the highest moral standards, one indisputable fact arises: *U.S. hospitals owned by investors with the aim of making money are less cost-efficient than non-profit hospitals, which includes virtually every facility in Canada.* This is not a left-wing pipe dream but the conclusion of a carefully monitored study by Dr. P. J. Devereaux, a cardiologist at McMaster University. The study reviewed medical results from hundreds of U.S. for-profit hospitals involving an estimated 350,000 patients.[11] Its initial findings were reviewed by researchers at Harvard Medical School, effectively neutralizing charges of anti-American bias by the Canadians. The Harvard reviewers estimated that the for-profit hospitals could save US$6 billion annually if they converted to non-profit operations. Even more remarkable, they claimed that patients would have received better care. "Investor-owned hospitals charge outrageous prices for inferior care," one member of the Harvard team stated. "The for-profits skimp on nurses but spend lavishly on their executives and paper pushers."[12]

Dr. Gordon Guyatt, admittedly not a supporter of the private-care option, provides a credible explanation for the poorer performance of for-profit health providers. In Guyatt's view, any efficiency advantage gained from private enterprise—and Guyatt is not prepared to admit that this occurs—is quickly absorbed within two layers that are essentially non-existent in the public sector. One is the need for private corporations to generate profit for their investors, usually to a target level of 15 percent annually. "So right away," Guyatt notes, "you're reduced to 85 percent of your potential." Along with this comes the impact of insurance companies that provide coverage for those not eligible for U.S. Medicare. "Insurance companies are always busy evaluating claims," he points out, "and frequently try to avoid paying them. They're also aiming for 15 percent annual profit."

Achieving profit margins for the insurers involves paying large numbers of people to review, question, assess, and negotiate the lowest possible payments, costs that are inevitably added to health care premiums. "In the U.S.," Guyatt says, "about thirty-two cents of every dollar invested in health care is spent on administration costs, which do nothing to treat patients. In Canada, it's about seventeen cents on every dollar, or barely half as much. Where is the saving?"[13]

PERCENTAGE OF NATIONAL HEALTH EXPENDITURES SPENT ON ADMINISTRATION AND INSURANCE, 2005

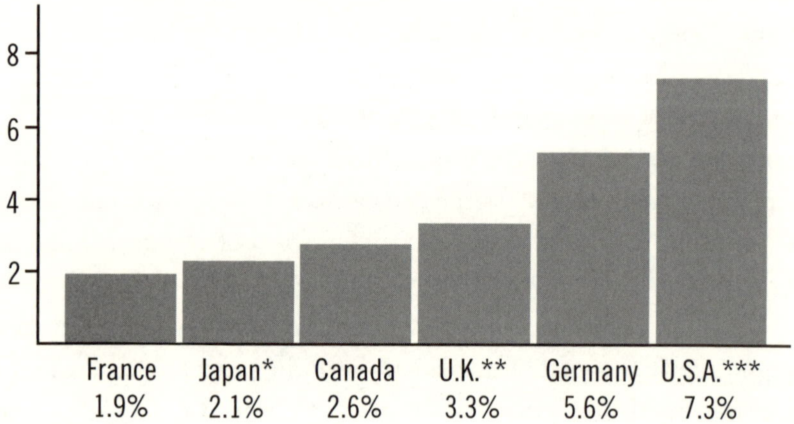

* 2002
** 1999
*** INCLUDES CLAIMS ADMINISTRATION, UNDERWRITING, MARKETING, PROFITS, AND OTHER ADMINISTRATIVE COSTS; BASED ON PREMIUMS MINUS CLAIMS EXPENSES FOR PRIVATE INSURANCE.

DATA: OECD HEALTH DATA 2005
SOURCE: COMMONWEALTH FUND NATIONAL SCORECARD ON U.S. HEALTH SYSTEM PERFORMANCE, 2006

Even the Fraser Institute does not propose shifting Canada to an exclusively private health care system based on the U.S. model. They widely applaud, however, the June 2005 Supreme Court of Canada decision declaring unconstitutional the efforts of Quebec to prevent its citizens from obtaining private insurance to pay for procedures covered under the province's public health care system.

The prospect of two tiers of coverage—public for everyone and private for those who choose to purchase it—remains the most hotly debated aspect of health care in Canada because everyone can grasp the concept and understand the positions of both sides. Those with allegiance to neither camp eventually begin feeling like the audience at a tennis match that has devolved into an endless rally delivered with equal power and accuracy from both sides of the net.

Advocates of two tiers of health care compare the concept with the education system. "You pay your taxes to support the public school system, and you pay extra for private education if you want your kid to opt out," argues Brett Skinner. "That's what happens with the European system, which works better at providing a higher level of resources than Canada."

Opponents of the two-tier idea argue it would weaken the public system because privately funded physicians and hospitals would accept only the healthiest patients.

So what? two-tier advocates say in effect. Any reduction in patient load on the public system will benefit those using the public system exclusively.

Not true, opponents rejoin. With physicians and surgeons moving to a private system, they submit, fewer will be left to treat those who cannot afford private care and must accept public coverage. This will lengthen, not shorten, wait times.

Advocates counter with sustainability, pointing out that no nation's economy can absorb endlessly increasing expenditures in any service, whether it's health care, education, defence, or another endeavour. Dismissing the publicly funded system's efforts to reduce expenses through better management and flatten the growth rates, advocates for a private-enterprise role say the results may represent progress but they are not yet reality. Nor does Brett Skinner expect them to produce a solution. "What's the alternative?" he asks. "Raising taxes? That hasn't worked in the past and would be an unacceptable drag on the economy. No one wants the huge deficits we experienced in the 1990s, and no one is prepared to accept rationing as a cost-saving method either."[14]

Opponents to the private concept point to studies that suggest for-profit hospitals offer lower-quality care.

Advocates contend that competitive markets yield wider selection, better cost-efficiency, and ultimate consumer benefits.

Opponents counter that shopping for a health care provider cannot be compared with choosing a laundry detergent—in health care the stakes are higher and the level of consumer knowledge is substantially limited.

Advocates note that a two-tier system provides wider choice.

Opponents claim the opposite—private insurance systems traditionally limit patients to specified primary care physicians and hospitals, and patients are frequently required to obtain second opinions from insurer-approved sources. Both restrict, not expand, choice.

And so it goes.

Perhaps the closest we'll come to a *coup de grâce* for this endless debate is to evaluate empirical evidence within and beyond Canada, an exercise that sidesteps theory and deals only with real experience. One of the mantras of the Fraser Institute is the phrase "If it matters, measure it." This certainly applies to rising levels of funding and lengthening wait lines in the Canadian health care system. It also applies to other aspects of health care here and abroad.

HOLDING ON TO MARKET SHARE IN A LIFE-OR-DEATH INDUSTRY

In the United States, a dated but largely undisputed 1999 study of patients with end-stage renal disease provided disturbing revelations. These end-stage patients were faced with two options to sustain their lives: enduring continued dialysis in a medical centre equipped to provide this treatment or receiving a kidney transplant, the universally favoured choice. Of almost 4000 patients undergoing dialysis and eligible for a kidney transplant, about two-thirds were receiving treatment at a for-profit facility. Following the patients' progress for as long as six years, doctors conducting the study reached a shocking conclusion: dialysis patients receiving treatment in for-profit facilities suffered a mortality rate almost 24 percent higher than those visiting non-profit clinics. There was no difference in the quality of care between the facilities. But in the words of those conducting the study, "The likelihood of being placed on the waiting list for a renal transplant was lower for patients treated at for-profit centers."[15]

The obvious conclusion: for-profit facilities were reluctant to refer patients for a kidney transplant because they would lose the income derived from providing the patient with dialysis services. In the packaged-goods industry, this is simply a matter of holding on to market share. In the health care arena, it could be construed as ghoulish.

Proponents of market-driven health care did not attack the study's techniques or its conclusions, but the "paternalistic, anti-market approach to medicine." They even managed to inject a dose of Reaganism into their argument, claiming, "A market-driven 'trust but verify' approach would arm patients with the understanding that health care providers have their own agendas, biases and imperfections and would give patients the information needed to evaluate competing physicians," adding that "a true market system would also require that patients pay for a significant fraction of the cost of their care, thereby giving them more control in healthcare settings."[16]

How many of the renal-failure patients who died as a result of not being placed on a transplant list, in order to boost the profits of the privately owned dialysis clinics, would agree?

A more recent study, this one conducted by the Harvard School of Public Health, measured the quality of care provided by for-profit health plans versus not-for-profit publicly funded facilities in four specific categories: breast cancer screening, diabetic eye examination, beta-blocker medication after heart attacks, and follow-up to hospitalization for mental illness. With a sample universe of more than 280,000 patients, 64 percent of them in for-profit health plans, the results should be considered significant.

On average, for-profit plans yielded a quality of care level 7.3 percentage points lower than that of not-for-profit plans for breast cancer screenings; 14.1 percent lower for diabetic eye exams; 12.1 percent lower for beta-blockers; and 18.3 percent lower for follow-up to mental illness treatment. In addition, the doctors conducting the study noted that for-profit health plans enrolled smaller numbers of patients aged 65 to 69 than not-for-profit plans, as well as fewer women and white and rural residents; for-profit plans had higher proportions of policyholders with lower educational attainment levels.[17]

One of the most fascinating sidebar stories to the U.S. experience with privately funded health care, seen in the light of the Canadian debate over funding, concerns the impact on private industry. It was long recognized that this country's universal health care system represented a primary factor behind Canada's enormous success under the Canada–U.S. Automotive Products Trade Agreement, dating back to 1965. Automotive plants in the United States, especially the union-dominated Big Three of Ford, GM, and Daimler Chrysler, were committed to providing, out of corporate profits, health insurance to all of their employees, a burden their Canadian plants did not carry. A recent revelation, perhaps apocryphal but not denied, claimed that General Motors spent more per vehicle produced on health insurance for its employees than it did on steel to build the car.

Nor was the automotive industry the only one decrying the situation. In 2005, the chairman of Starbucks Corporation announced that his firm was spending more each year to pay health insurance premiums for its employees than it was to purchase coffee for its customers. Joined by other CEOs from firms that included Costco and Verizon, Howard Schultz used a phrase dear to the hearts of critics in the Fraser Institute when he called the steep annual rise in private health care premiums "completely non-sustainable."[18]

The U.S. health care system, as the Fraser Institute is quick to acknowledge, should not be compared too closely with Canada's because the two systems vary widely in design and operation. More useful information can be gathered when different systems within our own borders are compared. One such study measured wait times for cataract surgery at both public and private clinics in Alberta.[19] The study was conducted in 1999 by the Consumers' Association of Canada—hardly friends to the advocates of for-profit health care—and examined wait times for cataract surgery in Calgary, Edmonton, and Lethbridge. Each city provided its own mix of facilities to conduct the procedure. In Calgary, for-profit clinics performed 100 percent of cataract surgeries. In Edmonton, only 20 percent of the procedures were handled by for-profit clinics, while Lethbridge public hospitals were responsible for all such procedures.

Advocates for for-profit care no doubt postulated that Calgary patients would wait the shortest length of time before surgery, and Lethbridge residents would face long waits for the same procedure. In fact, research results suggested precisely the opposite. In Calgary, patients waited between sixteen and twenty-four weeks for treatment, and in Edmonton the waiting time was five to seven weeks. Lethbridge residents requiring cataract surgery received treatment within four to seven weeks on average, a reasonable period for elective surgery.

These results ran counter to every prediction made by private health care advocates, and even those rigidly opposed to the concept, who preached that wealthier patients would buy their way to the front of the line. On the evidence this failed to occur. One explanation is that doctors are interested not in taking home bigger salaries but in having more leisure time with their families. If true, this suggests that private-clinic surgeons, who are paid more per procedure than those in the public system, may choose to perform fewer operations. They can take home the same amount of money for working fewer hours. In addition, patients at for-profit clinics were charged extra simply because the clinics were able to set their own fee schedules. Opponents of the for-profit alternative also point out that any complications that developed from procedures performed in private clinics were inevitably treated at publicly funded, not private for-profit, facilities.

In spite of such homegrown studies, it's to the international arena that the Fraser Institute prefers to turn when evaluating this country's public health care system, and here it produces compelling results. In a 2005 report,[20] the Fraser Institute ranked Canada third in age-adjusted health spending as a percentage of GDP among OECD countries with universal health care.*

When the Fraser Institute has gathered all the data, it makes some adjustments to the statistics it has assembled. Before releasing figures pitting Canada's performance against the performance of other nations, for example, it adjusts the data to account for differences in average age for each country. Age adjustments are common in assessing the incidence of specific diseases to avoid oversimplifying results skewed by other factors. In the United States, for example, Florida has a much higher rate of cancer than the state of Alaska. Does this indicate an overwhelming presence of carcinogenic materials in the southern state? No, it's because the average age of Florida residents is substantially higher than that in Alaska, and the incidence of cancer is age-related; without adjusting for this factor, the figures are dramatically skewed. When comparing Canada's fiscal performance to that of other countries, the Fraser Institute also adjusts its expenditure figures, according to its own formula, to reflect the average age of an entire country across every medical procedure. The action is based on the fact that elderly citizens draw on more of a nation's health care resources than do younger people. In 2002, Canada's seniors (age sixty-five and over) represented 12.7 percent of the population but consumed more than 44 percent of the system's resources. The older we get, the more health care we require; Canadians age eighty-five and over absorbed eight times the average per capita spending for all age groups.[21] When comparing health care costs between countries, we should expect nations with a greater proportion of citizens

*For the record, the country spending the highest GDP percentage was Iceland; the second highest was Switzerland, the nation that Fraser Institute health critic Skinner noted as a model for controlling costs through private insurance.

sixty-five and older to invest more in health care than countries with a younger population.

Among twenty-seven selected OECD nations—excluding the United States—Canada rated twentieth in average age, tied with Australia; countries near the top of the list had an older population average. (Italy had the largest proportion of citizens over age sixty-five, followed by Japan and Greece; Korea, with only 7.9 percent of its citizens over sixty-five years of age, was the youngest of the group.) The Fraser Institute submits that this places Canada in a more positive light than it deserves when measuring its health expenditures against those of countries with a larger proportion of elderly citizens. Without an adjustment determined by the institute's own formula, Canada spent 9.6 percent of its GDP on health care in 2002; implementing the age adjustment to account for a smaller proportion of aged citizens than most other countries, Fraser suggests 10.7 percent as a more realistic figure.

Other variables present enormous difficulties in assessing each nation's performance on a statistical basis alone. As an example, the Fraser Institute decries the low number of MRI units and CT scanners in Canada, as do many observers. Its 2004 report notes that Canada ranked fourteenth of twenty-two OECD nations (the United States excepted) in the number of MRI facilities per million citizens, and seventeenth in the same ratio for CT scanners. (Japan scored first in both categories.) In the same report, however, Canada held the twenty-second position among twenty-seven selected OECD countries when it came to the number of doctors per 1000 people. That's nothing to brag about, but it was better than Japan, in twenty-fifth place. Korea, which had rated second in ranking CT scanners per million citizens, was even worse than Japan when it came to the number of doctors per 1000 people.[22]

What does this tell us—that Japan and Korea place greater emphasis on technology than on physicians? That Canada is woeful in both? Or that statistics are malleable according to your point of view? Since this observation can be applied to both sides of the discussion, it may be more fruitful to approach the subject from another angle and examine the results of combining public access with privately funded facilities, as advocated by the Fraser Institute.

In 2000, the World Health Organization proclaimed France's health care system the world's best, an opinion supported by the institute and other proponents of a greater role for private enterprise. France indeed allows private for-profit insurance and hospitals, and the health system costs less, on a per capita basis, than Canada's. A key reason for this exceptional performance is the doctor–patient ratio which, when the WHO lauded the system, was 50 percent better than Canada's on a per capita basis. Adding substantially more doctors is an ideal way to improve the health of any nation's citizens, but how can France employ more doctors with less money per capita?

The answer is clear: lower salaries. In 2006, the average annual salary paid to doctors practising in France was about Cdn$70,000, or 40 percent lower than the amount paid Canadian physicians performing similar services.[23] This suggests that one way to improve health care for Canadians is to ask the country's physicians to accept a 40 percent reduction in income, an unlikely event.

Advocates for private care looked elsewhere and supposedly found support in, of all places, Sweden, long the beacon for socialization in the industrialized world. In February 2006, the *National Post* reportedly claimed that Sweden had privatized most health care in Stockholm "with dramatic results … sharply reduced wait times—on the order of 40 percent for most critical treatments."[24] But Daniel Cohn of Simon Fraser University, a research associate with the Canadian Centre for Policy Alternatives, had examined the Swedish experiment from a different perspective almost four years earlier.

Stockholm county, according to Cohn, had turned over operation of one hospital to a private firm and contracted patient care to several other facilities, a move launched by Sweden's Moderate Party (a right-wing political organization) as an example to the rest of the country.

With no national power, the Moderates used the privatization of one hospital as a showcase for their agenda. The results, as related by Cohn, were nearly disastrous. The private facilities were accused of cream-skimming (rejecting seriously ill patients and sending them to publicly operated facilities), and in 2001 Standard & Poor's slashed the county's debt rating. Soon after, a pro-business magazine published an article written by a leading heart specialist who claimed the decision to promote private care was jeopardizing the health of cardiac patients. The reason? According to the article, the council had created new spaces in the for-profit hospital to treat patients least in need of care with greater speed. The move cut funds to public hospitals; with less cash and more seriously ill patients to handle, their wait times extended substantially.[25]

Swedish voters were unimpressed. In September 2002, the Moderates suffered their worst defeat in almost thirty years. The winning Social Democrats promised to "stop the giant sell-off" in health care. Private enterprise continues to play a role in Sweden's social programs, but on a much reduced basis than before and in an atmosphere far different from the one portrayed in the *National Post* article.

Proponents of private care turned their eyes to Britain, whose National Health Service (NHS) was a model for universal health care. In 2005, it appeared that the NHS had embraced the private sector as its saviour from the same ills affecting Canada's system—endlessly escalating costs, lengthy waiting lines, unsatisfactory facilities, a shortage of physicians, and other problems. That year, the British government noted that private for-profit facilities permitted by the country's Private Finance Initiative (PFI) conducted about 5 percent of all non-life-threatening surgical procedures. On the basis of that success, Britain's Department of Health set a level of 15 percent to be reached by 2008, and Prime Minister Tony Blair declared that no upper limit should be set on the proportion of health care provided by private hospitals and specialized clinics, called Independent Sector Treatment Clinics (ISTCs). This was not a two-tier system; the private providers billed the NHS, and most of the procedures were for elective surgeries such as cataracts and joint replacements.

Sir William Wells, a senior director of the NHS, had no hesitation in promoting the idea of adding private-sector providers. In a comment made more astonishing because it came from a Labour Party–appointed official, Wells said, "The big trouble with a state monopoly is that it builds in massive inefficiencies and an inward-looking culture." His observation would resonate positively within the Fraser Institute. And this was not a mere experiment, Wells noted. "We've gone beyond experiment," he said. "There's now a consensus in both major parties that there should be a private agenda."[26] The motivation was basic and familiar: having raised government spending on the NHS from 6 percent of GDP to 9 percent, effectively matching the average of other European countries, the Blair government was reluctant to spend more money to correct serious failings in the system, including aging hospitals and clinics, a shortage of health care professionals, and long waiting times. The only remaining alternative was to open the doors to a profit-motivated second sector. According to Wells, procedures in private-sector facilities were heavily supervised; any clinic failing to meet NHS standards was closed down. More notable, the private clinics were guaranteeing a half-hour consultation, at Cdn$110, within an hour of each patient's arrival.

The Blair government refused to stop there. Surveying an NHS landscape that included crumbling, poorly equipped hospitals whose average age was older than the NHS itself, the Labour Party launched a program to construct 100 new hospitals, with private enterprise playing a partnership role in sixty-eight of them.

Several observers in Canada, including *Globe and Mail* columnist Jeffrey Simpson, hailed the British move while regretting the fact that nothing of the sort was being seriously considered as a solution to the woes of Canada's system. Meanwhile, those on the right wing of politics, who supported the Fraser Institute's demands for extensive involvement of the private sector in Canadian medicare, were turning the world on its head by praising a Labour Party initiative. Their explanation, of course, was that the concept was so rich with logic and promise that even left-wing Brits were buying into the idea.

All of this left the majority of Canadians, who valued the current system but agreed with the need to limit government spending, feeling confused. Both sides tossed statistics, case studies, research projects, and verbal brickbats at each other. So perhaps there is a need for presenting a few facts that both can agree upon.

Inserting private-care facilities into a publicly funded arena can be achieved in one of two ways. One is the discretionary approach practised in France and Germany. In these countries, your private insurance cannot be used to gain faster access to publicly funded health care; you are restricted to the private services offered by the insurance package you purchased. Both France and Germany, it should be noted, have shorter wait times for most procedures.

The other is the British example, replicated in Australia and New Zealand, where private enterprise invests in facilities to employ health care professionals who receive most or all of their income from the public purse, just as their colleagues do. Private insurance enables citizens in these countries to effectively buy their way to the head of the line, ahead of those who depend solely upon their tax-purchased coverage.

Of these alternatives, Canada, should it officially adopt a private-enterprise role for hospitals and surgical clinics on a grander scale than practised today, would more likely follow the British system. The U.K.'s experience provides a real-world example of this concept that both sides have studied and reported upon. Unfortunately, the real-world experience in the United Kingdom generates a dialogue similar to that being conducted in Canada, where extending private-care facilities remains hypothetical. At least the arguments on both sides are based somewhat more on fact than fancy. Here is the case privatization proponents make on eight claimed benefits and the response from those favouring a public non-profit solution:[27]

PRIVATE CLAIM	PUBLIC RESPONSE
ISTC surgery patients choose the date and time of their appointment; wait times and hospital stays are shorter.	ISTCs enjoy contracts with guaranteed income at costs to the government 40% higher than NHS facilities.
More beds and spaces are available for surgical procedures.	PFI hospitals and ISTCs "cherry-pick" easy, uncomplicated cases.
Operations proceed as planned and are not cancelled or postponed to accommodate emergency situations.	Only NHS hospitals accept emergency patients, increasing their load.
Patients are treated under NHS rules and standards.	But who is training new medical personnel in complex cases? Not PFI.
Patients have a choice of providers.	Consumers prefer good local hospitals over "shopping around."
PFI hospitals and ISTCs are pioneering new clinical practices, such as wider use of local vs. general anaesthesia to reduce length of post-operative stay.	Innovation is driven solely by profit; it is commercialization, not privatization, with many ISTCs "owned and staffed by foreign concerns."
250,000+ patients by February 2006.	The NHS remains responsible for continuity of care for *all* citizens.
NHS providers are inefficient, often unionized civil servants.	Private providers may go bankrupt.

ISTC=independent sector treatment clinics
NHS=National Health Service
PFI=private financial initiative

The private sector, the Blair government, and the U.K. Department of Health praised the initiative, the latter supporting its position with glowing testimonials from Brits extolling PFI hospitals and ISTCs. NHS supporters attacked every aspect of the program, including the fact that private enterprise paid more than the U.K. government to borrow money, an extra expense that must be passed along to patients. (The government responded by stating that "value for money is not simply about comparing interest rates," noting that additional borrowing costs are offset by the private sector's ability to innovate and make more efficient use of resources.)

Meanwhile, back at the Fraser Institute, Brett Skinner outlined the organization's multi-faceted solution to Canada's health care financing crisis, which included a new, wider role for private health insurance and the introduction of service fees for virtually all publicly funded procedures. Skinner offered these benefits to the idea:

1. Brings new funds into the system.
2. Offloads responsibility for current expenditures onto the private sector.
3. Introduces incentives for rational, responsible use of health care and for efficient allocation of resources, which is not available under a centrally planned system.
4. Encourages patients, via service fees, to step back and ask if they actually need the procedure they are demanding. If a physician suggests the need for a diagnostic test and outlines the various alternatives and relative costs involved, for example, the patient may be able to choose between the latest, more expensive test and one that the physician knows to be just as effective but much less costly.
5. Improves public sector health care, which would service fewer patients and thus be equipped to proportionately spend more on each.

Nothing in real-world experience suggests that points 4 and 5 will occur in the manner that Skinner suggests.

6

AGED CARE
THE COMING TSUNAMI

After a long and generally uneventful life, Fanny Albo achieved a degree of fame as a result of an exercise of bureaucratic cruelty. If it were any consolation to her and her family, her example drew attention to a fear that concerns all Canadians of a certain age and forced governments and citizens alike to focus on the final stages of government's role in caring for our physical conditions.

Fanny and her husband, Al, spent most of their seventy years of marriage in the Kootenay region of interior British Columbia. At ninety-one, Fanny suffered from congestive heart failure and counted Al, ninety-six years of age, among her caregivers. In early 2006, Al suffered an injury while caring for Fanny and was admitted to the Kootenay Boundary Regional Hospital for treatment. Within a few days, Fanny herself had suffered a fall and was admitted to the same hospital. Given their age and Fanny's serious heart problems, both were placed in the facility's acute care unit.

It's worth pointing out that nothing to this point reflects any lack of access to quality medical care. Living to ninety years and beyond may be a measure of good genetics, but it also suggests that when medical care was needed, the system met the challenge. The experience of Al and Fanny Albo demonstrates that we have as much right to quality care at the end of our lives as we have during all the preceding periods.

It was obvious to both hospital officials and the Albo family that Fanny would not survive for long. Problems with her failing heart could not be corrected. Al required something less than the high-tech acute care unit, however, something more suitable to keeping him comfortable and supplied with food and medication.

In the parlance of hospital administration, Al and Fanny were bed-blockers, patients who occupy beds that might be made available to people with needs more appropriate to the facilities. In Fanny's case palliative care, not round-the-clock monitoring and attention, was called for. Someone in the health care bureaucracy noted this and assigned Fanny to a "first available bed" listing, meaning that she was to be moved to a palliative care facility as soon as the next bed became available in the region.

And she was. On a Friday morning in February 2006, two attendants transferred Fanny from her bed to a gurney and rolled her briefly past her husband, Al. "They said, 'Say goodbye to your wife,'" their son Jim recalled with barely restrained outrage. "My poor dad never had time to really hold my mother's hand or to cuddle with her or not even a private moment together, and they turned around and wheeled her out the door. And my poor father just absolutely broke down."[1]

Transferring Fanny across town would have been understandable, even if the process appears to have been conducted with a disturbing lack of sensitivity. But Fanny was trundled clear out of the Kootenay region to the first available bed in Grand Forks, a ninety-minute automobile journey along winding roads. She died within forty-eight hours of being admitted. Al followed her in death barely two weeks later.

The story of the Albos spread across Canada and into the United States with all the speed and impact of a national disaster, leading critics on both sides of the border to decry the entire health system. The president of the B.C. nurses' union claimed the province "has moved into active euthanasia. If the health authority just wants not to spend money on the care of seniors, then why don't they just be honest about it rather than send them to an early death?"[2] *The B.C. government launched an inquiry that produced a report from the province's deputy minister of health; the report included six recommendations reflecting classic bureaucratise: "undertake an expedited process involving senior medical leaders ... conduct a comprehensive review ... implement, in conjunction with the Ministry of Health, a trial program.... " An expansion of facilities to banish the problem of bed-blockers and permit patients to receive the care they need instead of being moved about like luggage was quickly targeted as a rather obvious solution. All well and good, but nothing in the report's recommendations addressed the core problem that needed not a deputy minister's ministrations but a humane outlook constructed around a single quality: compassion.*

DEPENDING ON your point of view, statistics regarding the increase in population among Canadians age sixty-five and over are either comforting or disturbing. It is comforting to think that more of us are surviving into the fabled "ripe old age"; it is disturbing to contemplate how the public health system will fund care for this increasing number of older Canadians and how comfortable their later years will be.

The growth in numbers of Canadian seniors, and the proportion of the overall population they will represent, are unprecedented. Seniors are and will be, well into the future, the fastest-growing population group in Canada, reaching almost 7 million by 2021, with much of the increase occurring among those eighty-five and over.[3] Based on this projection, almost one out of every four Canadians would be sixty-five or over within fifteen years of this book's appearance, compared with about one out of 7.5 Canadians in the 2001 census.

As robust and independent as we may be during the first seven decades of life, most of us will become dependent on support from others as time wears on. The most fortunate will become dependants of loving relatives, usually their own children, with the assets, skills, and empathy to provide home care, supported by personnel and facilities within the health care system. Some of us will possess enough assets to cover the costs of a retirement facility providing a high level of comfort and care. Many of us, however, will become totally dependent on the public sector for our care via tax-supported hospitals and long-term care facilities (LTCFs), often for treatment of age-related chronic illnesses including cancer, heart disease, diabetes, and arthritis. Virtually all of us, of course, will remain tied to the public health care system, where we will absorb eight times the expenditure per capita that we did during our youthful years.

Our health care system operates today in many ways as though it were addressing conditions that existed in our great-grandparents' day. In 1900, the life expectancy of North Americans was about forty-seven, and illness and disability could arrive at any age. Moreover, the most serious illnesses encountered a century ago tended to end life more abruptly than they do today. Ailments such as pneumonia, tuberculosis, cholera, and gastro-intestinal diseases could result in death within days or weeks, not years, as could childbirth.

Today, Canadians boast an average lifespan of eighty years, and most of the acute illnesses that ended lives circa 1900 have been controlled. We are far less likely to succumb to illnesses that plagued citizens of four generations ago and more likely to die from heart disease, cancer, stroke, diabetes, and chronic respiratory diseases, often complicated by the onset of dementia. Their lingering effects, and the resources needed to address them over extended periods of time, represent a cost that was non-existent until recent generations.

THE COST OF LONGER LIVES

	1900	2000
Life expectancy	47 years	75+ years
Usual place of death	Home	Hospital
Medical expenses	Paid by family	Paid by public health plan
Disability before death	Limited	2 years average

SOURCE: *LIVING WELL AT THE END OF LIFE*, RAND CORPORATION, 2003

On its own, this difference in fatal illnesses among the elderly and the burden it places on health care costs is a significant challenge to future funding, but it remains only half the story. Chronic health problems among the elderly may not be deemed a threat to life, but they must still be acknowledged and treated. Arthritis and hearing or vision problems require extensive, ongoing treatment from medical and social agencies. Various attacks on the function of organs such as the heart, liver, and kidney may be the natural result of certain body parts "wearing out," and addressing these concerns is again a complex, drawn-out procedure. Finally, the frailty of older people, both their susceptibility to falls and broken bones and their lack of energy reserves to battle hitherto less serious health challenges, imposes another layer of expense and demand on facilities.

Yet Canada's health care system, like those in most of the industrialized world, works most effectively on preventing diseases, engineering dramatic rescues from illness or injury, and generally tackling the needs of those under sixty years of age. It is, all things considered, rather good at meeting that challenge. It is still adjusting to the health needs of the aged.

THE VERDICT OF TODAY'S SENIORS ON HEALTH CARE: NOT BAD AT ALL

While critics of the country's health care system regard with alarm the coming wave of seniors who will be drawing on the system, their warnings should be tempered with the reality that in 2006 seniors rated the quality of the services they received from Canada's health care system as very high.[4] Almost all had regular access to a family physician and prescribed medications, and most took advantage of influenza immunization programs. An earlier, more broadly based survey had reported that 35 percent of Canadians were dissatisfied with their access to home and community care,[5] suggesting a substantial improvement in the system's delivery capability, problems in delivering home care to the under-sixty-five age group, and general statistical variations between research techniques and audiences.

On the whole, our current seniors may be substantially healthier than any generation preceding them; those age-related chronic diseases will continue to strike, but they are likely to be felt later in life and be subject to much greater control. Notwithstanding the tragic experience of Al and Fanny Albo, we appear to be facing the baby boomer tsunami from a position of some strength. How well equipped are we to maintain this level of satisfaction without imposing excessive pressure on the system's shaky finances? Much of the answer can be found in the balance struck between home care and institutional care.

Home care remains by far the most attractive option for seniors by every measure, and research figures reflect the steady growth of this type of care. In 2006, an estimated 730,000 Canadians received home care services, and that figure is expected to have increased by almost 150,000 by 2016.[6] With less drain on the system's finances and requiring no new bricks-and-mortar facilities, home care has many benefits. Its integration into the federal health care system received across-the-board support from provincial and territorial premiers at a 2003 conference on the subject. They promised to provide by 2006 a single point of access for home care and residential services, broader technology for use by home care providers, general support and assistance to families and other caregivers, and a range of other services.

Whatever good intentions spawned these and other initiatives at the conference, they proved less than effective in reality thanks to a sequence of events tied for the most part to federal-provincial-territorial jealousies. As they signed the agreement, provincial premiers grumbled that they were receiving only half of the funding recommended in the Romanow Report. None of the territories accepted the deal because federal funding had been calculated on a per capita basis that failed to account for the higher costs of delivering health care in remote regions. Within a few months, Prime Minister Paul Martin had called a federal election, sparking debates over health care that served only to muddy some already opaque waters. And two months after the election, Martin convened a three-day first ministers' conference on the subject, a generally unproductive session made more feckless when Alberta premier Ralph Klein packed his bags and went home after the first day.[7]

Even if the federal and provincial governments lived up to their 2003 commitment regarding care for the aged, it is unrealistic to expect that home care alone will satisfy future demands placed on the system. We will still require a combination of home care and professional services and facilities, plus, as the Romanow Report describes it, "ongoing communication ... to prevent the revolving door effect of patients transferring back and forth between levels and types of care."[8]

Many aging Canadians fear ending their lives in a nursing home, which they consider end-of-life residences, similar to palliative care facilities but without the degree of specialized attention the latter provide. In many ways, the fear is justified—nursing homes are warehouses for the aged just as our prisons are warehouses for lawbreakers. The quality of care provided by nursing homes varies widely. Small wonder, then, that many seniors for whom home care is not possible resist the idea of a nursing home.

But by examining one institution that represents perhaps the pinnacle of the art, we can find inspiration for a new way of thinking about and refashioning nursing homes. In Toronto, the Baycrest Centre for Geriatric Care boasts facilities and programs for the aged so advanced and recognized that many specialists in geriatrics refer to it simply as the Model.

CAN "THE MODEL" BE REPLICATED ELSEWHERE? NOT LIKELY

Baycrest spreads across 7.3 hectares (18 acres) in northwest Toronto, encompassing several modern buildings that include a 300-bed hospital, 472-bed Jewish Home for the Aged, 204 supportive housing and assisted apartments, and an additional 120 life-lease condominium-style apartments designed for independent seniors. As well as providing care and services for an estimated 2500 people each day, Baycrest conducts research on subjects closely related to the challenge of an aging population. As one example, it features a clinical research program in geriatric neuropsychiatry. Much of this work is undertaken in conjunction with Baycrest's Rotman Research Institute, considered one of the top brain research centres in the world, and the Kunin-Lunenfeld Applied Research Unit (KLARU), which conducts research in geriatric medicine, nursing, social work, psychology, psychiatry, nutrition, and communication disorders. Baycrest is also affiliated with the University of Toronto, providing training for practitioners in several disciplines.

"Many facilities serving the elderly may have the elements we have," Baycrest president and CEO Steve Herbert notes, "but they may not be organized in the fashion that we are, and as a result they cannot deliver total continuum of care." Herbert, who has spent his entire career in hospital administration, the last seventeen as head of Baycrest, responds to questions in a slow, reflective manner, as though concerned with appearing too boastful of its success. He admits, for example, that "the Model" may not be easily replicated elsewhere in Canada because the wide range of services Baycrest provides, in a homogenous environment, would have to come from diverse sources working smoothly together.

"We were founded on the basis of volunteerism," Herbert explains, "when we opened our doors as the Toronto Jewish Old Folks Home in 1918. Today, we have about 6000 volunteers [who] can be divided into three groups: policy volunteers, who sit on boards and committees; hands-on volunteers, who work with clients and families throughout the facility including palliative care, eating assistance program, gift shops, and elsewhere; and fund-raising volunteers."

Volunteers, of course, can achieve only limited goals without funding, and the financial demands of maintaining Baycrest's facilities and services are substantial. Where does the money come from? Herbert identifies various sources. "To cover our research costs, we rely on federal and provincial sources, grants from U.S. agencies, and endowment funds to be used for research infrastructure. The lion's share of our costs to care for clients comes from government. We are also required to charge for some services, and we sell some services to other organizations. Plus, we receive support from our foundation." In 2006, the Baycrest endowment fund boasted assets of $100 million.

Despite this, Herbert feels Baycrest is underfunded. "I've been involved in reducing costs since 1977," Herbert adds with some frustration, noting that government funding may increase by 3 percent annually, "but that doesn't cover all cost increases." Improving the efficiency of electronic communications through updated computers and software is ongoing at Baycrest. "The banks in Canada spend hundreds of millions of dollars on this function alone," Herbert laments, "but the governments won't fund that kind of investment for health care facilities."[9]

AN ALTERNATIVE TO CENTRALIZED FACILITIES

If Baycrest, with its broad base of volunteer support and the impressive bundle of cash in its endowment fund, encounters funding problems, is there any chance of replicating its success elsewhere in Canada? Not likely. But other models may exist, and one of them demonstrates that a centralized facility is not the only way to deal with care for the aged. Launched in the early 1970s to assist elderly Chinese in San Francisco, On Lok SeniorHealth represents a contrasting model to Baycrest, one that has proven easier to replicate with less drain on public funding.

On Lok focuses its efforts on assisting nursing-home-eligible seniors to remain within the community, providing them with preventative, primary, and acute medical services as well as long-term care. While its name reflects Chinese origins—*On Lok geui* is Cantonese for "abode of peace and happiness"—it serves an entire cross-section of races, including Filipinos, Italians and other Caucasians, and African-Americans.

More impressive than its multicultural composition has been On Lok's strategy of assisting seniors to remain healthy, active, and involved within a vibrant social structure. Rejecting the notion of warehousing seniors within near-hermetically sealed chambers, On Lok employs multidisciplinary teams to help their clients remain secure and comfortable in their own homes. The teams consist of physicians, nurses, social workers, dieticians, physical and occupational therapists, transportation staff, home care workers, and recreational leaders.

Instead of making a sudden turn from independence within familiar surroundings to dependence on others in an institution, clients of On Lok and various adaptations of the original concept depend on the organizations for a range of services, including the following:

- Primary medical care and specialty care as needed (cardiology, neurology)
- Routine preventative care (audiology, dentistry, optometry, and podiatry)
- Rehabilitation therapy (physical, occupational, speech)
- Recreational therapy
- Home health care, as needed
- Social services
- Nutrition services and home-delivered meals, as needed
- Transportation and emergency medical transport
- Acute hospital and nursing home care
- Health monitoring
- Health care equipment and supplies

On Lok is paid by Medicare for those clients who qualify for the coverage and are able to continue living in the community without jeopardizing their own health and safety. Seniors not covered by Medicare are charged a flat monthly fee based on their personal income and assets, and the organization benefits from periodic fundraising programs. The financial benefits to the health care system are impressive: only 22 percent of On Lok's budget is spent on facilities and services closely associated with elderly care, such as hospital stays, laboratory tests, X-rays, prescription medicines, and specialist fees. In addition to requiring less hospital care for its clients than the average for citizens over sixty-five, On Lok invests almost eighty cents of every dollar in quality-of-life components, including day programs and social activities, and primary care from family physicians.[10]

Other savings have been noted as well. According to On Lok, fully two-thirds of family members caring for elderly relatives without access to a support program take substantial unpaid (and often unauthorized) time from work to care for these dependants.[11] This is reduced or eliminated entirely for families of On Lok clients.

A secondary but hugely beneficial aspect of the On Lok program has been its "single portal" access to essential services for seniors. In our more active years, we have little difficulty identifying and accessing a wide range of services. We can schedule visits to optometrists to have our eyesight tested and to opticians for corrective lenses and glasses, arrange visits to sights or events that interest us, and consult multiple sources for needs ranging from menus and diets to an annual flu vaccination. Age brings frailty, limited mobility, reduced social circles, and cognitive problems, reducing our ability to obtain assistance on a timely basis from multiple sources. Moreover, the delivery of service through several unconnected sources is often not influenced by the patient's needs, leading to excessive wait times, redundant evaluations, inappropriate use of resources, failure to transmit and receive critical information, and assumptions that "some other people" will provide needed services. The importance of a single portal to connect seniors with a network of important services cannot be discounted.

On Lok's success was duly noted by Ontario, which adapted many of its premises for organizations such as Ontario's Community Care Access Centres (CCACs). (Other provinces have yet to launch such a comprehensive program.) In the United States, it led to the creation of Programs of All-inclusive Care for the Elderly (PACE). Applying the principles of On Lok on a national basis, PACE now operates almost 100 programs from its headquarters in Virginia, ensuring that several hundred thousand U.S. seniors remain as healthy and active as possible. That's an impressive achievement made even more remarkable because the cost of caring for PACE participants is about 5 percent less than providing traditional, less fulfilling care.[12]

The success of PACE inspired the launch of similar programs in Canada, with encouraging results and at least three warm, inspirational names: CHOICE, Eden, and NICE.

NON-GOVERNMENTAL PROGRAMS THAT MEET A HEALTH CARE NEED FOR SENIORS

CHOICE (Comprehensive Home Option of Integrated Care for the Elderly) is an On Lok–inspired program. Founded in Edmonton through a partnership of the Capital Care group, a private not-for-profit company that operates seniors' homes, and the Good Samaritan Society, a Christian non-profit organization, CHOICE replicates the On Lok approach with enhancements that include overnight stays at a CHOICE centre for clients receiving treatment for short-term illnesses and respite care, giving home caregivers a break from their responsibilities for a few days. Candidates for CHOICE must be at least sixty years old with a history of complex, chronic medical conditions. Like similar programs, CHOICE relies on contributions in time and energy from volunteers and contributions in cash through fundraising activities, supplemented by monthly fees of $120 for non-health-related services. (Dispensed medications are billed through Alberta Blue Cross or other plans with patient copayments capped at $100 per month.) CHOICE bears all the hallmarks of success in reaching its goal of enriching the lives of the elderly without burdening the public health care system. Comparisons in hard dollars between CHOICE and traditional seniors' home accommodation are unavailable, but the proportion of seniors who enter hospital after becoming part of the CHOICE program is at least measurably lower than for those outside the program.

Elsewhere in Alberta, the Calgary Health Region has launched a similar PACE-based program entitled Comprehensive Community Care, or C3, featuring both a daycare centre and home care. Alberta Health Care Insurance provides up to $2950 per month to cover C3 charges; a small fee is charged for homemaking and companion services.

While PACE, CHOICE, C3, and similar progeny of the On Lok concept continue to appear, traditional nursing home facilities are undergoing changes to yield the same two-fold benefits of more fulfilment in the lives of their residents and less ultimate drain on tax-funded financial resources. The most influential of these is Eden, a concept that originated with a physician specializing in geriatrics.

After watching elderly nursing home residents literally dying before his eyes, Dr. William Thomas and his wife obtained a grant to enhance the nursing home's environment with the goal of reducing the "three plagues" of loneliness, helplessness, and boredom. No matter how bright, modern, clean, and comfortable the facilities of a nursing home may be, and no matter how attentive and capable the workers looking after the residents, these "plagues" cannot be eliminated by medical care alone.

Calling their venture the "Eden alternative," the Thomases attacked the three plagues with obvious and effective cures. Residents were no longer strapped into the beds as a means of restraining them lest they become "difficult." They were encouraged to move about and socialize. Nursing stations were eliminated to create an environment that was less like a hospital and more like a vacation lodge.

Companionship proved a treatment for loneliness while giving aid to others who battled helplessness, and spontaneity was a remedy for boredom. These were the diagnoses and cures. The medications came in multiple forms, including live-in dogs, cats and birds, potted plants in every area, visiting schoolchildren throughout the year, staff retrained to enhance the changes, and other modifications to the previous warehousing techniques. These rather basic and even obvious enhancements delivered remarkable improvements in patient morale and happiness, leading to a reduction of 38 percent in the cost of medication for the residents, a 15 percent decrease in the home's mortality rate, and substantially less staff turnover.[13]

The Eden concept has moved through nursing homes across North America like a life-giving rising tide. About a dozen Eden-inspired homes operate in Canada, with more being added each year. Germany, Japan, Australia, and New Zealand have Eden homes. None uses restraints, and all employ staff who provide a range of services. Instead of being isolated within specific roles, as personal care aides, housekeepers, or food servers, for example, each member fulfils multiple roles, establishing deeper relationships with the residents. How well does the Eden alternative work across a range of nursing homes in various locations? Research conducted by Southwest Texas State University revealed a 50 percent reduction in decubitus ulcers (bed sores) among residents and a 60 percent decrease in difficult behavioural incidents, which in turn resulted in a 48 percent drop in staff absenteeism and an 11 percent decline in employee accidents.[14]

The Eden alternative remains an apparently successful, imported concept. Our home-grown approach to improving health care for seniors would undoubtedly be described by some as "typically Canadian": it is under study. The National Initiative for the Care of the Elderly (NICE), founded in 2006 and supported by the federal government's National Centres of Excellence program, is a resource for students and front-line professionals working in geriatric care. The strategy for developing and assisting workers to meet an anticipated future demand is sound and, according to NICE director Dr. Peter Donahue, makes good sense financially.

"When you have a better-trained staff equipped to deal with the needs and concerns of the elderly," he says in his downtown Toronto office, "you are better able to achieve this on a cost-effective basis." Working with major universities, NICE is busy developing curricula and programs for undergraduates seeking certification in geriatric care. If Dr. Donahue and his staff along with their counterparts at universities and learning centres across the country succeed, we should soon have a cohort of specialists to deal with the growing aged population in an effective manner.

Medical care can do nothing more than extend our lives to whatever limit awaits (or as one physician wryly noted, "All I can do is try to ensure that my patients die of something else"). Questions surrounding the massive cost of cancer treatments that may delay death by only a few months become complex. Another day of living may be precious beyond all calculation to a dying patient who would otherwise be in the prime of life. But should the public purse be tapped to postpone the inevitable among the elderly? The answer has been delivered not by steely-eyed bureaucrats but by the elderly themselves.

"Let Me Decide" remains a landmark study conducted by McMaster University's Geriatric Research Group in six Ontario nursing homes. During the eighteen-month study, competent residents and families of incompetent residents made health care decisions, most of them associated with end-of-life matters. Bureaucrats and health care professionals decided on procedures for a control group. The results were dramatic.

Residents in the control group spent more than twice as many days in hospital (5.86 versus 2.61) on average as those permitted to make their own decisions. Measured in dollars, the Let Me Decide (LMD) group cost the system less in hospital expenses ($1772 per person versus $3869 in the control sector) and total health care expenditures ($3490 versus $5239).

Somewhat surprising was the reduced number of deaths among residents who had taken control of their destiny via LMD. About 24 percent of residents in the LMD group died during the study, compared with 28 percent of the control group. Can power over your health care treatment create a greater will to live? It appears so.

"'Let Me Decide' increases patients' autonomy, takes families off the hook, and allows health care workers to give people what they want," comments Dr. William Molloy, professor of medicine at McMaster University's medical school and principal investigator in the study. "Otherwise, health care professionals feel obliged to 'do everything to prolong life,' when in fact they may be prolonging the dying process. This is not what most of us want."[15]

Nor what the system can afford. In 2006, an estimated 300,000 people occupied nursing homes in Canada. Even with the extension of in-home services for seniors, this figure can only be expected to increase over the next decade, and it will take programs such as Let Me Decide to enable the system to accommodate the cost.

"We are going bankrupt in health care providing resources to people who don't want them," adds Molloy, "and we have shown that they don't benefit from them. We need to empower people to take control of their own health care and make decisions for themselves."

WHAT HAPPENED TO Al and Fanny Albo has become a parable among critics of the health care system and its treatment of seniors. As tragic as their story may be, we may take some comfort in the fact that its dramatic power is rooted in its apparent uniqueness, and that it has inspired a broad cross-section of people in and outside of the system to ensure that it is not repeated.

More critical perhaps is the need to recognize the substantial change that will be required by the system to deal with seniors' health issues over the coming decade. It may be argued, with some conviction, that we need as much research on Alzheimer's disease and other causes of cognitive decline as we do on cancer, diabetes, and arthritis. In 2006, an estimated one in four Canadians over sixty-five was affected by various versions of dementia; within twenty years, one authoritative source suggests, "the number of cases is expected to reach epidemic stages."[16]

Other truths need to be acknowledged, including the fact that better social conditions for seniors lead to a reduced demand for health care services, and that the most effective economic and social means of dealing with our aging population is not to build more and larger nursing homes but to construct a social system that supports home care.

In the area of senior care at least, it appears that the most efficient means of providing health care has less to do with medicines, physicians, hospitals, and technology, and more to do with basic issues like compassion, understanding, and accommodation.

7

FROM OPERATING ROOM TO COURTROOM

PROTECTING PATIENTS AND DOCTORS

"The first time I saw Morgan Bystedt, I actually caught my breath," says lawyer Thomas Harding in his Surrey, B.C., office. "I had never seen a more beautiful child. She was three years old at the time. In the photographs I have seen of her as an infant she was so perfectly formed that I thought of her as a Gerber baby—she looked just like the one shown on their baby food jars."

Thomas Harding came to know Morgan Bystedt and her physical condition very well during the seven years after first meeting her. It took that long to obtain a legal decision finding her physician at fault for the effects of a horrific infection the little girl suffered as a baby, and to finally obtain the funds from the settlement agreed on in court. The doctor's negligence resulted in serious damage to Morgan's central nervous system. She is totally deaf and a spastic quadriplegic, a condition that the court ruled could have been avoided with a commonly used drug that Dr. Richard Hay, the family physician, should have prescribed as soon as he identified her ailment. But he did not.

"Morgan had herpes," Harding explains. "She was not born with it. It erupted when she was ten days old. That's when Morgan's mother took her to a physician and showed him a halo of blisters that had broken out on the crown of the baby's head after she had been taken home from the hospital. It was a classic case of the baby being infected during delivery."

Morgan's mother, Wylie, was a herpes carrier. Harding surmises she had an outbreak of the virus, probably on her cervix, at the time of Morgan's birth. As Morgan's head passed through the cervix, the herpes virus would have infected the otherwise healthy child; a week or so later, the virus caused the blisters on her head and began the attack on Morgan's brain that debilitated her.

"The doctor spotted the condition from ten or fifteen feet away when Wylie brought Morgan to see him," Harding says. "He never touched the child. All he said was, 'That's herpes. Keep an eye on that,' and gave her mother some cortisone cream for the blisters." Harding shakes his head. "Prescribing cortisone for herpes is an insane call. Standard procedures would have been to admit Morgan to hospital immediately, administer the proven anti-viral drug Acyclovir, and conduct a series of routine steps to stem the disease. Instead, she contracted encephalitis."

Harding was practising family law and had never pursued a case of medical malpractice when Wylie Bystedt sought his help. But the persuasive skills of Ms. Bystedt and Harding's outrage at the tragedy that had befallen the beautiful infant were so powerful he agreed to launch a suit claiming serious negligence against Dr. Hay. The decision cost Harding almost seven years of his career. During that period his income dropped so low that he had to mortgage his house to cover his living expenses. He ultimately won the case, but the experience left him with bitter feelings toward the lawyers representing Dr. Hay and the Canadian Medical Protective Association (CMPA), the organization that provided the physician's defence.

A review of the positions taken by the lawyers retained by the CMPA in arguing Dr. Hay's case reveals some remarkable statements, made more disturbing in light of the ruined life of an innocent child.

- *In their statement of defence, lawyers for Dr. Hay accused Morgan of being responsible for her own condition, charging the ten-day-old baby had "failed to mitigate her losses by failing to take all reasonable steps to avoid or minimize such injury, loss, damage or expense."*[1]
- *Dr. Hay's lawyers argued that Morgan had been infected in the womb. "Invariably, babies infected with herpes while in the womb are born dead, grossly deformed, or at the very least are covered in lesions," Harding points out. "Morgan was a beautiful, perfect child at birth."*[2] *In her judgment, Madame Justice Smith commented that "the defendant's theory of causation is like trying to fit a square peg in a round hole."*[3]
- *When witnesses called by Harding described Morgan as a happy, contented baby during the first two weeks of her life, then noted that she began wailing inconsolably and incessantly as though in pain after developing meningitis as a result of the herpes infection, Dr. Hay's defence team claimed there was no proof that babies felt pain.*

The court ruled that Dr. Hay was indeed guilty of gross negligence in the case and awarded Morgan and her family $2.7 million to fund ongoing care, but Hay's CMPA-hired defence team wasn't finished. They appealed the decision and lost. This time the court ruled that the CMPA should begin providing Morgan, who had received not a penny to this point, interim monthly payments of $9000. The CMPA fought this as well. Finally, after all the legal posturing, jousting, and appeals, the first interim payment arrived—just in time for Morgan's tenth birthday.

HARDING REMAINS ANGRY at the defence launched on behalf of Dr. Richard Hay. His attitude is unusual among attorneys, who rarely, despite the manner in which they are depicted in TV and movie dramas, express such a deep emotional response. Besides, now that the general public acknowledges that physicians and surgeons are highly skilled and trained professionals and not gods in possession of secrets of immortality, can't we assume that they are just as vulnerable as their patients when it comes to making mistakes at work? "Of course," Harding agrees. "But in this case the doctor was not found liable just for making a mistake; he was found liable for making a mistake so bad it should never have happened."

In most industrial societies, doctors are protected from claims of negligence involving mere errors of judgment. This acknowledges the imperfection of the science of medicine and the fallibility of human beings. If you visit a doctor complaining of flu-like symptoms, the doctor may agree with you and send you home with the usual directives to get some rest and drink plenty of liquids. But meningitis produces symptoms similar to influenza, and without proper and immediate treatment, it can kill. If that's the case, is the physician guilty of gross negligence?

Not usually. Adults rarely contract meningitis, and if no outbreak of the disease has been reported in your community it would be reasonable for the doctor to diagnose your ailment as influenza. This may be tragic for you and your family, and create feelings of distress and guilt for the physician, but it does not qualify in law as gross negligence. Nor should it.

Incidents of true gross negligence by physicians and hospitals occur, however. When they do, it is instructive to review how they are handled in both the legal and medical professional arenas, and to agree on methods to prevent a reoccurrence by the same physician.

In cases of gross negligence such as Morgan Bystedt's, Canadian physicians have the advantage of being supported in their defence by an aggressive ally financed in large part by public funds.

STACKING THE ODDS AGAINST YOU WITH YOUR MONEY

Thomas Harding's anger reflects his conviction that his adversary in this case went beyond accepted limits in defending a client, especially because it involved the permanent disability of a helpless baby. It is also a response to the vigorous defence launched as a result of the rare but disturbing incidents when physicians and surgeons turn away from their famed Hippocratic oath, and when claims by those who suffer from medical incompetence are fought by the Canadian Medical Protective Association. One lawyer who has duelled with the CMPA in court claims the organization "basically takes the view that anyone suing a doctor is in the extortion business."[4]

The association's belligerent attitude toward those with a substantive claim of malpractice effectively stifles many complaints. In the opinion of Thomas Berger, this tactic is a constant strategy by the CMPA. "It's, I think, coordinated across the country," says the former B.C. Supreme Court Justice. "It's intended to make these cases as difficult as possible for the plaintiffs."[5]

Supporting his view, Ontario lawyer Paul Harte, who once defended physicians for the CMPA and now acts on behalf of patients with claims of malpractice, suggests, "Probably one in ten legitimate cases of general malpractice goes forward because of the costs associated with them.... There [are] ... people out there who have been injured through no fault of their own [and] are not being compensated."[6]

As Thomas Harding noted, it's not a matter of charging your physician or surgeon with making a mistake; it's a matter of charging him or her with major mistakes that should never have been made. If you file a claim of malpractice against a CMPA member (an estimated 95 percent of all physicians and surgeons belong to the organization), you may become the target of challenges, scorn, and personal attacks similar to these:

- When sixty-eight-year-old Betty O'Reilly of Saint John, New Brunswick, suddenly collapsed and died, a coroner's report attributed her death to an overdose of Nortriptyline, an antidepressant. Mrs. O'Reilly had been following the directives of her psychiatrist, who had prescribed eight times the manufacturer's approved dose for patients of her age. When her husband, Mike, sought legal advice about launching a lawsuit against the doctor, he was told that his case was solid but the effort would require $40,000 to

$50,000 in legal fees with no assurance of success, and that he should expect the suit to drag on for years. Mike O'Reilly claimed he wasn't after money. "What I would like is an apology from the doctors," he said. But the prospects of risking $50,000 he couldn't afford, investing several years in a battle he was uncertain of winning, and opening the door to unknown allegations against him and his wife by CMPA lawyers was more than he could handle, and he dropped the idea.[7]

- Shannon Shobridge of Richmond, British Columbia, underwent surgery in September 1995 to relieve persistent pelvic pain, but for weeks after the procedure she felt even more discomfort than before. The surgical wound became infected, needing repeated draining of pus and blood, and remained sore and tender. Finally, almost three months after the original procedure, the same surgeon operated on Ms. Shobridge to remove an abscess and discovered, to the surprise and horror of the attending nurses, a six-foot length of gauze left in the patient. The surgeon, Dr. David Thomas, informed the OR nurses that "there will be no paperwork on this," directing them not to reveal the error responsible for the three months of agony suffered by Ms. Shobridge. When the truth was finally revealed, she sued Dr. Thomas for malpractice, claiming that the pain had cost her a management job in retail, among other problems. During the trial, the CMPA's lawyer suggested that she lacked a job not because of the discomfort she suffered but because she lacked intellectual ability (Ms. Shobridge is dyslexic). In the end, the patient was awarded $235,000, underwent more than a dozen operations to correct the original surgery, and required extensive psychotherapy.[8] Dr. Thomas was punished by the College of Physicians and Surgeons of B.C. with a three-month suspension, prompting Ms. Shobridge to note that she spent more time in hospitals recovering from the surgeon's mistake than he spent under suspension.[9]
- In another B.C. case, a surgeon performing gallbladder surgery spilled "hundreds" of gallstones within his patient's abdomen and

> closed the incision without removing them, causing the patient five years of pain and discomfort through many surgical procedures. During a malpractice hearing, the CMPA-hired lawyer attributed her suffering not to the enormous number of gallstones scattered among her intestines (one witness at trial described the scene as looking "like a gravel road") but to the patient's troubled home life.[10]

PHYSICIANS WILL POINT OUT, quite correctly, that their professional and financial status requires them to rely on a stalwart defence against those who might see doctors as potential targets of extortion (although the legal record provides precious little evidence that this represents a significant risk). As Mike O'Reilly's experience suggests, however, serious cases of malpractice and error may never get on the record due to the inhibiting actions of the CMPA when one of its member physicians is challenged. Any claim that patients launching malpractice suits are driven by greed is spurious. It is unlikely that any of the patients whose stories are told above believe that the suffering they underwent as a result of the medical errors was worth the monetary awards granted by the courts.

It is worth noting, in passing, that the CMPA remains one of the most powerful non-governmental organizations in Canada, especially when assessed against the public good. The association's war chest to fight judgments against its members exceeds $2 billion. With that amount of money in the bank, settlements of more than $100 million annually could be paid to aggrieved patients from earned interest alone, without drawing from the principal. And the association's balance continues to grow. During its 2005 fiscal year, the CMPA's revenues, almost entirely from membership fees and investment income, exceeded its expenses by $387 million. Among its $220-million expense bill were payments of $116 million to Canadians who successfully sued its memberships for malpractice and $115 million to its legal advisers and experts to fight the charges. For every dollar a

Canadian patient received because of a doctor's negligence, another dollar was paid to fight the claims.[11]

Each year, 60,000 CMPA members send the organization over $300 million in membership dues, which are calculated according to a sliding scale based on their practice and province. Teachers, researchers, and missionary doctors pay the lowest amounts; neurosurgeons and obstetricians are hit with the highest fees. The cost to family physicians for CMPA coverage is about the same as their automobile insurance.

In reality, many physicians and surgeons do not pay for the insurance coverage themselves—*you* pay for it. Or at least most of it. Ontario reimburses physicians for as much as 70 percent of the CMPA membership fees; some B.C. doctors are repaid 100 percent of their coverage costs by the province. So each Canadian who challenges a CMPA-insured physician or surgeon in court is paying at least a substantial portion of the legal fees for the other side to launch a defence that frequently attacks not only the patient's credibility but aspects of his or her personal life.

And the doctors hold the trump cards in this game. When the Ontario government, alarmed at the $52-million annual insurance subsidy to doctors, announced it would cancel the subsidy, obstetricians threatened to stop delivering babies, and surgeons threatened to cease performing high-risk operations. The province quickly backed down.[12]

PREVENTABLE ADVERSE EFFECTS IN HOSPITALS AND CLINICS

In a field of practice that deals literally with life-and-death issues, the legal choreography of fixing blame and assigning rewards is less important than the need to ensure that offending doctors do not repeat their errors and omissions on other patients. Unless a clearly criminal act has been committed, this duty falls into the laps of provincial medical bodies.

How well protected are Canadians from avoidable adverse effects (AAEs), ranging from transitory discomfort to death, when receiving treatment for health problems? And how effective is the system in identifying the source of the AAE and avoiding a repeat with other patients of the same physician, surgeon, or facility?

A 2004 landmark study[13] found that an estimated 9000 to 24,000 Canadian patients die each year following an AAE suffered in a hospital. This figure perhaps is not as startling as it first appears. The number of adverse events (not the death rate) in the study was estimated at 185,000, representing 7.5 percent of the 2.5 million hospital admissions recorded that year. Of these, the authors of the study estimated that perhaps 70,000 were preventable. (Non-preventable events include unanticipated reactions to an antibiotic or routine procedure.) Other countries measuring the rate of adverse events in their health care systems record annual rates ranging from 2.9 to 16.6 percent, placing Canada smack in the middle of the range. In addition, the majority of complications attributed to an AAE and leading to death appear to be related, not surprisingly, to critically ill patients who had experienced a heart attack, undergone a major surgical procedure, or were breathing with the aid of a ventilator.

Still, thousands of preventable deaths annually cannot be ignored, nor can the substantial number of Canadians who suffer pain, loss of mobility and income, and other consequences of AAEs. In an ironic twist of fate, their survival relegates them to a near-anonymous category, marked by their presence in a court of law, not a morgue.

Medical care will always carry risks, even when conducted in the best of hospitals. As one experienced physician and medical school lecturer wryly commented, "Hospitals are very dangerous places." The apparent malpractice of individual physicians and surgeons is a very different matter. When the same doctor commits similar errors year after year, leaving his patients maimed and inhibited both financially and emotionally from seeking a settlement, the situation demands attention.

These outrageous cases of multiple incidents of malpractice should not by any means suggest that Canadians are inundated with doctors who, were they employed at criminal instead of medical activities, would be quickly labelled repeat offenders. But though we may forgive a doctor for one grievous error, we should be concerned when medical professionals maintain a pattern of incompetence, misconduct, and apparent disregard for their patients over an extended period of time. In many cases, the patients are left scarred and humiliated. And a disturbing note: in virtually every case, the physicians are male and the patients female.

INCOMPETENT MALE DOCTORS AND SCARRED FEMALE VICTIMS

The still-unfolding tale of Dr. Errol "Sonny" Wai-Ping has echoes of Gothic horror tales in which a dominant male brutalizes innocent women in a dark, forbidding castle dungeon. Here, the male villain is a highly educated and qualified surgeon, and the castle dungeon is an operating room in a small suburban hospital.

Born and raised in Trinidad, Dr. Wai-Ping obtained a science degree at the University of Toronto, returned to Trinidad to earn his medical degree at the University of the West Indies, came back to Canada to intern at Toronto's Mount Sinai Hospital and the Hospital for Sick Children, and received specialist training in obstetrics and gynaecology at the University of Saskatchewan, all highly regarded institutions. In 1992, he opened an office and clinic in the Toronto suburb of Whitby and earned privileges to practise at a hospital in nearby Ajax.

Almost from the beginning, patients began filing complaints against Dr. Wai-Ping's abilities and attitude. According to documents filed in legal proceedings and with the discipline committee of the College of Physicians and Surgeons of Ontario (CPSO), the surgeon compounded errors with an often abusive bedside manner, as demonstrated in these cases:[14]

- Patient A, age thirty, arrived at the hospital with severe haemorrhaging. Dr. Wai-Ping diagnosed her as suffering from cervical cancer

* Patient names have been concealed in response to requests from the CPSO.

and performed a hysterectomy. The surgical procedure was not well handled, leaving the patient bleeding and in pain for several days. Biopsy results indicated the woman's cervix was normal and non-cancerous.

- Patient B, age twenty-four, suffered from menorrhagia, excessive menstrual bleeding. Instead of pursuing other treatments, including prolonged progestin therapy and various medical and conservative surgical options, Dr. Wai-Ping performed a hysterectomy. (Commenting on these two cases, the CPSO evaluation of Dr. Wai-Ping noted they had to undergo subsequent ovarian surgeries, thus "both women were surgically castrated by age thirty.")
- Patient C, age twenty-seven, had undergone only two months of therapy with birth control medications to treat painful menses before Dr. Wai-Ping performed an abdominal hysterectomy.
- Patient D, age twenty-eight, took clomiphene, a medication prescribed to assist women to conceive. When she complained of pain, Dr. Wai-Ping noted two ovarian cysts and conducted an abdominal hysterectomy and removal of her ovaries. Clomiphene is known to cause benign cysts, a side effect that the surgeon either was unaware of or ignored.
- Patient E, age thirty-five, suffered from dysmenorrhoea (painful menstruation). Instead of exploring less drastic and invasive treatment, such as antibiotics to treat infection, surgery to remove fibroids or polyps, or low-dose oral contraceptives to prevent ovulation, Dr. Wai-Ping informed her that her only option was a total abdominal hysterectomy, which he performed.
- Patient F, age twenty-nine, was diagnosed with simple endometrial hyperplasia, the thickening of the walls of the uterus. Rejecting the normal procedure of prescribing progesterone or conducting a simple D&C procedure, Dr. Wai-Ping performed a vaginal hysterectomy.
- Patient G, post-menopausal, had been consulting her gynecologist about bleeding problems. With her regular specialist on vacation,

she was examined by Dr. Wai-Ping, who prescribed and conducted an immediate hysterectomy despite the absence of any proof of the need for urgent care.

- Patient H, age thirty-three, underwent an ultrasound procedure that appeared to identify a hemorrhagic ovarian cyst without active bleeding. Normal response to this condition is to consider it benign and treat with analgesia and observation. Dr. Wai-Ping performed surgery. During this procedure, the right fallopian tube was damaged, but no note was made of this in the operative record.
- Patient I also underwent ultrasound on her ovaries. Although the ultrasound report said that the right ovary was not convincingly seen and that no abnormal mass was demonstrated, Dr. Wai-Ping's pre-operative note stated that it showed a 3.7-cm cyst on the right side, and he removed the right ovary.
- Patient J gave birth and suffered post-partum bleeding. Dr. Wai-Ping instructed the nurses by telephone to pack the vagina with sponges and did not assess the patient until the following morning, when he inserted another pack. The patient required multiple blood transfusions and a D&C. Wai-Ping was in the hospital when he gave the order for the pack, but he did not assess the patient.
- Patient K requested an epidural during delivery of her child, but Dr. Wai-Ping performed a vacuum extraction and forceps delivery after one hour in the second stage of labour without the use of analgesia.

The above list may appear extensive, but it represents a fraction of the cases in which Dr. Wai-Ping's surgical record extended beyond incompetence to suggest, in the minds of many, butchery. The CPSO found him incompetent in forty-seven cases they investigated, although more than 150 women filed complaints against him. When word spread of their investigation into his record, *225 women* claimed similar sufferings at his scrubbed-and-gloved hands, joining a $25-million class-action suit against him and the hospital that had granted him operating privileges.

As horrific as the cases of unnecessary and incompetent surgeries might appear, the college's charges against Dr. Wai-Ping also included record-keeping that often appeared designed to conceal his actions. Many female patients charged that his attitude toward and response to their concerns were abusive. One patient, a qualified nurse, knew that her post-operative condition involving hemorrhaging and fever indicated serious problems. When she contacted Dr. Wai-Ping by telephone from her hospital bed to request that he assess her condition, he hung up on her. She immediately had herself transferred to another hospital, where she was diagnosed with an abdominal abscess that would probably have proved fatal had it been ignored much longer.

In March 2004, more than ten years after the first complaint was recorded against Dr. Wai-Ping, the College of Physicians and Surgeons of Ontario cancelled the surgeon's licence, preventing him from practising medicine in the province and, effectively, anywhere else in Canada. An examination of his records revealed that Dr. Wai-Ping's patients suffered post-surgery infections at four times the rate of other patients in the hospital and received hysterectomies at ten times the rate for other surgeons in the facility.

Wai-Ping may have lost his licence, but he still had the CMPA to defend him with vigour against charges laid by former patients. Some cases dragged on for more than five years thanks to court delays, failed attempts at arbitration, and repeated appeals filed by CMPA lawyers. The association's legal team, comprising more than a dozen attorneys from the prestigious firm McCarthy Tetrault, billed the CMPA as much as $525 per hour; one estimate claimed that the physicians' association had spent over $2 million defending Dr. Wai-Ping by the spring of 2006, with the clock still ticking on billable hours.

Not all of the doctor's legal expenses are covered by funds drawn out of the CMPA accounts. In April 2006 the disgraced surgeon demanded $32,000 from one of the former patients who was suing him to cover his own legal costs.

Over the same period that Dr. Wai-Ping was performing unnecessary and poorly executed surgeries on female patients east of Toronto, another obstetrician-gynecologist was facing similar problems in a western suburb of the city, in a case with disturbing parallels of serious infliction and questionable discipline.

Dr. Sankar Vaidyanathan, who practised at the Humber River Regional Hospital in Etobicoke, faced allegations from forty-seven women that he had been incompetent in his treatment of them. Most claimed that he displayed a lack of knowledge, skill, and judgment, or exhibited blatant disregard for their welfare. Of these charges, twenty-six cases were investigated by the hospital and the CPSO in early 2001.[15]

One patient was diagnosed with spontaneous rupture of membranes when she was thirty-four weeks pregnant. The first physician to examine her prescribed a medication to assist the fetus to develop lungs and antibiotics to prevent possible infection as a result of the broken membranes. When Dr. Vaidyanathan assumed care of the patient a few days later, tests and the patient's comments suggested that the baby's movements had "slowed down." Three days later, when the patient returned for an examination, Dr. Vaidyanathan told her the baby was dead. Despite the fact that the patient had delivered her first child via caesarean section and had been expected to deliver the second child in the same manner, a fact noted on her chart, Dr. Vaidyanathan tried to induce labour naturally. Only when this failed, with excessive suffering for the patient, did he perform a C-section delivery. The CPSO investigation ruled that the baby's death had been preventable, the doctor's documentation was faulty, and the patient was never made part of the decision regarding her treatment.

In another case, Dr. Vaidyanathan assured a patient in her thirty-second week of pregnancy that her unborn child was normal, despite the patient's complaints of decreased movement by the fetus. A week later, another visit to the hospital confirmed that the baby was dead, and Dr. Vaidyanathan attempted to induce labour with misoprostol, a drug normally used for the treatment of duodenal ulcers. Around midnight the woman complained of chest pains, and tests revealed an elevated heart rate and very low blood pressure. Vaidyanathan ignored increasing concern from the nurses until the morning, when he consulted an internist, who determined the patient was in shock. A quickly scheduled operation was needed to repair her ruptured uterus.

Other incidents add to the picture of a physician with apparently little concern about the health and welfare of his patients. He admitted falsifying records to conceal incorrect treatment of a pregnant patient, ordering nurses to stop administering medication prescribed by another physician even though Vaidyanathan was unfamiliar with the patient's history, and maintaining substandard documentation.

Despite the seriousness of these allegations, it took the OCPS more than three years from the first complaint about Dr. Vaidyanathan's antics to complete its report and specify penalties. Of twenty-six documented charges of malpractice, an OCPS investigating committee confirmed the essential facts in sixteen of them. Despite finding that the doctor had been incompetent, dishonest, and unreliable, and had demonstrated little remorse for his actions, the investigating committee refused to revoke his licence. Instead, they suspended the doctor's licence for twenty-four months, backdating it to the day he voluntarily withdrew from practising medicine. Even then, the suspension period would be shortened by eighteen months if the doctor completed a series of training courses, sought psychiatric assistance to manage his stress levels, and returned to practice gradually under supervision.

The doctor's aggrieved patients and their representatives on the committee had asked for a complete revocation of his licence as the only safe means of protecting the public. They had to satisfy themselves with a de facto six-month suspension plus $12,500 in costs to be paid by Vaidyanathan who, the committee's report noted, "even when declared incompetent in regard to the cases at issue in this hearing, was indeed capable of rehabilitation."

Or was he? In October 2005 another OCPS investigation heard that Dr. Vaidyanathan had removed a patient's healthy ovaries without her consent, punctured a patient's bowel and uterus during a bungled internal procedure, and performed a tubal ligation on a woman without determining that she was already pregnant. A new investigation by the OCPS ruled that he was not guilty of incompetence but only of "[failing] to meet the standard of practice in his care of six of the women."[16] Two months later, the doctor was punished with a recorded reprimand and ordered yet again to adhere to various terms, conditions, and limitations on his practice. During all of this period, there is no evidence that Dr. Vaidyanathan's privileges at the hospital were lifted.

HOW MUCH PROTECTION FROM MEDICAL INCOMPETENCE CAN CANADIANS COUNT ON?

These may be exceptional cases, and their existence should not suggest that the level of physician care in Canada is noticeably worse than it was ten or twenty years ago. Reduced hesitation by patients to assess the quality of care provided by physicians may in fact suggest that health care professionals are subject to wider and closer scrutiny than before. In 2000, one in twenty-five Canadian physicians was the subject of a new legal action, and between 1995 and 1999, the number of malpractice cases going to trial doubled.[17]

Patients reading about the cases of Wai-Ping, Vaidyanathan, and others understandably question the accountability of doctors who fail to measure up to standards, leaving their patients suffering physically and emotionally. It is not unreasonable for them to wonder how often serious errors by physicians are dismissed as unfortunate and unavoidable aspects of the disease or injury being treated. The frequency and impact of such errors remain essentially unknowable, and to question every death or serious consequence of medical treatment on the basis that the physician or surgeon may have been incompetent would be a form of paranoia. It would also defy the reality that medical diagnosis and treatment depend on both art and science (if "art" means the unique abilities of each practitioner). In that sense, the medical profession may claim "To err is human" with at least as much validity as any other group.

It is reasonable, however, to expect the medical community to be held to a clearly defined standard, a task that many Canadians may be surprised to discover is not directly maintained by government bodies. Medical professionals are evaluated, approved, and supervised by self-regulating provincial organizations (SROs), not by government bodies per se. A practical alternative to this arrangement may not exist, given the training, demands, and expectations placed on physicians and surgeons. But as patients, we have to trust that the SROs are putting the interests of the patients on at least the same level as the interests of the doctors. In the case of Dr. Vaidyanathan, concerns have been raised about the CPSO's actions. Could it have been more responsive to earlier complaints?

Similar questions were asked in the notorious case of another Toronto-area physician, neurologist Ronald H. Wilson. He and a technician operated a series of clinics providing electroencephalography tests, tracking electrical activity within the brain. Descriptions of the conditions in Wilson's clinics would astonish anyone with a rudimentary understanding of anti-infection procedures. Needles inserted into the scalps of patients were used over and over again without any serious attempt at sterilization. Blood often poured from scalp wounds where the needles were inserted, and the wounds were rarely treated against infection or even bandaged. Patients who complained of severe pain from the process were bullied by Wilson's technician, and any clinic employee critical of the hygiene standards was dismissed. Records confirmed that the infection rate for Wilson's patients was 600 times higher than normal for this procedure.

The results were both predictable and appalling. An estimated 15,000 patients of Wilson's clinic either contracted deadly hepatitis B or were suspected of having acquired the disease. At least one patient died; hundreds more live with the effects of the viral infection, and are at greater risk of contracting diseases such as cancer and cirrhosis of the liver. Yet it took eleven years from the first infection for the CPSO to complete its investigation of Wilson, find him incompetent, charge him with performing unnecessary tests (for which he billed the provincial health system), and set a penalty hearing date. And over most of those years, he continued to practise medicine.

Doctors elsewhere in Canada grew concerned about another development: the court gave its approval for Wilson's patients to launch a class-action suit, a rare procedure in Canada. The suit, originally seeking $100 million in damages and punishment, was settled for $27.5 million, paid by the CMPA.[18] The original claim of $100 million represents the total amount paid by the CMPA for all physicians in Canada for an entire year. Clearly, the CMPA and physicians generally fear the impact of class-action suits if they become widespread.

One response has been for Canada's medical schools to address the reality of possible legal action against physicians. The Faculty of Medicine at Newfoundland's Memorial University includes a course called "The Importance of Medical-Legal Education" in its curriculum to sharpen not the diagnostic and therapeutic skills of its students but their understanding and appreciation of risky decision-making. Included in a test on the subject are questions such as the following:

- A first-year resident has been dating a patient whom he briefly examined in a clinic. Is this okay?
- A patient has requested a copy of her file, but an orthopaedic surgeon who did an assessment of the patient is refusing to permit the resident to provide a copy of the orthopaedic's consult, which is part of the file. What should the resident do?
- A pregnant schizophrenic woman is refusing prenatal care. What should be done?
- An elderly patient was admitted with a diagnosis of cholelithiasis (gallstones) but died within twenty-six hours of hospitalization.

The patient had not undergone surgery. Should the residents call the coroner?[19]

The test recognizes that, in recent years, many complaints about physicians have related as much to ethical and moral issues as to questions of professional competence. In fact, according to data from provincial medical colleges responsible for licensing and disciplining doctors, a patient is more likely to suffer the effects of sexual exploitation than malpractice at the hands of a physician, especially in a female patient–male physician encounter. In late 2006, the College of Physicians and Surgeons of Nova Scotia published the results of thirteen disciplinary hearings involving its members. Of these, six related to charges of sexual exploitation; only three touched on questions of competence. (The others involved alcoholism, drunk driving, writing an excessive number of prescriptions for narcotic drugs, and breach of confidence.)[20] Similar ratios can be found in the records of other provincial medical colleges that make such information public.

Not all do. Your ability as a patient to assess allegations and disciplinary actions against your physician or surgeon depends on your place of residence. Canadians in Newfoundland and Labrador, Nova Scotia, Ontario, Manitoba, and British Columbia have internet access to documentation that includes a description of the charges (patient names are always concealed), the physician's defence, the college's findings, and the limitations, if any, imposed on the doctor's practice. Those in Prince Edward Island, New Brunswick, Saskatchewan, and Alberta have no such access. New Brunswick reports on incidents but conceals both the physician and patient names; Quebec posts its findings in French only.

Provinces that publish highly detailed descriptions of charges laid against doctors, as well as the resulting decisions and penalties, if any, do so in the interests of patients. Physicians, of course, note that information revealed to patients can virtually destroy a doctor's credibility, not to mention his or her social and political status in the community. This complaint should be viewed as a secondary issue, and not a very important one at that. Professional financial advisers, to cite one example, may find details of charges and assessed penalties, including any suspension of their right to remain in the profession, made publicly available. Canadians have at least as much right to information regarding their health care as they have to the care their investments are receiving.

Dr. Dale Mercer agrees. As the president of the College of Physicians and Surgeons of Ontario (CPSO), he represents more medical professionals than anyone else in Canada. "The college is open to providing information to the public that is related to a doctor's practice," Mercer emphasizes. "Even more information on the physician register may be made public in the future as the public seeks more aspects of what we do at the college."[21]

In the summer of 2006, twenty-six Ontario women suggested it was too late for them. All claimed to have suffered serious abdominal injuries at the hands of a Toronto-area obstetrician/gynecologist; these injuries included, in several cases, perforated bowels and bladders. As a result, the women had to wear plastic bags to collect urine and stools, and most had launched malpractice lawsuits.

None of the claims had been proven in court, but the CPSO must have been suspicious of so many claims against the same physician, alleging similar incompetence and injuries. If so, anyone accessing the CPSO website would never have known because the physician's name remained in place, with no hint of the pending claims.

While this reflects the honourable notion of innocent until proven guilty, it compromises the expectation of patients that a pattern of unacceptable behaviour will not be allowed to continue. The hospital where the surgeon practised did not make public any information regarding claims against the doctor. The lawyer representing several of the women in their lawsuits asked, "Why would the doctor's right to hide [serious charges of incompetence] supersede your right to know that doctor has a track record where there's been a number of complications?"[22]

Thomas Harding, who maintains that Canadian physicians found guilty of incompetence frequently avoid appropriate penalties for their acts, has a wry view of control and punishment. “In the U.S.A.,” Harding notes, “they would be put out of business. Not by the professional regulator but by the insurance companies—their premiums would rise so high that the doctors would give up their practice.”

8

HOSPITALS
DOES TOYOTA HAVE THE ANSWER?

She is known only as Mrs. Grant, a pseudonym, but she has become famous among those who decry how the medical profession treats its patients and those who are dedicated to improving the state of patient care in hospitals, especially when the need for improvement is prompted by simple, avoidable tragedy.[1]

The sixty-eight-year-old non-diabetic woman had entered hospital for elective cardiac bypass surgery. The procedure resulted in a number of complications common among patients undergoing this operation, including ventilator-acquired pneumonia, and she remained in an intensive care unit longer than normal while she recovered.

Two weeks following her surgery, Mrs. Grant's condition had stabilized and her primary physician noted during his rounds that she was feeling comfortable; her attitude was positive, and her physical condition had improved to the point that he recommended imminent transfer from the ICU to a regular ward bed before discharge from the hospital and an anticipated complete recovery.

At 6:20 the next morning, Mrs. Grant awoke, sipped some orange juice, and fell asleep again. Nothing untoward was noted by the night nurse. About half an hour later, an alarm alerted the night nurse that an arterial line was blocked, probably from a blood clot. The nurse flushed the line according to standard procedure, noted it in his report, and left Mrs. Grant sleeping soundly.

By 8:15, the day nurse had assumed her duties in the ICU. Suddenly Mrs. Grant's body began flailing uncontrollably in a series of violent seizures. Over the next five hours every available resource and procedure was applied, including a CT scan, which revealed no brain haemorrhaging or other apparent cause. Blood test results, however, indicated that Mrs. Grant was suffering from acute hypoglycaemia, and the next several hours were spent attempting to raise her blood sugar level without success. Mrs. Grant, now in a deep coma, remained in that state for seven weeks before her family agreed to withdraw life support.

In the midst of the controlled chaos surrounding Mrs. Grant, the day nurse noticed an empty vial of insulin on the medication cart outside her room. The conclusion was obvious: instead of administering Heparin, a standard blood thinner, to clear Mrs. Grant's blocked arterial line, the night nurse had injected insulin, which caused hypoglycaemic shock that proved irreversible.

MRS. GRANT'S TRAGIC DEATH substantiates the observation that hospitals indeed are dangerous places. The dangers exist not only in the risk of transfer of viruses and bacteria, but in the potential for disaster as a result of easily avoided human error. The detailed report on this incident, presented in a leading medical journal, revealed the extent of these errors and suggested a promising, if unconventional, means of averting them in the future.

Mrs. Grant's two-week stay in an ICU was well beyond the normal period required for her procedure, but it was necessary because of the pneumonia she contracted from the ventilator used to assist her breathing. Even in an ICU, where we might expect to encounter higher standards of hygiene and a lower incidence of potential exposure to sources of infection, secondary complications take an enormous toll in human life and health care costs.

A German study found that of 103 long-term patients in a fourteen-bed ICU over the year-long duration of the research, 48 percent developed one or more attacks of ventilator-acquired pneumonia.[2] The majority of these cases involved *Staphylococcus aureus*, a bacterium highly resistant to antibiotics that has become widely known as "the hospital germ" because of its presence in hospitals everywhere in the world.

To a patient recovering from an operation as intrusive as heart bypass surgery, pneumonia introduces an alarming level of risk and complication—not to mention cost, especially in an ICU setting.

Mrs. Grant's unfortunate death can be evaluated two ways. It represents an unnecessary loss of life, which is especially ironic, given that Mrs. Grant survived a delicate cardiac bypass procedure only to succumb to foolish human error. The technology employed to repair critical arteries feeding the heart would have been categorized as science fiction a generation or two ago, yet perhaps 35,000 Canadians annually undergo the procedure, with the vast majority recovering free of complications. Surviving their hospital stay, especially in ICUs, is another matter.

This is the other measure of the case, for while Canadians express concern about the growing cost of universal health care, they assume the solution lies in providing more money. The greatest returns, however, are promised by improving management of the system—in this case, hospitals—to attain greater levels of efficiency. The potential rewards of modernizing hospitals to slash unnecessary costs are enormous, even if the hospitals move from an efficiency level of the 1920s, where they now function in many ways, to an equivalent level of immediate pre-computerization in the early 1960s. Changes that cost pennies to correct could produce savings of millions of dollars each year.

Hyperbole? Not a bit, considering the level of expenses involved. Each ICU bed costs $1800 per day; medical ward beds cost something over $1000 per day.[3] If a relatively small hospital treats 5000 patients annually, and 10 percent of them remain in hospital an average of ten days beyond their normal recovery period as a result of errors, inefficiencies, injuries, and preventable secondary infections, the avoidable extra cost (measured by extended accommodation alone) is $9 million annually. Add inevitable other expenses and the annual drain on revenues will easily top $20 million for a single hospital.

While no detailed analysis of preventable hospital expenses is available for Canada on a national basis, a U.S. study that measured hospital errors, and their cost in dollars and human suffering, estimated that as many as 987,000 patients were injured annually, leading to between 44,000 and 98,000 deaths.[4] Even the minimum estimate of deaths exceeds the number of Americans killed in motor accidents every year.

The monetary costs to hospitals alone, according to the study, was estimated at $17 billion to $29 billion each year. No figures exist to suggest that Canadian hospitals are better at avoiding these preventable errors than their U.S. counterparts, so that translates into a drain on the health system's resources of between $1.7 and $2.9 billion each year. These estimates are considered very conservative by most observers. In fact, when it comes to hospital-acquired infections, such as the one that extended Mrs. Grant's stay and led to the human error that cost her life, Canadian hospitals are considered substandard. A 2003 benchmark study[5] suggested that half of all such illnesses are preventable, and 80 percent of Canadian hospitals "fall seriously short in preventing patients from getting hospital infections."

"This is a tragedy and very disturbing," said the report's author, Dr. Dick Zoutman, who, in addition to his position as epidemiologist at Queen's University, serves as director of infection control services at Kingston General Hospital and was chair of the Ontario SARS Scientific Advisory Committee. "The results clearly show that we need to be doing a lot more to prevent hospital-acquired infections. Our hospitals are not safe enough."

Dr. Zoutman quotes the Community and Hospital Infection Control Associations of Canada, which in 2003 estimated that each year about 250,000 patients experience infected surgical wounds, blood infections, and infections of antibiotic-resistant organisms while in hospital. Of this number perhaps 8000 will die, and the treatment price will exceed $1 billion. (For more on this subject, see Chapter 9, "Treatment: How Much Care Can We Afford to Offer?")

These are statistics. But it must be remembered that we are discussing human tragedies, often the result of stunning mismanagement by individuals whose profession is literally a matter of life and death. In the summer of 1996, Jeffrey Brown, thirty-three, was being treated for a kidney infection at Leamington District Memorial Hospital, in southwestern Ontario. A nurse prepared to give him an injection of furosemide, a diuretic that would flush extra fluids from his kidneys. Brown had received similar injections several times and fully expected this to be a routine procedure. As soon as the fluid entered his veins, however, he knew it was not. Screaming with pain, he pleaded with the nurse to stop, pulling his arm away. Instead of stopping, the nurse placed her weight on the arm and forced the medication into his body. Losing consciousness, Brown died within minutes. Instead of the essentially harmless diuretic, the nurse had forced into her patient 20 cc of concentrated potassium chloride, the chemical used in many U.S. prisons to perform executions via lethal injection.[6]

The experiences of Jeffrey Brown and Mrs. Grant are not unique, but neither are they evidence of an entire system staffed with incompetents. With an estimated 1.5 million hospital admissions annually in Canada, errors, even monumental errors like the one that doomed Mr. Brown, will sometimes occur. If we predict that 0.1 percent of annual hospital admissions will result in errors of substantial magnitude, we should expect 1500 serious incidents every year. In fact, studies suggest that the health of at least 1 percent of all patients entering a hospital will seriously deteriorate, not from complications of the original reason for being hospitalized but from incidents suffered within the care facility. The vast majority of these, thankfully, are not nearly as egregious as the one that doomed Jeffrey Brown.

Most are the result of acquiring an infection within the hospital environment.

Are hospital-acquired infections inevitable? Not necessarily. True, hospitals have become the residences of choice for *Staphylococcus aureus*, the bacterium that infected Mrs. Grant. As a result of the excessive use of antibiotics, *S. aureus* is now resistant to methicillin, once the standard antibacterial treatment for such infections. This gives the nasty little bug virtually free rein to leap from patient to patient in hospital settings, where it is frighteningly effective at invading lungs, blood, bones, skin, and joints. Given its wide distribution and the difficulty of controlling it, *S. aureus* represents a far greater risk to human life—not to mention cost for treatment—than SARS, West Nile virus, or most other virulent dangers.

That's the bad news. The better news is that the majority of *S. aureus* infections in hospitals are preventable. The basic step of insisting that hospital staff improve their hand-washing routines could reduce such infections by as much as 35 percent.[7] Even the relatively simple act of increasing the separation between beds in ward settings from 1.9 to 2.5 metres would cut infections dramatically. If a 2006 study by the Pennsylvania Healthcare Cost Containment Council is correct and applicable to Canada,* each hospital patient who avoids acquiring *S. aureus* during his or her stay represents a reduction in total hospital costs—ICU or bed, medications, physicians, nurses, technicians, lab tests, etc.—of almost US$90,000.[8] Here's another, more direct measure from the same study: of patients with a hospital-acquired infection, about 15 percent die as a direct result of the ailment, compared with less than 2.5 percent who expire because of other preventable causes, such as faulty diagnosis, wrong medication, and equipment failure or malfunction.

*Our reliance on U.S. studies stems from the abysmal attention paid in Canada to these kinds of statistics. Even the country's auditor-general calls Canada "surveillance poor" on health statistics generally.

The solution to these problems is well within the reach of most hospitals. By simply modifying their designs, layouts, and methods of operations, hospitals could bring about great savings in dollars and lives, yet they do not. The reason has little to do with either ignorance or disregard, and everything to do with operating philosophies.

Hospital staff, like employees in most complex organizations, assume a dual approach to their work best described as "Make do" and "Work around it." Most of us understand and apply these twin methods of dealing with challenges in our own work and domestic chores. The light on the basement stairs is burnt out and you have no spare light bulbs available? *Make do*—just be careful descending into the cellar. Your dinner guests are arriving in an hour and your recipe calls for a double boiler and you loaned yours to your sister-in-law? *Work around it* by heating the sauce gently in a bowl or pot set over hot water.

The consequences of this approach at home can range from a ruined dinner to a serious fall downstairs; the consequences from the same approach when applied to hospital operations are often fatal and, at the very least, lead to an enormous increase in costs. In fact, hospitals may actually "make do" and "work around" problems more frequently and on a more widespread basis than other organizations because they often lurch from one life-or-death crisis to another. The primary goal is to save the patient, and in an ICU environment a decision made under pressure may well involve a life-or-death outcome. This "make do/work around" philosophy almost ensures that easily corrected errors will occur again and again *because those in the system lack the will, the time, the resources, and the process to eliminate them.*

Let's return to the errors that led to the unnecessary deaths of Jeffrey Brown and Mrs. Grant. Mr. Brown's death was attributed to human error, and nothing further was recorded except verbal assurances that it would not happen again.

A remarkably detailed investigation into Mrs. Grant's death revealed that other nurses had come very close to injecting a patient with insulin instead of Heparin, and vice versa. In those instances, the nurses corrected themselves quickly, almost by reflex, and administered the prescribed medication but *never drew attention to the error.* Why should they? Their professional training and dedication to the patient's safety had kicked in and avoided a potential tragedy. (The investigation of Mrs. Grant's death suggested that timing had been a factor in her incident; it was the end of an evening shift, the nurse was fatigued, and the light in the ICU, dimmed to encourage sleep for patients, made it difficult to read the vial label.)

Nurses admitted they had often noted the similarity between the vials of insulin and Heparin, but none had suggested that the labels or containers be altered, or even that the vials not be placed adjacent to each other in the cart. Aware of the risk, they simply increased their level of vigilance and "worked around it." One nurse described this practice as "confronting the same problem every day for years and treating it as just another irritation, another inefficient way of doing things, then moving on."

The problem with "making do" and "working around it" in a hospital environment is that the underlying problem is rarely, if ever, solved. Like the mistake that cost Mrs. Grant her life, an error is addressed only when the problem yields a disaster. Meanwhile, preventable errors in hospitals, as extrapolated from U.S. estimates, cause 5000 to 10,000 deaths annually in Canadian hospitals and drain billions of dollars from an overtaxed system.

This is perhaps where the P4P proposal that is gaining support in the United States fails to hold promise. If individual performance represents the prime measure for each patient, especially in a complex hospital environment, where a dozen or more providers are involved in activities, no one will feel compelled to step away from a problem, examine the underlying cause, and impose a corrective procedure unless an incentive is offered for such diligence. There is a limit, then, to "market-based solutions," especially in the context of publicly funded health care.

The ultimate means of reducing human error and avoidable secondary infections while tackling steady increases in hospital expenses may lie not in the realm of public funding but in the enlightened environment of private industry, according to progressive quarters of the free-enterprise-based U.S. health care system.

In Pittsburgh, Pennsylvania, twenty-four local hospitals managed to reduce the incidence of bloodstream infections, caused by intravenous catheters placed in blood vessels leading to the heart, by more than 50 percent (some achieved a 90 percent reduction). Central line associated bloodstream (CLAB) infections pose a serious risk for already-weakened patients, with one of the surveyed Pittsburgh hospitals recording a 40 percent mortality rate from these infections. An average 50 percent reduction of infections among two dozen hospitals applying a similar system to tackle the same problem represents a major breakthrough. And where did the system originate? At a Japanese auto plant.

Most manufacturers in the world have implemented some lessons from "the Toyota Way." More than any other element, Toyota's management principles and business philosophies, which have been adapted by the firm's suppliers and competitors alike, are responsible for Japan's domination of the global automotive market and Toyota's position as the world's largest and most profitable car manufacturer. The Toyota Way requires fewer man-hours of production and lower levels of on-hand inventory while producing higher-quality vehicles at less cost. On that basis, it qualifies as the most important manufacturing advance since the Industrial Revolution and deserves consideration as a tool not just for manufacturing operations but for management of any complex system. Including health care.

THINGS THAT AN AUTOMOTIVE ASSEMBLY LINE CAN TEACH A HOSPITAL

Patients can be thought of like automobiles if we recognize that the systems managing these two very different "products" are similar. Of the fourteen principles that make up the Toyota Way, at least five can be adapted by virtually every system of management, given sufficient will. They include:

1. Eliminate wasted time and resources
2. Find low-cost yet reliable alternatives to expensive options
3. Build a learning culture of continuous improvement
4. Base management decisions on a long-term philosophy, even at the expense of short-term financial goals
5. Do the right thing for everyone concerned: the company, its employees, its customers, and society as a whole[9]

The first response of most hospital operational and administrative staff, when it is suggested that they adapt a system born on an automotive assembly line, is to roll their eyes and shake their heads. Engineering an automobile and slapping identical parts together to create a million replications of the same product can hardly be compared, they will point out, with treating a million patients, each distinctive from the other in gender, age, ailments, attitudes, and so on. Besides, they will add, caregivers must not be categorized as assembly-line workers; patients are sensitive and vulnerable human beings, and they deserve individual care and treatment.*

This attitude suggests a failure of the medical profession to change its mindset. While the practice of medicine inspires and welcomes technological advances, from MRI machines to artificial hearts, its systematic approach often seems deeply rooted in a time when patients were invited, if not directed, to treat physicians and surgeons

*All well and good, until you discover that orthopaedic surgeons routinely schedule knee replacement operations on alternate days—right knees today, left knees tomorrow, right knees the day after, and so on. They may emphasize that this lessens the possibility of performing surgery on a healthy knee, and it does. One cannot help being reminded, however, of an automotive assembly line at the sight of several patients lined up outside an OR, waiting to move through the stages of preparation, anaesthesia, surgery, and recovery with the same team of surgeons and nurses, each with a distinct and specified function to be repeated.

as infallible demigods whose training and abilities were beyond reproach.

Imagine those five Toyota principles adapted to hospital applications:

1. Eliminate wasted time and resources spent duplicating or correcting overlooked procedures
2. Find low-cost yet reliable alternatives to expensive treatments, tests, equipment, and facilities
3. Build a learning culture of continuous improvement by eliminating "make do/work around" attitudes
4. Base management decisions on a long-term philosophy, even at the expense of short-term financial goals, with the objective of saving future lives and future dollars
5. Do the right thing for everyone concerned: the hospital, its staff, its patients, and society as a whole

Now the approach sounds acceptable, if still somewhat alien to hospital applications. But the Toyota philosophy produced the dramatic reduction in CLAB infections recorded in the Pittsburgh-area hospitals, saving dozens of lives and hundreds of thousands of dollars. The hospitals employed a range of small process enhancements—not loudly trumpeted "breakthroughs"—to achieve their impressive reduction, with each hospital adapting procedures according to its own needs and situation. These included such apparently mundane steps as

- changing the standard disinfectant to a more potent formula;
- using transparent dressings to keep wounds visible and eliminate the necessity of removing the old dressing, exposing the wound to the air for inspection, and covering with a new dressing;
- changing bloodstream lines for all new admissions;
- ensuring hand-washing compliance among all caregivers;
- permitting medical residents to place and change lines only under supervision until fully trained;

- investigating, identifying, and tracing each infection as it is discovered;
- initiating identification of positive cultures and identifying sources.

None of these is revolutionary, but in a "make do/work around" environment, especially one focused on cost control as much as patient care, none would be easily implemented unless the focus was shifted from this month's (or this quarter's or this year's) budget restraints to more significant long-term savings. Transparent dressings are more expensive than traditional materials, changing lines for every new admission is time-consuming, and restricting the activities of resident interns may be difficult to justify on an immediate cost-effective basis. But compared with the expense of treating hospital-acquired infections, especially those caused by CLABs, it is a penny's worth of prevention to save a pound of cure. Saved lives, of course, are inestimable.

Seeing these kinds of advances strictly in terms of single applications in reduced cost is not the point. Constant improvement demands a changed mindset, one applied across the entire system. So far, where it's been executed with commitment, it appears to work.

Consider the pre-surgery nursing unit at Pittsburgh's Western Pennsylvania Hospital ("West Penn"), where an average of forty-two patients are prepared for scheduled surgery each day. After a unit secretary enters the patient's data into the hospital's computer system, a nurse accesses the patient's medical history, conducts a physical examination, and draws a blood sample for testing. The results of these tests are passed along to the surgical team.

In some instances, the nurse conducting the physical examination would draw the blood. At other times, the nurses would call on a technician to carry out the procedure. If the nurse's attention was diverted by some unexpected intrusion, blood sampling and testing might be overlooked completely. On other occasions, blood work was delayed by an absence of supplies. In fact, one in six patients, or more than 15 percent of those scheduled for surgery, would arrive at the operating room without having their blood work completed, and the operation would have to be delayed until the information arrived.

The cost of these delays was enormous—about $300 per minute that the OR remained idle. In many cases, procedures were delayed or even cancelled, meaning that all the preparatory work to that point would have to be repeated the next day. Patients with serious ailments and those who had fasted prior to the scheduled procedure experienced a good deal of anxiety.

Most hospitals throughout North America recognize this kind of bottleneck as just one of dozens of similar hurdles facing staff. The deeply ingrained approach is to reschedule, shuffle, and improvise. In other words, to "make do/work around it."

West Penn decided to implement the continuous-improvement approach in this one area as a test before adapting the Toyota concept throughout the facility. The goal was not only to ensure that blood work was done in a timely and efficient manner but to improve the procedure as a whole. Much of the program was based on the elimination of ambiguities, and the activity proceeded in this manner:

1. Introduce visual indicators to confirm that blood has been drawn (these consisted of coloured stickers attached to charts and to the patient's bed).
2. Designate one individual per shift to draw blood samples and monitor and maintain supplies.
3. Carry out the blood work as soon as the patient is registered.
4. Indicate patients for blood work by placing a card on a rack as soon as the patient's registration is completed. A glance at the rack by the assigned nurse would show how many were awaiting the procedure.
5. Convert a small storage room into a designated area for drawing blood samples. Fresh bright paint and lighting, plus a comfortable

chair for patients, reduces anxiety. Only supplies necessary for the blood work should be stored in the area.

6. Arrange for patients to change into hospital gowns only when a bed is ready for them.

These steps were not taken in one overnight revolution. They were achieved over several weeks as a result of incremental advances or continuous improvement, and they extended well beyond the blood work process. Each time progress was made, methods of improving the process even further were proposed, tested, assessed, and implemented in a "rapid experiment" approach until the entire pre-surgery process had changed. The elimination of ambiguity of task and the rejection of a "make do/work around" philosophy produced the results shown below.

WEST PENN PRE-SURGERY PROCESS

PROCEDURE	BEFORE	AFTER
Time between signing in and registration	Up to 2 hrs	None
Time to register patients	12 to 60 minutes	3 minutes
Time assembling patients' charts	9 hrs daily	2+ hrs daily
Charts with unstamped pages each day	35 (average)	Less than 1
Nurses' time wasted re: above	70 minutes	Negligible
Number of gowned patients waiting in hallway	4 to 7	None
Number (average) of incomplete lab results	7	None
Availability of supplies for blood work	Varies	Complete
Number of unnecessary blood bank reports issued	10 to 11 daily	None

SOURCE: REPRINTED BY PERMISSION OF *HARVARD BUSINESS REVIEW.* FROM "FIXING HEALTH CARE FROM THE INSIDE, TODAY" BY STEVEN J. SPEAR, SEPTEMBER 2005.

Individually, these are incremental moves. This is totally in keeping with the Toyota philosophy; large-scale, dramatic breakthroughs rarely occur in manufacturing plants, hospitals, or our own lives, for that matter. The idea is to break overwhelming problems into small tractable units that, once dealt with, can produce spectacular results.

Lest doubt still exists that the hard-hearted automotive industry can teach lessons to a profession based on Hippocrates and compassion, academic studies have encouraged hospitals and health care providers to examine the idea more closely. Unfortunately, the profession often appears convinced that nothing "outside the box" holds promise for it. Again, with all due respect to the sanctity of the medical profession and the elevated position of its practitioners, where system management is concerned, the industrial world may offer more practical, hard-nosed solutions than any phalanx of white-coated physicians, no matter how bright and dedicated.

Consider the vexing question of extended wait times for hospital admissions. Is funding for Canada's health care system so thin that our hospitals cannot afford to purchase sufficient beds and hire sufficient staff to accommodate patients? Surprisingly, the answer is almost always no. Beds and staff exist. We may simply be looking at the wrong problem.

A more telling area is not facilities but flow, meaning the peaks and troughs that every service operation undergoes. Again, private industry has dealt with this question for generations. Perhaps, instead of gnashing their teeth and seeking more funding, those both in and out of health care should follow three reasonable steps: examine, evaluate, and adapt.

First, the examination. As Dr. Michael Rachlis points out,[10] fate may choose whom to strike with illness, but except for viral pandemics, it does so with remarkably little variation in degree. "In other words," Rachlis suggests, "the system creates more variation than does fate."

Where hospitalized patients are concerned, examination of the system reveals that physicians routinely make their rounds perhaps two or three times each week in some hospitals. A patient may be ready for release today, but her physician may not visit until tomorrow or the day after. Until then, she remains occupying a hospital bed. And even when the physician determines that the patient is ready to be released, the orders may not be supplied to the hospital until late morning or mid-afternoon, creating backlogs among the hospital pharmacists to fill prescriptions and among orderlies to move patients off wards. Meanwhile, with many surgical procedures scheduled for mornings, patients are normally scheduled for admittance in mid- or late afternoon. Now the traffic jam involves people coming and going, as attendants rush to prepare beds for new patients.

Now evaluate the impact. The fractured flow may appear to be only a minuscule cause, considering the scope of the problem—can horror stories of cots in corridors and eight-hour waits for ER admission really be caused by poor traffic control? For an answer, recall the last time you were delayed on a six-lane highway, with vehicles moving at tortoise speed, only to discover that the problem was not construction or a road blockage but a minor accident that had occurred much earlier. The damaged cars were pulled off the highway, the drivers were scowling, the tow trucks were idling, and the police were investigating. The lanes were open, but the flow was disrupted by these relatively minor diversions. If you gather a handful of such diversions in any passageway, whether a highway, a major blood artery, or a hospital corridor, expect a similar result.

The stumbling block most often appears when a system is challenged to use new ideas to solve an identified problem. Here is how one facility managed to do it:

In an effort to eliminate chronic overcrowding that had existed for years, Piedmont Hospital in Atlanta, Georgia, scrapped a system of booking beds based on telephone calls and faxes from physicians. In its place, the hospital installed an electronic system that posted real-time data, listing bed availabilities on its website and on electronic signs in doctors' parking lots. Physicians quickly learned to dispatch patients to the hospital when they knew there would be no waiting time or to hold patients back a few hours until bed availability was certain.[11]

When I described this system to someone in the travel industry, he shrugged and said, "Hotels have been working that way with travel agents for over twenty years. What's the big deal?" The big deal for Piedmont, and for physicians with privileges to admit patients there, was a reduction in ER diversions of 60 percent and a 3 percent increase in patient capacity. Hospital records confirmed that more than 90 percent of patients were assigned a bed within an hour of a physician's request; only a year earlier, this figure was fewer than 20 percent.

CANADIAN HOSPITALS: LESS ADVENTUROUS—OR JUST UNMOTIVATED?

U.S. hospitals appear to demonstrate a greater willingness to examine, evaluate, and adapt solutions spawned beyond the hospital grounds than their Canadian counterparts. Or perhaps it's a question of our hospitals aiming too low, as suggested by the actions of one Canadian hospital attempting to hit a budget target through multiple incremental improvements.

With about 300 beds, Royal Victoria Hospital is the largest facility of its kind in Simcoe County, north of Toronto. Along with Ontario's other 151 hospitals, the Royal Vic was informed in 2004 by the province's Ministry of Health that, beginning March 31, 2006, it could no longer operate in a deficit situation. Already on the province's list of the ten Ontario hospitals running the largest deficits, the Royal Vic considered the challenge overwhelming. With an annual deficit floating around $16 million, the hospital was already stretched to the limit. Based on the population within its large and expanding patient base, the Royal Vic should have had the capacity to handle 60,000 patient visits annually, but it could accommodate only 17,000. Cancer patients undergoing chemotherapy treatment had to be treated as outpatients, not an ideal arrangement for many. And while the province's Ministry of Health had promised $250 million for a badly needed expansion program that would enable the Royal Vic to function as a stand-alone cancer treatment centre, the funds wouldn't arrive until 2010. Meanwhile, there was that matter of the $16-million deficit to be erased.

This dilemma illustrates the challenges faced by hospitals that depend on government funding to cover some costs but are expected to handle other expenses on their own. These include keeping the lights on and the rooms warm, purchasing and maintaining supplies, and paying the salaries of nurses and other staff members.

With sixteen months between the order to erase the deficit and the March 31, 2006, deadline, Royal Vic's CEO, Janice Skot, faced the daunting task of finding a new way to save $1 million every month. "There weren't any no-brainers," she commented. "We tried to turn over every stone."[12] Among the steps she and her staff took were

- raising rates for parking and for private rooms;
- replacing parking lot attendants with automated meters;
- eliminating staff discounts in the cafeteria;
- requiring new mothers to provide their own diapers for newborn babies;
- joining with sixteen other hospitals to form a large buying group, earning volume discounts on purchases of surgical and other supplies.

When none of these measures succeeded in erasing the budget deficit, the hospital requested a peer review that brought three Toronto-area hospital executives to Barrie, where they spent six weeks poring over Royal Vic's operations. The group's report offered twenty-nine recommendations, including the adoption of bylaws preventing the hospital from operating at a deficit—an unnecessary move given the province's earlier directive—and from expanding its patient-care services without the aid of government funding.

Despite these efforts, the hospital was still almost $10 million short of its objective with three months remaining before the March 31 deadline, and many of its 2000 employees feared losing their jobs. On January 9, however, Ontario's minister of health, George Smitherman, rode into town with his saddlebags filled with $9.7 million, enough to restore fiscal balance on the target date.

Incredibly, both the hospital and the ministry celebrated this as a victory. Claiming he was proud of the Royal Vic's accomplishment, achieved with the assistance of outside hospitals and his own largesse, Smitherman declared, "I call it the system helping the system."[13] How could success be celebrated when Smitherman, who had delivered the ultimatum, provided the vast majority of funds out of his own budget? And how much might actually have been saved if the Royal Vic's administrators had focused on guidelines from the Toyota Way, especially those dedicated to continuous improvement and basing management decisions on a long-term philosophy, even at the expense of short-term financial goals?

Both the hospital's and the health ministry's actions reflected the familiar "make do/work around" philosophy, used in this case to achieve an objective that was only surface in nature. Smitherman himself noted that "[Ontario] can't sustain health care in an environment where spending is increasing ten or twelve percent a year."[14]

No hospital in Canada, the United States, or elsewhere has achieved the distinction of being called "the Toyota of health care." This will require a wide application of the philosophy of continuous improvement until it becomes a mindset maintained by staff members at every level. Such an attitude will lead to experiments to test improvements, sharing learned knowledge via collaborative work, and persuading staff that "working around" and "making do" are options to be employed once only, under circumstances where the patient's health and comfort are at risk.

Can Canada's hospitals adopt such a revolutionary stance, given the singular nature of health care and its unique needs? The easy answer: Why not? Health care professionals are among the brightest and most dedicated workers produced by our culture and educational systems. Who would be better qualified to first recognize and then realize the promises of such a strategy? Yet a substantial level of suspicion and doubt remains regarding the potential benefits of a system born from a crass industrial application. One hospital CEO commented that hospital administrators "are very good at managing their facilities, but not so good at managing the system."[15] And a physician who is a prominent member of a leading teaching hospital questioned the whole approach by suggesting that "advances in medical systems and administrations tend to reflect the dedication and leadership of inspired individuals, not systems." Is this reasonable?

The medical profession is constantly assessing and accommodating technological advances. The future of our hospitals, measured in both dollars and patient safety, may rest on the ability of these same people to adapt to a proven management and operational strategy. One, admittedly, that began with a need to create better automobiles at less cost.

9

TREATMENT

HOW MUCH CARE CAN WE AFFORD TO OFFER?

Mrs. Hunter had not known the cause of her ailment for some time. She only knew that she suffered unbearable pain along her spine, pain that analgesics could not ease and that normal procedures to relieve discomfort could not cure. Finally, the source was determined: a benign tumour had invaded the roots of nerves along the woman's spine. Mrs. Hunter was eighty years of age.*

Surgery to eradicate the tumour from her spine was categorized as high-risk a generation ago. The procedure would include removing a portion of her spine, which could cause severe damage to her spinal column or to the intricate system of nerves serving as the tumour's habitat. She could be left paralyzed, devoid of feeling below her waist, or suffering various other effects of the operation.

But this wasn't 1975. It was 2006, and the skills, equipment, and techniques to perform the procedure were available. That summer, Mrs. Hunter was admitted to Toronto Western Hospital, where a team of three surgeons, a neurophysiotherapist, an anaesthesiologist, and several nurses occupied Operating Room 1. For almost six hours, fifteen highly

---

*A pseudonym.

skilled professionals supported by several million dollars' worth of exotic equipment, ranging from a TV camera tiny enough to probe the patient's innards to a gamma knife costing over a million dollars, used their exceptional abilities to improve the quality of Mrs. Hunter's life.[1]

Together, the health care team, the multimillion-dollar equipment, and the small army of nursing and support staff in Toronto Western provided Mrs. Hunter with pre-operative and post-operative care over a recovery period taking several days. She awoke from the operation feeling a new discomfort, this one from the incisions made by the surgeon, but it would fade with time. A week later she went home to resume her life, finally free from debilitating pain for however many years remained to her.

The operation performed on Mrs. Hunter may have been complex and demanding, but it was hardly unique; Toronto Western had performed about 300 similar procedures before the year was over. The cost of each would easily nudge $100,000, absorbing $30 million of the province's annual budget.

THE STORY OF MRS. HUNTER is both heartening and disquieting. The idea that, regardless of socio-economic status, we can expect relief from chronic pain that would have crippled and immobilized our ancestors, represents a benefit of universal health systems that place cure above cost.

This medical advance becomes disquieting, though, in the face of certain fiscal realities. Two or three generations ago, few people survived long enough for tumours such as the one that caused Mrs. Hunter so much pain to develop. Over the next decade and into the foreseeable future, Canada's health care system will be inundated with a need to provide similar relief to an aging population. Many of today's eighty-year-olds are more active than sixty-year-olds in the mid-twentieth century, but the devastating impact of age-related ailments on our health care system remains a concern, as we've seen. Canadians aged sixty-five and over account for only 15 percent of the country's population but consume almost half of the nation's health care costs.[2] So when the question is asked, with brutal honesty, if it is worth

$100,000 to remove the source of back pain in an eighty-year-old, the answer is likely "Of course." Mrs. Hunter had every right to expect and even insist that the health care system she and her spouse had supported with taxes during their working years deal with her serious ailments. The problem arises when the system is asked to do the same for 1000 eighty-year-old Canadians each year. Or 10,000, or 100,000. Will this be practical?

There is no reasonable answer to that question. There is only this realization: *We are funding a medical system that has been structured to deal with acute illnesses and injuries, yet each passing year sees more of its resources diverted to handle chronic ailments and conditions that were once considered untreatable.* Buried among the panic-stricken cries that our publicly funded system cannot continue to consume a growing proportion of our GNP each year—cries backed by charts and statistics—is that one enlightening fact.

We have changed our visions and expectations of medical care over the years. We have not changed the structure of funding it, however, and this represents a serious obstacle to controlling costs, especially those related to hospitals.

Our grandparents considered hospitals a resource for treating injuries or acute illnesses. To put it bluntly, when you entered a hospital you either got better or died. Today, hospitals deal with a multitude of complex challenges, including treatment of heart disease, cancer, and diabetes, as well as surgeries to improve appearance, relieve discomfort, and other procedures.

Some observers suggest that hospitals themselves have complicated the situation through their own policies. Michael Rachlis notes that hospital administrators "watch their case severity indices more closely than your broker watches the TSX. The case severity index indicates the average sickness of the patients and, therefore, the resources that are needed to manage them. Hospitals strive to have the highest possible severity index to demonstrate that they have the sickest patients who need the most resources."[3]

IF YOU BUILD IT, THEY WILL (PROBABLY) COME ... AND BUY IT

When hospitals can justify new resources, they usually acquire them. Once acquired, the new resource is used. No one doubted the value of X-rays in diagnosing illnesses and injuries in hospital patients, so every hospital installed facilities to provide them. When CAT scans, which provide a 360-degree view, were seen as a major advance over X-rays, hospitals scrambled for funds to purchase the necessary equipment. These were followed by MRI machines, remarkable devices for viewing internal body structures, and most recently by PET (positron emission tomography) scans, to evaluate the functioning of brain and heart tissues.

These represent near-miraculous advances in technology, and they arm physicians and surgeons with patient data that once could only be discovered or confirmed in a post-mortem examination. We should all be thankful that we live in a time and a society that makes such advances available to us. But miracles come with a price, and the miracles are paid for by the public health care system.

That's one measure of the fiscal impact. Another is the changing mindset of doctors and patients alike. In many ways, our fascination with new technology has skewed our perception of medicine to the point where, as one observer commented, "health is simply a state of inadequate diagnosis."[4]

You don't need to suffer from a life-threatening disease to appreciate the situation. Consider the change in preventative medicine over the past thirty years. If you were sufficiently conscientious in the 1970s, most of your attention to health issues involved getting an annual physical examination that included a few probes and questions from your physician plus a urine test. Mature Canadians today expect to undergo, depending on their gender, PSA tests for prostate cancer, Pap smears for cervical cancer, BRCA tests for ovarian cancer, mammograms for breast cancer, and other procedures. If the test results suggest something untoward, patients are directed to any of a series of specialists, each one juggling waiting lists according to various criteria.

Medical developments once considered miraculous are commonplace today. Hip and knee replacements solve disability problems among seniors, and cataract surgery avoids blindness. Childhood leukaemia is no longer a tragic death sentence, and the success rate for heart bypass surgery is as high as that for appendectomies. These are medical services that citizens value highly, and they deal with commonplace problems, not exotic ailments. If the technologies and skills exist to correct them, should responsible governments limit their availability to those who can afford to pay for them directly or provide them according to need, whatever the cost? This is the crux of the constantly expanding public-sector financing of health care in Canada and around the world.

These procedures save lives, relieve pain, and prevent healthy productive citizens from becoming bedridden and a drain on the system. No one suggests they be restricted. The idea that we are living longer and more productive lives than our forebears is admirable, but the price to attain such longevity can be substantial. This fact needs to be acknowledged by critics of our publicly funded health care system on both sides of the political spectrum. The system is not broken, and perhaps not overwhelmed. It simply trails the technology. Thanks to technology, we have the means to extend lifespan substantially, but we lack the funding to provide it universally.

This truth throws concerns about health care funding into perspective. If the skills and technology to extend a productive life and relieve the agony of chronic pain exist, will the sole measure of their use be the patient's ability to pay, either directly or through an ensuring third party? (Raising another issue: Will an ensuring party agree to pay for a procedure to solve a condition that is not directly life-threatening?) In Canada, as in most industrialized nations, the answer is no.

Critics of our publicly funded system will suggest that we cannot continue escalating our health care costs to infinite levels, and they are correct. The most acceptable solution may lie not in restricting the level of funding but in controlling the demand. Like the Toyota system, this strategy is based on managing the system first, and it permits the funding, in effect, to cure itself. To Chicken Littles who perceive every ER delay and every cot in a corridor as evidence of an oncoming apocalypse, this lacks sufficient drama to be newsworthy.

It is always newsworthy, of course, to make a straight-line projection on growing health care costs and follow the line all the way to fiscal hell. It is not nearly as headline-grabbing to demonstrate that the curve is levelling off, but this appears to be the case. Consider Canada's position among ten selected industrialized countries when it comes to per capita expenditures and share of gross national product, both of which offer very different perspectives on the matter.

HEALTH EXPENDITURES, PER CAPITA, IN US$ 2004

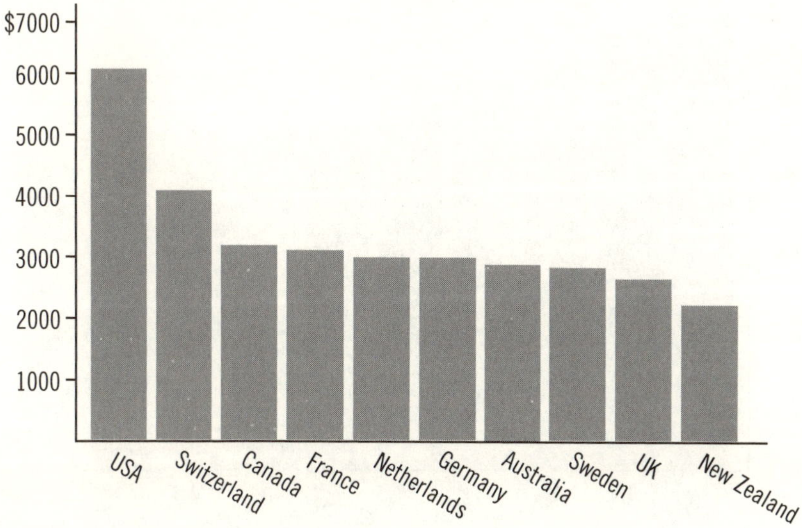

SOURCE: ORGANIZATION FOR ECONOMIC CO-OPERATION & DEVELOPMENT, JUNE 26, 2006

In 2004, Canada spent $3165 per capita on health care, including both public and private expenditures. About 70 percent of the spending was public, placing us very close to France, the Netherlands, Germany, Australia, and Sweden. The United States spent $6102 per capita during the same period. Only about 40 percent of that was from the public sector, yet an estimated 45 million U.S. citizens lacked health care coverage.[5]

For another perspective on the cost factor, compare health expenditure as a share of gross domestic product (GDP) in the same countries for the same period:

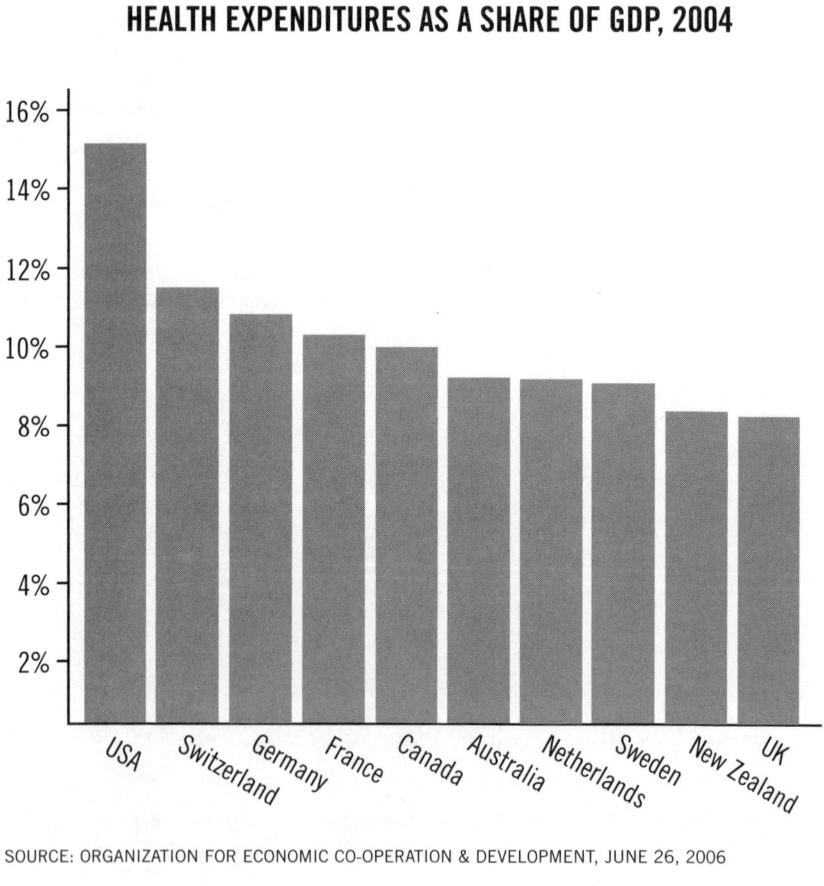

SOURCE: ORGANIZATION FOR ECONOMIC CO-OPERATION & DEVELOPMENT, JUNE 26, 2006

Again, the United States led all OECD states, spending 15.3 percent of its GDP on health care in 2004. Canada's share was less than 10 percent, which placed us with Australia, the Netherlands, and Sweden (the average across all OECD countries was 8.9 percent).

Within Canada, per capita costs vary by province. Projections for 2006–07 indicate that Alberta residents paid almost $800 more than those in Quebec:

PER CAPITA PROVINCIAL/TERRITORIAL GOVERNMENT HEALTH EXPENDITURES (CDN$) 2006–07

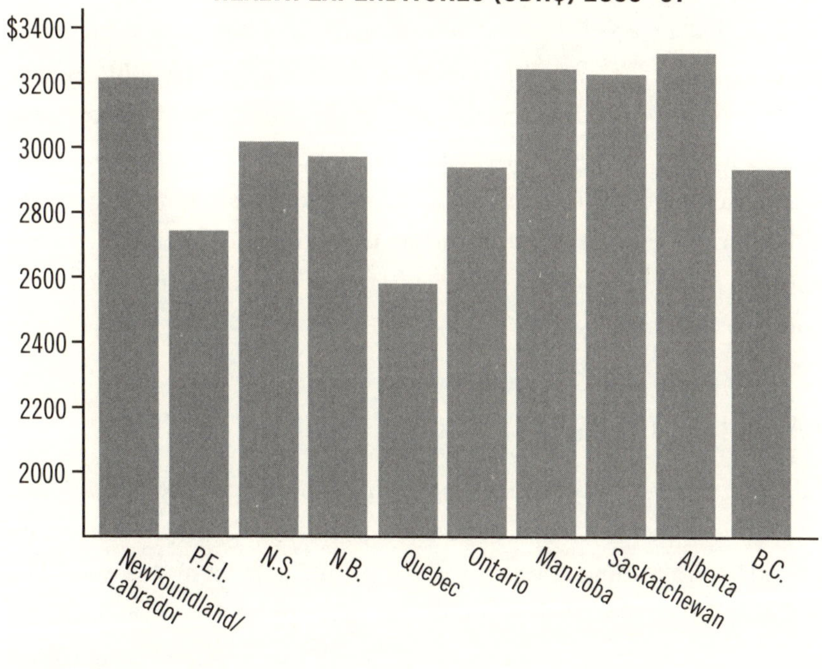

SOURCE: CANADIAN INSTITUTE FOR HEALTH INFORMATION, NOVEMBER 1, 2006

Higher health care costs in the territories skew the national average somewhat. CIHI figures for this period suggest that per capita spending for 2006–07 in these regions is as follows: Yukon Territory, $4,508; Northwest Territories, $5,404; Nunavut, $7,610.

The rate of annual increase of health care costs is beginning to flatten, suggesting that we may at some point link it to inflation. For the 2006–07 period, average spending by provincial and territorial governments increased by 5.7 percent over the previous period, which is a significant reduction from the 6.5 percent for 2005–06 and from the 7.0 percent annual increase during the years from 2001 to 2004.

The challenge will be to continue flattening the curve even as the number of aging Canadians rises with the oncoming wave of geriatric baby boomers. Can it be done? Only if the paradigm of treatment is altered in ways that lower the cost of care while continuing to change the means of delivering it. No fixed pattern exists for this process, although the P4P debate and the adaptation of management systems derived from the Toyota experience may well blossom into more concrete methods.

PHYSICIANS THEMSELVES CAN HELP HEAL THE SYSTEM

Fortunately, the system may be repairing itself, not in a top-down, government-dictated style but in a bottom-up approach where care providers are finding ways to make a greater impact at less cost. The individual benefits of each innovation may appear small when placed against the enormous annual cost of health care in Canada, but their cumulative impact cannot be ignored, as we saw in the case of the hospital in Pittsburgh.

Without suggesting a Pollyanna feel-good response, the examples below demonstrate both the scope and the impact of a movement that ultimately may achieve the goal of providing better health care at less cost.

In Victoria, British Columbia, a quick response team (QRT) was introduced in 1987 as a means of assessing frail seniors who arrived at a hospital too shaken or bruised to manage on their own. Formerly, such patients had been provided with a hospital bed for several days, a move that proved expensive for the health care system and hazardous for the patient (because, once again, hospitals can be very dangerous places, especially for older people with existing health concerns). In the new procedure, the QRT assessed each situation and offered alternative care, where suitable, that was equal to or better than a hospital stay, such as short-term twenty-four-hour home care. Over the years, the QRT program has proved so effective at freeing hospital beds that it has been extended to cover enhanced services for all individuals in crisis situations and was adapted by Alberta and Saskatchewan, where it has proved equally successful.

In Calgary, a comprehensive palliative care program provides terminal patients with the opportunity to end their lives at home rather than in the confines of a hospital. Across Canada, about 70 percent of terminal cancer patients die in hospitals; in Calgary, the figure has been reduced to 40 percent.

In Sault Ste. Marie, Ontario, the Group Health Centre pioneered a program for the treatment of congestive heart failure, or CHF, based on a concept originally inspired by employees at Algoma Steel almost fifty years ago. Patients suffering from CHF represent a substantial portion of all hospital admissions across Canada each year. A generation ago, CHF patients may have remained in hospital for up to three weeks before discharge; today the stay is reduced to perhaps ten days. Group Health Centre patients with CHF are visited in their homes by nurses who, using a three-level assessment system easily grasped by the patient—green for good, orange for concern, red for professional care—aid patients in monitoring and gauging their own condition. The program has reduced the readmission of CHF patients by 60 percent. The Group Health Centre, described by an admiring Roy Romanow as the "jewel in the crown of Medicare," also managed to cut the time between a patient's mammogram and her resultant diagnosis from 107 days to eighteen.

In Hamilton, Ontario, the number of patients treated for mental health problems rose by 900 percent in the first year of a new program, yet referrals to a regional psychiatric clinic dropped by 70 percent. As a result, substantially more people were being treated at substantially less cost to the system. The secret? The program involved teams of counsellors, family physicians, and psychiatrists working to determine the best treatment for each patient rather than taking a one-size-fits-all approach.[6] A similar program in Saskatoon enables mental health patients to return to their homes sooner and avoid re-admittance through home care services.

In Vancouver, pharmacists enrolled in a physicians' education program visit doctors to review the relative costs and efficacy of various medications, identifying those that represent a combination of best effects and best value. Reviews of the program estimate that the provincial government saves two dollars in pharmaceutical costs for every dollar invested, a benefit that has inspired group health care to launch similar programs in Ontario and elsewhere.

The Drug Evaluation Alliance of Nova Scotia (DEANS), whose members include medical and pharmacy school faculty as well as practising physicians and pharmacists, identifies major drug issues with the goal of reducing dependence on and expenditures for pharmaceuticals. The group's activities include management of chronic non-cancer pain, expanded self-monitoring of blood glucose for Type 2 diabetes, and reducing the use of medications in nursing homes. As with many relatively small innovations in health care, the incremental savings from simple steps are impressive and easily replicated. In one recent example, DEANS managed a switch from the use of masks for certain asthma and emphysema sufferers to portable inhalers. Capital cost savings to the province were estimated at $1 million annually. Actual savings from improved efficiency and reduced transmission of disease from contamination may be at least that much.[7]

In Toronto, yet another pharmaceutical-related program teams a University of Toronto professor of pharmacy with the family practice department of St. Michael's Hospital to assist physicians in the management of complex (and expensive) drugs.

These are just a sample of perhaps hundreds of similar initiatives occurring across the country. The two most important aspects of such undertakings are that they directly involve hands-on medical care professionals, eliminating a layer of academics and bureaucrats to get at the heart of the matter, and that they were conceived, designed, and executed by local community-based providers with nary a federal or provincial government official in sight.

These actions should be heartening to those who believe in our publicly funded system but are disconcerted by tales of eventual financial collapse. For the most part, they represent a practical resolution to the dilemma of rising costs in an aging population.

DYING IN A PLACE WHERE YOU SHOULD GET BETTER

Within a single generation, the average length of hospital stays has been reduced by one-half or more, a development that strikes some people as a miserly method of reducing costs. But the reduced time is related more to technology than to economy. Twenty years ago, removing a gallbladder involved major abdominal surgery and substantial trauma, as well as a week or more of hospitalization. Today, the same operation is a laparoscopic procedure involving three or four small incisions and, for most patients, an overnight stay. Other procedures that once required a week or more in a hospital ward, including normal childbirth without complications, have been reduced to a day or two. Many people interpret this as a bureaucratic assessment of economy over humanitarianism. "They throw you out on the street in half the time as before" is a common complaint, especially among seniors. The observation is true, but the risk to a patient's well-being is reduced, not increased, by shorter hospital stays, and the older the patient, the greater the risk.

Health care professionals have known this for generations, but it took a recent study of elderly patients in a Sherbrooke, Quebec, hospital to generate an accurate—and frightening—picture of the dangers and consequences of hospital stays.[8] The study targeted *Clostridium difficile*-associated disease (CDAD), which causes diarrhoea so severe and difficult to treat that many patients succumb to its effects. And these patients are not always the elderly; in one U.S. case, an otherwise healthy thirty-one-year-old woman, fourteen weeks pregnant with twins, battled the disease for six weeks before aborting the fetuses and dying two days later.[9] Similar cases are becoming more and more common with time.

CDAD has reached an endemic stage in hospitals across Canada, partly because the disease bacillus is growing resistant to traditional means of control. In 1995, CDAD was noted in 3.6 out of 10,000 hospital patient-days nationally; within ten years, the incidence exceeded fifteen cases per 10,000 patient-days in Quebec. In Sherbrooke, the number of CDAD cases among those sixty-five years of age and over approached 900 per 10,000 patient-days; almost all of them were transmitted among hospital patients. Statistics in one Sherbrooke hospital revealed that almost one-quarter of patients who contracted the disease died within thirty days of the diagnosis.

In addition to demonstrating a growing resistance to standard antibiotics, the CDAD bacillus has become mobile as well. In late 2006, thirteen patients died after being infected from the same evolved strain in a St.-Hyacinthe hospital, and seventeen were infected in one ward of a hospital in Joliette, seventy-five kilometres north of Montreal.

CDAD is an example of the risks associated with hospital stays, and medical studies can identify at least a dozen others. The virulence of CDAD demonstrates the two-fold benefit of reducing the time patients spend in a hospital environment: it saves lives and it saves money. The Sherbrooke study noted that each case of CDAD contracted in the hospital led to an additional ten or more days in the facility where the disease had originated.

Cutting the average number of days spent in hospital by patients will clearly reduce the capital costs needed to build new facilities and to cover operational expenses, and will likely save lives. Encouragingly, this policy has become well-established across the system. The next level of cost reduction lies in refining the extraordinary number of unnecessary tests performed on patients both in and out of hospitals.

WE ARE TESTING MORE AND DISCOVERING LESS

It is neither redundant nor demeaning to point out that physicians are human beings subject to the same weaknesses as the people whose health they monitor and treat. Among their faults is the temptation to use all available technology on the basis that, in medicine as in any other science, there is no such thing as useless information. The result has been millions of unnecessary tests and procedures that do nothing except drain the financial resources of the system. Batteries of tests may satisfy both doctor and patient, but satisfaction rarely cures ailments. To put it bluntly, physicians need to become better consumers.

Technicians who operate diagnostic equipment and perform lab tests tend to agree. At least one group, the Canadian Association of Radiologists (CAR), actively supports the idea of providing its members with less, not more, work. "Better management of diagnostic imaging could greatly reduce, if not end, waiting lists for imaging across Canada," states CAR president Robert Miller.[10] According to CAR, about 35 million radiological examinations—X-ray, ultrasound, and fluoroscopic—were performed in Canada during 2004, or more than one for every man, woman, and child in the country. Applying a different yardstick, the average radiologist conducts 17,000 such examinations each year.

The Atlantic Health Sciences Centre, an integrated health network in New Brunswick, conducted a pilot study to determine how many of these examinations are a waste of time and money. The initial study, conducted in 2004, estimated that 14 percent of radiology examinations ordered during a six-month period were either inappropriate or unnecessary. Blending this data with their own experience, radiologists identified three basic causes for this wasteful use of diagnostic imaging:

1. Repeating a process already completed because the original report, examination, or image was either lost or not immediately available. (Many of these instances will be addressed, it is hoped, by the widespread implementation of electronic patient records, discussed in Chapter 2.)
2. Replacing a low level of resolution in a diagnostic image with a second procedure to yield greater detail. This not only adds cost but may also expose the patient unnecessarily to more radiation and its attendant risks.
3. Ordering tests that are unlikely to affect patient management, or ordering the wrong procedure for the patient's condition. CAR recognizes that physicians may be pressured by increasing workloads, the legal imperatives of medical liability, and indeed by patients themselves, to perhaps err in prescribing more tests than required. The association also acknowledges that doctors cannot realistically be expected to maintain a full understanding of radiology technology, noting that almost 2 million scientific articles are published and over 300 clinical trials are launched every year.[11]

These findings inspired another study, conducted in Manitoba, to evaluate new software installed on every physician's computer. The program helps eradicate unnecessary procedures by instantly informing doctors if they are ordering the most appropriate radiology test given the patient's symptoms, the physician's preliminary diagnosis, and the information being sought. Whenever the program encounters an inappropriate lab test or diagnostic procedure, it will identify the conflict and ask the physician to reconsider. With provincial governments adding more multimillion-dollar MRI and CT scanners each year, these units should be used only when most appropriate and not for "what if...?" situations.

Radiology, of course, is only one of many test procedures that physicians should use with a much higher level of discretion, on a purely financial basis. If the money wasted on the 14 percent of inappropriate and unnecessary diagnostics were applied to lab tests and similar procedures instead, upward pressure on our health care financing could easily be relieved for good.

THE EXPERIENCE OF MRS. HUNTER, and the fiscal wisdom of investing $100,000 to relieve pain in an eighty-year-old woman, is a touchstone in the ceaseless debate on funding Canada's health care system. The "on this hand ... but on the other hand" dialogue pits limited resources against (supposedly) unlimited demand, and often leads to the conclusion, that we must either (a) make heartless decisions, penalizing the few for the good of the many, or (b) endure continual increases in health care funding that threaten to stifle economic stability.

Yet as we saw in this and previous chapters, the same technology that provides an extended lifespan for Canadians, and the consequent rising demands on the system, can be employed to improve the system's efficiency. Perhaps the two absent and most important ingredients in the debate are the will of health care professionals to implement changes and the ability of health care consumers to adapt to them.

Unfortunately, few observers consider incremental change made within the system a means of survival for universal health care. Some propose rescuing the system with private health care, like a knight riding in on a white horse to free the binds of public funding. Others see the private option not as a galloping white horse but as a looming *bête noir* set to destroy universal health care. Worshipped by advocates and reviled by adversaries, the private option is rarely evaluated strictly from the point of view of the health care consumer, something we will endeavour to achieve in the next chapter.

10

OF CABBIES AND CONSUMERS

Every eighteen months or so, Joseph and Cecilia McGuire drive from their home in Burlington, Ontario, to an airport outside Hamilton, where they board their private aircraft for a forty-minute flight to Michigan. Joseph, sixty-six, owns a small but highly successful industrial machinery company and has been a private pilot since his teenage years; his wife, Cecilia, owns a few small apartment buildings in the Hamilton–Burlington area. Despite their wealth, they live a generally modest lifestyle.*

Landing at Oakland County International Airport on the outskirts of Detroit, Joseph and Cecilia clear U.S. customs and board a waiting limousine that carries them to an attractive building set among landscaped grounds near Grosse Pointe, Michigan. They enter a lobby and are welcomed as old friends by a receptionist who escorts them into a private room, where they are served tea and snacks before changing into patterned hospital robes and placing their jewellery and other valuables in a small safe.

After completing a few forms, they are escorted to an anteroom. Joseph remains there—"She always goes first," he says with a smile—as Cecilia follows a technician into a low-ceilinged area. The light is dim and the air somewhat cooler than elsewhere in the building. Soft music plays in the

*Pseudonyms.

background. A technician helps Cecilia onto a cushioned table and confirms she is comfortable, then leaves the room. Within a few moments he speaks to her through hidden loudspeakers, and Cecilia responds that she is ready. The cushioned table begins to move slowly forward, and Cecilia is subjected to a full magnetic resonance imaging (MRI) body scan. When her scan is completed, she returns to the anteroom to read her book while Joseph undergoes the same procedure.

The scan has not been motivated by any health concern, nor was it recommended by Joseph and Cecilia's family physician back in Ontario. The decision is entirely their own.

With Joseph's MRI scan completed, they return to the change room, get dressed again, and walk to a small dining area where other people about their age are being served a lunch of soup, sandwiches, dessert, and coffee. Most have preceded Joseph and Cecilia and are relaxing, chatting among themselves. Some have a glass of wine with the meal. Joseph and Cecilia strike up conversations with the others, sharing stories of vacation destinations and grandchildren.

After lunch, Joseph and Cecilia meet with a radiologist who displays the images captured by the MRI scan and compares them with results from their previous visit. He notes two cysts on Joseph's kidneys, assuring him they are not an issue. The fatty deposit near Joseph's liver has enlarged since his last scan, however. "Need a tighter diet," Joseph responds with a grin. Cecilia is relieved to learn that no tumours appear in her breasts and no polyps are seen in her colon. Her mother succumbed to colon cancer. "She's deathly afraid of contracting it," Joseph says. "More than anything else, she wants to make sure she is free of cancer, especially there."

Joseph pays for the procedure with his credit card and steps outside just as the limousine requested by the receptionist arrives to carry them back to the airport.

The previous year, Joseph and Cecilia had timed their spring visit to catch a baseball game—Joseph is a lifelong Detroit Tigers fan—before returning home. But baseball season is over. Within an hour of leaving the clinic, they are winging their way home again. The MRI images are tucked in an envelope, to be added to others in their files. "The flight home is always a relief," Joseph comments. "It's a little like feeling that we're safe and healthy for another eighteen months."

Cecilia closes her eyes and smiles. The sky is blue, the flight is comfortable. Joseph is a good pilot. Her body is free of any visible problems on the inside. All she has to worry about are those darn lines on her face ...

NOT EVERY CANADIAN can afford scheduled visits to a private MRI clinic to enjoy the peace of mind that $3000 buys them. For that matter, not every American can either. Nothing prevents the McGuires from taking advantage of this service, and no one suggests that a medical Berlin Wall be erected to stop it. Their experience, however, gives the lie to any claim that Canada provides universal health care within a single-tier system. Health care facilities are always available to those who can afford to pay for them and, like the McGuires, are willing to travel beyond the country's borders to obtain them. Those who can afford the cost will always buy their way to the front of the line, either within the country or beyond it. And with each passing year, Canadians need less reason to cross an international border for private health care, because more opportunities are presenting themselves to those who choose private care over the public system.

This country's assertion that it is the only industrialized nation with a functioning single-tier health system within its borders is constantly being challenged. One by one, provincial bulwarks are crumbling, their foundations being shattered by things like the decision of the Quebec Supreme Court on Dr. Chaoulli's challenge and the bluster of former Alberta premier Ralph Klein.

The quiet insurgency of operations such as Vancouver's Timely Medical Alternatives Inc., a private medical brokerage, may be doing more damage to the concept than either Chaoulli or Klein. Richard Baker, president of the Vancouver-based operation, delights in highlighting the faults of Canada's single-payer health care system. And why not? He has built a profitable operation by exploiting these flaws, matching patients to private health care providers and pocketing a fee in the process. In early 2007, hundreds of Canadians were accessing Baker's website daily to locate private clinics, often finding one within a few blocks of their home. If the number of clinics and Baker's services continue to expand, the McGuires may soon choose to forgo their periodic 200-mile treks to Detroit and simply drive across town to purchase their body scans.

Some Canadians are almost provoked into choosing private health care over their tax-supported public system. Ontario retiree Lindsay McCreith documented one such experience and promoted it with great drama in a video titled *A Short Course in Brain Surgery.* Premiered at the Fraser Institute and posted on the Timely Medical Alternatives website, the video provides dramatic support for foes of the public system.

Diagnosed with a potential brain tumour in February 2006, McCreith was told he faced a four-month wait for an MRI scan to confirm and pinpoint the size, location, and characteristics of the tumour, and another four-month wait before surgery could be scheduled. Waiting more than eight months while a potentially malignant tumour grew inside his skull was horrifying to McCreith, as it would be to anyone. In addition to wondering if he would survive the lengthy delay, he would continue to suffer worsening headaches and dizzy spells. Yet within a day of contacting Baker's firm, McCreith was in Buffalo, New York, for an MRI and, a few days later, surgery to remove the tumour. He paid $28,000 for the procedure; his request for OHIP to reimburse him for the private surgery was refused because he had not received advance permission.

McCreith's case is an example of bureaucratic inflexibility gone mad. The video, gleefully promoted by the Fraser Institute and Baker's firm, warns Americans of the folly of government-sponsored health care, inserting a brief clip of political disturber and *Fahrenheit 911* filmmaker Michael Moore, whose presence and provocative commentary were certain to infuriate opponents of public health care.

Advocates for Canada's public health system were appalled, not only by McCreith's experience but by the way campaigners for private health care exploited the incident to attack the entire system. No one makes videos, they point out, detailing everyday successes of the public system in such a dramatic manner.

McCreith's experience may be rare, but it is not an exception, as the success of Rick Baker's operation proves. Whatever your position on the question of Canada's single-payer system of health care, Baker has clearly identified sectors that are credible in their logic but bizarre in their execution, as the experience of Heidi Bozek, another client of Baker's Timely Medical Alternatives, shows.

Bozek suffers from tumours on her knees and right hand, an affliction that causes her substantial pain. Told by her physician that she would have to wait four months for an MRI procedure at Vancouver's publicly funded St. Paul's Hospital, she paid $1400 to Baker's firm and received the same three-hour procedure at the same hospital within days.[1] The experience left Bozek grateful, confused, and perhaps guilty. "I couldn't quite understand how a public facility could be contracted out to a private organization for me to have my MRI," Bozek said. "I do believe I've pushed people out of the queue."

Although Baker refused to reveal the mechanics of obtaining almost instant access to MRI facilities his clients had been told would not be available for months, a spokesperson for St. Paul's admitted that it accepts about fifty patients annually from Baker's firm. The figure represents fewer than 1 percent of all the MRI procedures conducted at the hospital. When Bozek's story was reported in the press, British Columbia's health minister promised a full enquiry into the matter, but six months later nothing had been released, and Timely Medical Alternatives continued to flourish.

So how does Baker's firm shoehorn its clients into a facility supposedly booked several months in advance? It appears to gain access to the MRI during off-hours—the equipment is not scheduled to operate twenty-four hours daily—which means paying a technician a fee to conduct the procedure. And since the hospital spokesperson affirms that St. Paul's "only accepts patients who have received a requisition from a doctor,"[2] physicians may in some instances be paid to issue the necessary paperwork.

If Bozek feels guilty about obtaining her MRI procedure ahead of others, she should not. The system routinely pushes people aside to make room for politicians (former federal cabinet minister Alan Rock received treatment for prostate cancer at breakneck speed), RCMP officers (in many ways, including this one, the force operates outside federal limitations placed on the citizens it protects),[3] and federal prisoners (health care critics love sharing the tale, possibly apocryphal, of a man who intentionally committed a crime in order to be sentenced to a federal prison, where a chronic painful condition affecting both elbows was treated within days).

"Justice should not only be done," British politician Gordon Ewart wrote, "but should manifestly and undoubtedly be *seen* to be done." If justice must be seen to be done in our courts, how can we expect anything less than just treatment for health care consumers, especially where life-and-death issues such as brain tumours are concerned?

STRIVING TO IMPROVE Canada's public health system is both admirable and achievable. Striving to perfect it is neither.

We are hardly short of champions, all of them drawn until now from the ranks of politicians and health professionals. Both sides engage in tussles like two adversaries seeking access to a bank vault: politicians have the combination, and health professionals want the contents. The Chaoulli decision has added the courts as a third participant; despite the Supreme Court decision limiting the impact of this ruling to Quebec, Canadians who are denied out-of-country surgery for critical health matters will undoubtedly use Chaoulli as a means of forcing other provinces to modify their rules. "Chaoulli has created a new paradigm for the delivery of health care," noted Patrick Monahan, dean of Osgoode Hall Law School, "one that includes the right of patients to timely medical care. Governments and health care administrators will now have to keep such rights front and centre as they plan needed reforms, or be forced to do so by the courts."[4]

Politicians speak in platitudes, lawyers in abstracts, and medical professionals in nomenclature reflecting the science of their profession. They all, of course, claim to speak for health care consumers. Perhaps it is time to submit views that are not influenced by extended wings of the political spectrum or slanted sermons of politicians and professionals in law and medicine. For the moment, let's challenge the opinions of these groups with two undeniable facts: publicly funded health care systems in other countries accommodate the private sector so they can maximize the benefits of the arrangement; and Canadians assume that their lauded public system will not commit bungled acts, generating shocking anecdotes to be traded smugly among critics of universal health care.

Proposing these concepts when I have no link with the political, medical, or legal community may appear presumptuous, but I am guided by, of all things, a story told by comedian Bob Hope with some glee.

The day after Hope's first television special aired in the early 1950s, he hopped into a New York taxicab for a ride to the airport to catch his flight back to California. The toothpick-chewing cabbie watched Hope in the rear-view mirror for a few blocks before saying, "Hey, you're Bob Hope."

"That's right, I am," Hope said, beaming. "Did you see my TV show last night?"

"Yeah, I saw it," the cabbie replied.

"So what'd you think of it?"

The cabbie shrugged. "It was okay."

Hope's ego was bruised. "So what are you, a TV critic?" he sneered.

The cabbie pulled to the curb, and in classic New York fashion, he twisted in his seat and gestured at Hope. "Hey, I'm the people," he said. "I'm the people. You forget about me and you're nothing, right?"

You and I are not New York cabbies, and Canada's health care system rates dramatically higher on a scale of substance than a television show broadcast over fifty years ago. But the lesson continues to apply. We pay for the health care system. We use it. We benefit from it when it succeeds and suffer when it fails. We have a right to debate the means of improving it. And we should not require a medical degree, a political position, or a courtroom to do so.

"I WANT IT *NOW*!"—WHAT IS A REASONABLE WAIT TIME FOR HEALTH SERVICES?

The question of wait times remains the most controversial topic among Canadians discussing the value of their public health care services. Yet the assumption that extended wait times are the result of inadequate funding and resources is generally incorrect. As we have seen, everything in health care over the past fifty years has changed except for the way we manage the system.

Why should a woman who has had a mammogram wait six months before being wheeled into an operating room for necessary surgery, as frequently occurs?* Because if the mammogram suggests further investigation is warranted, she will be scheduled to receive an ultrasound. If the ultrasound reveals evidence of a tumour, she will be scheduled

*A 2006 report indicated that 10 percent of Canadians surveyed waited three months or more before seeing a cancer specialist. Post-diagnostic treatment can be just as delayed; in the same report, it was revealed that 0.6 and 12.9 weeks passed between referral for radiation therapy and actual treatment for Ontario residents. One of the challenges of measuring wait times is that each province determines not only the criteria to be used but also the extent of the information to be revealed. All of this makes federal assurances of reduced wait times ring hollow and suggests that wait times for cancer treatment are as unpredictable as winning lottery numbers. (*Waiting for Health Care in Canada: What We Know and What We Don't Know*, Canadian Institute for Health Information, 2006.)

for a biopsy. And if the biopsy proves positive for cancer, she will be scheduled for surgery.

Each step in this maddening dance requires time for medical staff to assess patient records, prepare equipment, and book the clinic location, among other things, often employing much of the pre-computer technology that private industry abandoned a generation ago. Inefficient scheduling, not inadequate facilities, is at the core of the system's wait-time problems. Imagine having to stand in line and purchase tickets from four different sellers before you can enter a sports stadium. There may be enough seats to accommodate everyone, but the entry system means most people will be late for the game. That's the problem with our health care scheduling system.

Solutions exist. In Sault Ste. Marie, Ontario—a city, as we have seen, that has much to teach communities elsewhere in Canada—wait times between mammogram and diagnosis were slashed by as much as 75 percent at the city's breast health centre by compressing the early steps. A woman could receive a mammogram, have it assessed, and be scheduled for the ultrasound procedure and even the biopsy all in one day. It wasn't a matter of throwing more money at the problem, but of applying logic to the process.[5]

Ushering patients into the OR without excessive delay involves matching facilities to procedures. Again, a number of models exist that can be emulated with almost assured success. Do we need massive public hospitals for many elective surgery procedures, such as hip and knee replacements? Probably not. Toronto's Trillium Health Centre, which has the largest free-standing day-surgery facility in North America, performs these procedures with great success, winning a number of national and international awards for innovation and overall excellence. The Shouldice Hernia Clinic, just north of Toronto, has achieved worldwide fame, through articles in the *Harvard Business Review* and elsewhere, on both its surgical procedures and its business operations. The clinic is a private business, but residents of Ontario have the cost of their operation covered through the provincial health plan. Critics of Shouldice note that it accepts only patients with no complications that may require additional procedures beyond hernia surgery alone. While true, this does not negate its remarkable success rate, nor the fact that it relieves local hospitals of their patient loads.

In a dramatic demonstration of inflexibility, in March 2007 the Ontario government rejected a proposal by the Don Mills Surgical Centre, a private for-profit clinic, to perform knee replacement surgery for at least $1000 less than a community hospital receives for the same procedure. In addition to saving Ontario an estimated $1.6 million annually, the proposal would almost certainly reduce wait times, which were stretching up to a year for knee replacement candidates.

Was the government's dismissal of the proposal based on a question of competence or fear of setting a precedent? Apparently not, since the same facility was already performing cataract and orthopaedic procedures funded by the province's health care program, as well as cosmetic surgery and prostate cancer therapy. Moreover, British Columbia, Alberta, and Manitoba were contracting out similar surgeries to private providers in an effort to reduce wait times. Nevertheless, Ontario health minister George Smitherman rejected the proposal out of hand, declaring he would never support the funding of knee operations for a private for-profit hospital.[6]

Surely the private option deserves more serious consideration as a means of reducing wait times, because experience suggests that mere tinkering with the system relocates the problem without solving it. When a 2004 agreement between Ottawa and the provincial governments imposed wait-time limits on five selected procedures—cancer surgery, heart operations, cataract removal, hip and knee replacement, and diagnostic imaging—wait times for other procedures lengthened as a direct result. Patients requiring hysterectomies, colonoscopies, and gallbladder removal were asked to wait longer than before the policy was introduced. In a reaction that public advocates would expect from the greedy private sector, hospital administrators paid special attention to financial incentives proffered by the federal and provincial governments. Shifting resources toward the targeted procedures generated additional funding, so operating rooms, anaesthetists, and nurses across the country were assigned to accommodate patients requiring surgery for cancer, heart problems, joint replacement, and cataracts, and money arrived to purchase diagnostic-imaging equipment. In the end, little was solved.[7]

EMERGENCY DEPARTMENT WAIT TIMES—OUTRAGEOUS INEFFICIENCY OR URBAN MYTH?

Emergency rooms draw the most criticism where extended wait times are concerned. Tales of people spending three, four, five hours or more waiting to receive attention in an ER are legion and get reported with apparent glee in the tabloid press. While all such delays are regrettable and, in a few cases, disastrous, ERs themselves are just *symptoms* of problems.

All ERs operate on a triage principle. Arrive with severe chest pains and breathing difficulties, and you receive (or should receive) immediate attention; show up with a runny nose and a headache, and you will be asked to wait.

Delays in an ER may be caused by a lack of facilities in other areas of the hospital or by a sudden surge of influenza cases in the community. Influenza is hardly enjoyable, and in some instances, with the very elderly or those suffering from some other medical condition, it can be life-threatening. But the overwhelming majority of flu patients will improve more from following the familiar dictum of getting bed rest and consuming liquids than they will from hanging around a busy ER.

ERs suffer from the same "make do/work around it" syndrome encountered in Chapter 8. As a leading Canadian medical publication noted, hospitals can find ways to deal with ER overcrowding when they design and implement disaster plans because "the approach in such plans is to spread the workload evenly throughout the institution, thus doing the most good, and the least harm, with whatever resources are available." Do we need larger, better-equipped ERs? The same source suggests that we do not, noting that "the overwhelmingly greatest single cause of ER overcrowding is our inappropriate and unsafe approach to dealing with a lack of hospital capacity (not the lack of capacity itself)."[8]

Still, the horror stories continue, proving the power of anecdotes over statistics. No statistics exist to provide a meaningful comparison between provinces and territories, or between the Canadian experience generally and that of countries with similar systems. This prompted the comment from a team of ER specialists that "it is little wonder that the majority of information regarding ER overcrowding in Canada is anecdotal when the collection of this critical health information is so variable."[9]

THE CRUMBLING WALL AGAINST PRIVATE CARE—SHORE IT UP OR KNOCK IT DOWN?

Few aspects of the health care debate are as easily delineable as the question of tiers. Do we maintain a single-tier–single-payer system, an approach shared only with Cuba, North Korea, and China among all the other countries offering universal health care? Or do we open the doors to a wider role for private enterprise in our search for shorter wait times, reduced expenditures, and greater satisfaction?

Here are the primary debating points, pro ("adding private care will save the system") and con ("adding private care will destroy health care as we know it"):

1. **PRO: We already have a multi-tiered system.** If you are sufficiently wealthy with easy access to the United States, are employed by an arm of the federal government, or are a prison inmate, you will receive health care services faster than others, via private clinics if necessary. Within the public system, various

levels of service remain available for those with the wherewithal to access them. Access is never a question of government policy; it is always a question of money. The highly regarded Trillium Health Centre in Mississauga, Ontario, offers three levels of accommodation, as do many similar operations. Standard accommodation consists of four beds in a traditional ward-room layout. Those with sufficient private insurance coverage or sufficient cash in their wallet can choose to recover in a semi-private or private room instead. The medical treatment may be identical for everyone, but the post-surgical environment varies according to choice and ability to pay.

A significant development in the move toward supporting private providers occurred when Montreal marketer Jason Wright formalized the process of finding and patronizing private clinics through a website (www.findprivateclinics.ca). By January 2007, Wright's website listed 250 private clinics across Canada, categorized by location and specialties. Informed of the website's existence, a spokesperson for Ontario's health ministry declared that the province would refuse to accept the presence of private clinics, "passive or otherwise." But the private clinics continued to operate, and Wright's firm continued to direct patients their way.[10]

Did Ontarians represent the first line of defence against privatization of the health care system? If so, they appeared to be no more vigilant on the matter than residents of British Columbia, Alberta, and Quebec, who also seem tolerant of the development. When the residents of Canada's four most populous provinces consider privatization either a positive development or no big deal, how confident can we be in the immutability of a single-tier system?

2. **CON: The move would likely be irreversible.** Opening the door to a greater role for private enterprise would be a permanent modification to the country's forty-year-old medicare program.

That's not simply an opinion; it reflects rules embedded in the country's free trade agreement with the United States. Among the firms eager to participate in a move toward privatization would be U.S.-based insurance companies, chains of clinics and hospitals, and other privately owned businesses. They would arrive promising greater efficiencies, more attractive surroundings, shorter wait times, and other solutions to headline-grabbing disaster stories. Under the terms of the North American Free Trade Agreement (NAFTA), corporations may sue a foreign government if they believe its measures reduce, challenge, or limit their profits. As it stands, the public, not-for-profit nature of our system minimizes the risk of a NAFTA challenge. If Canada were to open the door to private health care suppliers, any attempt to close it in the future would spark a chain of complaints from foreign firms who had invested in the delivery of health care. This may or may not be a concern. To the Canadian Union of Public Employees, it represents an unacceptable threat; to groups such as the Fraser Institute and the Montreal Economic Institute, it is a non-issue.

3. **PRO: Private care is inevitable.** The system, in the vernacular, is already a little pregnant. The extent of its condition depends on where one resides in Canada. In British Columbia, private health care facilities spring up like daffodils, accommodating clients who wish to use them, professionals who seek to practise within them, and politicians who find ways to ignore them. False Creek Urgent Care Centre, everyone agrees, violates both the spirit and the letter of the law by operating as an alternative to emergency rooms in publicly funded hospitals in the Vancouver area. The provincial government first threatened to shut down the operation, then agreed to permit it to accept patients under a modified scheme. In Alberta, Edmonton's Northeast Community Health Centre functions along similar lines, providing ER service but no beds. And

Quebec continues down its own road toward greater activity by the private sector. More and more, the anti-private care policy of many provincial governments resembles the Vatican's stance against birth control; the priests may preach, but the congregation keeps using condoms.

4. **CON: The single-payer system provides an opportunity to control spending.** For all of its faults, the public system enables the federal government, as the single largest source of revenue, to control health care expenditures when necessary. This occurred between 1992 and 1998, when Ottawa managed to reduce by a full percentage point the portion of our GDP directed toward health care costs. Dr. Gordon Guyatt, an outspoken opponent of private funding, states, "That extraordinary decrease, without parallel in any other industrialized country, occurred because governments could put the brakes—hard—on health care spending. Only a single-payer system allowed that kind of discipline."[11]

5. **PRO: Instead of a single national program, we have ten provincial, three territorial, and one federal system.** If you are a resident of Quebec, you are not likely to receive free health care services when presenting your provincial medical card to an Ontario-based physician or hospital. Instead, you will be asked to pay cash because of widely differing payment schedules between the two provinces. Ontario health care providers will not perform services at Quebec's fee levels. How does this support the premise of portability for Canadians where health care coverage is concerned?

6. **CON: A two-tier system will extend, not reduce, wait times.** While advocates for introducing private medicine declare that it will relieve pressure on the public system, supporters of the single tier argue that wait times will grow longer for those without private coverage. They are probably correct as long as Canada has a shortage of physicians and nurses. With increased enrolment in

our medical schools and a promise from provincial colleges of medicine to reduce the backlog of immigrants with certified medical qualifications, this shortage will clearly grow less critical.

7. **PRO: Hospital bed capacity could be expanded without cost to the system.** Among the most common horror stories attributed to the inadequacies of our health care system is the one that depicts patients lingering on cots in hospital corridors because beds are unavailable. In a two-tier system, private hospitals could be required to provide a proportionate number of new beds to accommodate patients treated by physicians who have opted out of the public system, leaving more beds in the public sector. Opponents argue that the private quarters would likely be more posh than those provided for publicly funded patients, which may be true but is also irrelevant as long as the quality of care for both meets fixed standards. We continue to have class distinctions on aircraft, in hotels, at sports events and concerts, all based on ability to pay. As long as minimal standards are met and bed capacity is increased without cost to the public sector, is this really an issue?

8. **CON: Private health care providers will place profits ahead of patients.** We saw examples of this concern in Chapter 5, where private dialysis clinics avoided placing patients on transplant-eligible lists in order to maintain the clinics' income levels. Any formal move toward private health care will invite close government scrutiny and tough enforcement measures where necessary. Switzerland, for example, requires each citizen to carry private health care coverage but monitors the insurance companies to prevent abuses. Here at home, the province of British Columbia has reached accommodations with private providers who, despite various restrictions, still appear eager to do business.

9. **PRO: Face it—the wealthy already benefit from a two-tier system.** In December 2006, pharmaceutical giant Roche Canada

announced that five drugs for cancer treatment not covered by provincial drug programs would be made available to patients across Canada. The program, administered by McKesson Canada, a health care management consultancy, requires patients whose condition could be improved by the medications to visit one of eighteen branches of Bayshore Infusion Clinics Inc. The clinics are managed by Bayshore Home Health, the largest home care agency in Canada, on behalf of Roche, which is funding the operation. Among the Roche drugs available at the clinics is Avastin, which prolongs the lives of patients with incurable colorectal cancer. The cost of the therapy, borne by the patients, ranges from $22,000 to $40,000; patients who pass a means test qualify for a discount.[12] We thus have two kinds of cancer patients: those who can afford the best treatment, and those who cannot (perhaps with the exception of the near-destitute).

10. **CON: A balance cannot be struck between equity and efficiency.** Profit-making private insurers will seek to attract only healthy clients ("cream-skimming") to maximize profits and will reject, via inordinately high premiums and other means, those who represent a higher risk. This will shift high-risk patients to the public system, effectively erasing any gains expected from dividing services among two tiers.

ONE FACT REMAINS: TWO-TIER PUBLIC-AND-PRIVATE HEALTH CARE SYSTEMS WORK EVERYWHERE ELSE IN THE WORLD

Do we take pride in the fact that Canada is the only democratic country with a universal health care system that insists on a government-sourced single payer? Or do we ask if perhaps we are missing something? Both sides of the private-public debate make their cases with passion and conviction, to the point where consumers usually decide the match is a draw. A draw solves nothing, but a study commissioned by the CMA and completed in 2006 appears to tip the scales. The study, which examined "regulatory frameworks to safeguard patient access to health care in an environment of increased private finance for health care," reviewed two-tier systems in Australia, Ireland, New Zealand, and the United Kingdom. It concluded:

> The experiences of these countries ... suggests that access and choice [are] enhanced for those who can afford private health insurance, and that for those who rely solely on the public sector their health status is not compromised when there is an enhanced role for private finance. It appears that a parallel system of private health finance will not threaten the integrity of the public health-care sector as long as appropriate regulations on insurers and providers are in place and enforced. All OECD countries have implemented various regulations and policy options to promote access to PHI [private health care], and to protect access to and enhance the quality of publicly ensured care.... Canada would be wise to do the same.[13]

11

STEAL THE BEST AND INVENT THE REST

Examining Canada's health care procedures from a consumer's point of view is difficult enough; dissecting the systems of other countries is a near impossibility owing to complexity and scale, and the fact that countries constantly tweak their systems in response to perceived failures. This year's wildly acclaimed new development in public health care may be next year's abandoned failure. Several ideas, however, appear to work in many different systems, and those that have been proven over time and circumstance at least deserve consideration for Canada.

A quick review of various countries and their health care systems reveals concepts worth copying and others that we might be wise to avoid.[1]

Australia: Introduced in 1984, Australian Medicare is funded in part by a tax levy of 1.5 percent on income and is designed to cover the cost of medical services, pharmaceuticals, and public hospital care. (Canadian health care costs are financed from general revenue collected for the most part by the federal government.) All citizens are entitled to free public hospital care, but may elect to be treated as private patients in public hospitals or to use private hospitals where they (or their insurance provider) are responsible for medical costs. Private hospitals provide about one-third of hospital beds.

The Pharmaceutical Benefits Scheme covers patient costs for an agreed list of prescription drugs; only drugs that have been evaluated as clearly beneficial for specific illnesses and that represent the best value among other alternatives are included in this coverage. About half of all Australians carry private health insurance. Almost all of them are also covered for out-of-hospital care and services, including physiotherapy, dental treatment, and prescription eyeglasses.

Australian Medicare pays 100 percent of scheduled fees for out-of-hospital general practitioner services and 85 percent of fees for services such as specialist consultations, diagnostic imaging, and pathology (in this case, specific diagnosis regarding a contracted disease). Physicians are permitted to charge more than the standard Medicare fee; patients pay the difference. The cost of government-supported health care is divided between the federal government, which pays about 68 percent, and state, territory, and local governments, which absorb the balance.

Interesting point: Australians are actively encouraged to purchase private health insurance coverage, which preserves Medicare as a universal safety net. But the government has also reduced services for the public system, and has introduced a means test for access to public hospitals. A substantial number of physicians are concerned about the declining quality of services in the public sector, a situation blamed on the current conservative government's apparent intent, in the words of one group, to create "a health system destined to rival the United States in its inequity and inefficiency."[2]

Advocates for improving the country's health care system propose a shift in emphasis from hospital care toward primary care and preventative measures, and away from fee-for-service payments to physicians toward salaries or hourly wages supplemented with extra payments according to the procedures conducted. They have also called for a commitment that public and private providers will maintain equal levels of service quality.[3]

France: Public health insurance, which provides coverage for over 96 percent of French citizens, is funded by direct taxes on salaries (making up 60 percent of fund requirements) and indirect taxes on alcohol and tobacco products. About 80 percent of French citizens receive supplemental private health insurance from employers. More than 185,000 physicians were practising in France in 2001, providing the country with three doctors for every 1000 inhabitants (versus 2.1 per 1000 in Canada). Over 40 percent of French physicians are female, as were more than half the medical students in 2005. Salary levels for French physicians, as we have seen, are substantially lower than those in most other OECD countries.

Hospitals and clinics are either publicly funded, private for-profit operations, or private not-for-profit facilities. By law, private clinics are required to share medical files with all health care providers and must belong to a medical care commission that dictates evaluation procedures. Private not-for-profit institutions were originally denominational facilities that continue to rely largely on endowments for their financing. In 2005 public hospitals numbered 1032, providing 315,700 beds; 2139 private for-profit and not-for-profit facilities offered 170,400 beds.

Interesting point: Private medical care conducts more than 50 percent of surgeries and treats more than 60 percent of cancer cases.[4]

Germany: Employees contribute 7 percent of their gross earnings to fund the German system, a figure matched by employers. Over 300 non-profit organizations provide government-funded health services, and every citizen with an income below about Cdn$72,000 is obliged to join one of them. Those with incomes above this amount may opt out, if they wish, and choose private insurance, but these premiums are risk-related, rising with age and the individual's medical history.

The government health plan provides several more health-related services than in Canada, paying for all prescription drugs, dental care, diagnostic services, rehabilitation treatment, home nursing, and income support during sick leave. User fees ranging from Cdn$7 to

Cdn$20 may be levied, with an annual cap on the amount patients are required to pay. Physicians generally charge more for privately insured patients, but all medical providers are required to provide identical levels of service.

Interesting point: In December 2006, the country endured a widespread strike by physicians and pharmacists protesting federal government plans to slash spending, including a reduction of €500 million for medications. Government representatives claimed the overhaul was necessary to rein in spiralling medical costs; physicians and pharmacists argued the move threatened their livelihoods, and would result in staff shortages and long wait times for critical treatment.[5]

Japan: Universal insurance was achieved through the 1961 National Health Insurance Act, which established three categories of coverage: employees and their dependants in firms with 700 or more employees, who operate society-managed insurance whose boards are divided between management and worker representatives; employees and dependants of firms with fewer than 700 employees, who are automatically enrolled in a government-run small business national health plan; and a "citizens insurance program" covering retired and self-employed citizens, administered by municipal governments.

No restrictions are placed on an individual's choice of hospital or physician, and no preauthorization is required or user fees applied. Hospitals are either large government-owned facilities or smaller (fewer than twenty beds), often family-owned clinics operated by independent doctors. All hospitals must, by law, operate as not-for-profit entities.

Drug prices are determined by comparing new medications with similar drugs already on the market; drugs shown to be more effective or innovative than existing drugs are priced higher. If no comparable drug exists, the price is determined by manufacturing cost and the price of the drug in other countries. Prescription drug costs are paid by insurers.

The policy of paying physicians for each prescription they write and each lab test they order, rather than for time spent with patients, resulted in runaway costs in recent years. Efforts to change the system were not successful because both physicians and patients objected—physicians' incomes, tied to tests and prescriptions, would drop, and patients measured their service by the number of tests and prescriptions they received. Meanwhile, Japan's rapidly aging society is producing a financial crisis that has yet to be adequately addressed, in the opinion of many observers.

Interesting point: Hospital stays are much longer than in Canada, averaging thirty-three days per person, but surgery occurs only about one-third as often, owing to a resistance in Japanese culture to invasive procedures. Other social values affecting health care include a lack of emphasis on preventative care (until recently, the government was the country's largest tobacco retailer); a reluctance to discuss sexual activities, which has led to a slow but steadily increasing rate of HIV infections; and limited voiced dissatisfaction with the health care system, the result of the Japanese hesitation to express displeasure. Concerns about rising costs and quality of care are slowly eroding this latter trait.[6]

New Zealand: New Zealand has one of the longest histories of providing public health care to its citizens (it dates back to 1938), and many of its original features were emulated by the United Kingdom and Canada.

Health care budgets, established annually by the national government, are allocated to twenty-one district health boards (DHB), along with broad guidelines for the services the DHBs must provide. (This is similar to Canada's federal–provincial funding arrangement.) Each DHB either purchases these services or establishes facilities to do so, working within the budget figures. Some DHBs operate public hospitals and preventative programs, while others depend, to one extent or another, on various private profit and not-for-profit suppliers.

Citizens normally access the system through a primary-care provider (usually a family physician) and pay a user fee of between Cdn$15 and $40. Specialists can be accessed only through the primary-care provider. Low-income earners may apply for a community services card (CSC), which provides a subsidy for access to physicians and a subsidy for prescription drug purchases. A high-use health card, for patients who need to consult their GP more than twelve times annually, offers further subsidies. Among the services provided without a user fee are treatment in public hospitals, visits to primary-care providers for children under six years of age, laboratory tests and X-rays, dental services for schoolchildren, and breast cancer screening for women aged forty-five to sixty-nine.

The government agency PHARMAC makes some prescription drugs eligible for full or partial payment under the government plan. Before a drug can be added to the approved list, its marketer must demonstrate that the medication is both more therapeutically effective and more cost-effective than similar products.[7]

Interesting point: In a 1990 general election, the conservative National Party assumed power and converted hospitals to Crown Health Enterprises with government-appointed boards of directors. Much of the system's funding was generated from market-driven competitive contracting by private providers, a radical departure from the country's established system. Eight years later, when the promised benefits of the monetarist reforms failed to arrive, a Labour government was elected and promptly began reversing the new procedures. Since then, the government has found it necessary to raise various taxes to increase funding levels for the system.

Sweden: Public health care is somewhat broader in Sweden than in Canada, and extends to home visits by doctors, payment for all prescription drugs, and dental care to those nineteen years of age or younger While the national government sets policies and provides a portion of funding, services are managed and delivered through a decentralized system of twenty-six county councils and 288 municipalities. The county councils assume full responsibility for the management and delivery of health care services within their jurisdiction. About 70 percent of the cost is obtained from taxes set by council members, who face election every four years; many election issues relate to a council's health care management ability. Municipalities are responsible for financing and managing a specific list of services, including home care and nursing homes for the elderly, the disabled, and long-term psychiatric patients.[8] The councils own and run the hospitals, health centres, and other health institutions, including those supplemented by private providers, such as diagnostic clinics. Most councils charge individual user fees of between Cdn$7.50 and Cdn$45, although these are capped at $150 annually for physician and hospital services, and $300 annually for prescription drugs.

Private insurance is legal and growing rapidly as a means of sidestepping waiting lists in the publicly funded system. In 2002, more than one out of four medical providers were in the private sector, and nine private for-profit hospitals served patients who either enjoyed coverage from private insurance firms or paid directly for their treatment.

Interesting point: About 90 percent of physicians are salaried employees of the county councils. The balance operate as private practitioners but are contracted by the county councils, who assume the role of local regulators.[9]

United Kingdom: Having achieved almost the status of a religion among U.K. residents, the country's National Health Service (NHS) is centrally managed beyond the scope of other nations' health systems, with comprehensive care extending to prescription drugs, dental care, and optical services (the latter subject to user fees). Its 1.3 million employees qualifiy the NHS as the largest single employer in Europe and one of the five biggest in the world. A senior member of the Blair government, in defending the NHS, claimed "its founding principles—a health service paid for by all, with treatment free to everyone—reflect the best British characteristics of fairness, decency and respect."[10]

Private health care is available through employer-sponsored insurance and individually purchased policies. While the vast majority of Britons rely on the NHS to provide health care, an increasing number over the decade between 1995 and 2005, primarily as a response to growing waiting lists for elective surgery, chose to purchase private insurance, entitling them to services from physicians, surgeons, and clinics operating outside the NHS. (Insured patients can also access treatment in NHS facilities via "pay beds," which effectively enable them to "jump the queue" ahead of uninsured patients.) By 2006, more than 11 percent of citizens owned private health insurance, usually to avoid waiting for elective surgery.[11]

Extended wait times, deteriorating facilities, escalating costs, and growing public dissatisfaction made necessary a general overhaul of the NHS under the Blair government through 2006. In April of that year, fees for prescription medicines were set at £6.65 (Cdn$15), although these were waived for people under age sixteen and over sixty, and for patients with special medical conditions or in a low-income bracket. Those requiring repeated prescriptions could purchase a single-charge certificate permitting unlimited refills at no cost over the term of the certificate.

Prescription costs, especially expensive medications for cancer treatment, have created an ongoing debate. In 2006, British courts declared that women who met necessary clinical criteria could receive the breast cancer medication Herceptin at public expense. This decision is expected to cost the NHS Cdn$225 million annually to treat 5000 women.

With an annual deficit of £7 billion predicted for 2010, the NHS needed to improve efficiency and reduce expenditures, goals that required it, among other steps, to open more doors to the private sector. From the Blair government's point of view, greater involvement by the private sector (the U.K. government prefers the term "independent sector") will achieve three goals: increase capacity, support patient choice, and "improve value for money by raising productivity and innovation."[12] It should be noted that this declaration was accompanied by a doubling of the NHS budget.

It is difficult to isolate the impact of greater involvement by the "independent sector" on NHS operations, although, as we saw in Chapter 5, there is no shortage of criticism over the move. Improvements have been made, but according to the government's own watchdog, the results have been modest. During an eight-year period between 1998 and 2006, maximum wait times for hospital treatment fell from eighteen months to about six months. Wait times for cataract operations were cut to a maximum of three months, and the NHS targeted eighteen weeks as the longest wait period between a GP referral and hospital treatment. Other improvements, including a claim that death rates from breast cancer in women and lung cancer in men are falling faster in Britain than anywhere else in the world,[13] may be due at least as much to changing lifestyle habits as to modifications of the NHS.

Interesting point: The United Kingdom, under the banner of expanding patient choice and influence, sets specific targets for the NHS and publishes its achievements or failures. Many of these goals are associated with the organization's proactive tactics to improve the general health of Britons. In 2004, the following goals were announced, along with several others that could be measured and assessed between then and the target date of December 2010:[14]

- Increase life expectancy at birth to 78.6 years for men and 82.5 years for women.
- Reduce mortality rates from heart disease, stroke, and related diseases by 40 percent in people under seventy-five.
- Reduce mortality rates from cancer by at least 20 percent in people under seventy-five.
- Reduce mortality rates from suicide and undetermined injury (via improved mental health treatment) by at least 20 percent.
- Reduce adult smoking rates to 21 percent or less by 2010.
- Halt the rise in obesity among children under eleven, as part of a broader strategy to reduce obesity in the population as a whole.

THE SEARCH FOR AN IDEAL SYSTEM IS OBVIOUSLY FOLLY

No national health care system can hope to satisfy all of its citizens, or even a majority of them, all the time. France rates highly among many observers, but only at the cost of unacceptably low incomes, by North American standards, for physicians and the least-developed system of electronic data storage and transfer among all OECD countries. The United States scores best for short wait times, but it has the highest total health care cost measured as a percentage of GDP, plus astronomic administrative expenses and no coverage at all for 15 percent of its citizens.

Revamping the system in a country as geographically and culturally diverse as Canada presents an exceptionally challenging task. If we were to formalize the two-tier system by legislating limited private care, the experience of other countries suggests that we adhere to these guidelines:

1. *Provincial choices.* Provinces that select the private option must follow rules (such as those below) to qualify for support.
2. *No means test.* Citizens should choose, according to their own standards of preference, between private and public care.
3. *Strict enforcement of equal levels of service quality in both public and private systems.* Either federal or provincial governments would establish and review levels annually, releasing findings and proposing means of correction.
4. *Full access to patient records between public and private systems, with no restriction or fees.* This will become essential (and easier) with the establishment of electronic records.
5. *Expansion of dental care under the public system to children under six and adults over sixty-five.* In these age categories, dental care is as much a medical issue as it is a cosmetic one.
6. *User fees, with an annual cap for individuals and families, as a means of limiting unnecessary GP visits and bridging the funding gap.* We can charge $15 per GP visit with an annual $50 cap for individuals

and $100 for families. These fees can be waived for those who qualify for specified social services as a result of economic distress.

7. *Set, announce, and measure progress toward specific targets, replicating the British system.* In addition to representing a proactive approach to health care, measured targets provide Canadians with some indication of the system's effectiveness; without a baseline, it is impossible to measure improvement.

FEDERAL AND PROVINCIAL GOVERNMENTS

Governments at both levels remain the guardians of health care no matter how far the private sector encroaches into the system, and the involvement of those levels of government via funding can provide necessary equity. Based on international experience and our national situation, the federal and provincial governments should consider the following:

1. *Formalizing the entry of the private sector into our health care system.* This requires a redrafting of the federal act, a process that should include the establishment of strict guidelines for access and maintenance of service quality as a means of avoiding unacceptable claims by foreign providers under NAFTA.
2. *Setting a maximum percentage of GDP as the federal contribution toward public health care.* Every system benefits from fiduciary limits, within reason. Canada has achieved a GDP level of health care funding that should be frozen, providing the private sector with incentive and opportunity.
3. *Continuing to modify the fee-for-service payment system to doctors.* Inflexible fee-for-service payments may work against the concept of providing comprehensive care and, when beneficial to the patient, teamwork.
4. *Avoiding any attempt to manage the enrolment at medical schools.* The concept of central planning to control supply and demand is as old and unproductive as Lenin's tomb. Canadians should be

encouraged to obtain medical degrees according to their abilities and ambition, not discouraged or rationed. If nothing else, this would assist in ending the scandalous situation of attracting foreign physicians to fill a need artificially created by government decree and often leaving the homelands of these immigrants underserviced. About 40 percent of the practice certificates issued annually by the College of Physicians and Surgeons in Ontario, for example, are awarded to graduates of medical schools outside North America, about the same proportion awarded to those with degrees from Ontario medical schools. (The remainder are graduates of schools elsewhere in Canada and in the United States.) Moreover, the trend has been steadily growing. In 1995 the college issued 419 certificates to immigrant medical graduates; by 2005 the figure was well over 1000.[15] It's time to end our reliance on foreign-trained physicians (which remains ridiculously ineffective—see below) and produce our own medical professionals in sufficient numbers.

5. *Providing necessary funding for nurse practitioners to conduct routine procedures traditionally assigned to physicians.* The benefits of reducing time constraints on primary-care physicians may prove substantial (see below).
6. *Tracking experiences at emergency rooms to separate dramatic anecdotes from hard facts.* Too many tabloid-style headlines enlist ER horror stories as evidence that the entire health system is crumbling. Let's obtain and publish hard statistics according to diagnoses, time of day, and other factors for a clear picture that consumers can grasp and administrators can address.
7. *Shaping a program for aging Canadians with an emphasis on home care and day hospitals.* This will require a switch in funding, substantially raising the portion of each province's health budget dedicated to home care, but savings should ultimately accrue. Each dollar spent on day hospitals, for example, saves an estimated $2.16 in overall health care costs.[16]

8. *Eliminating interprovincial differences as a source of restraint on true portability of health care coverage.* Provinces will defend with great passion their right to establish pay rates for physicians and other health care suppliers. This should not prevent individual Canadians from expecting the public system to provide services of equal quality with no exceptional out-of-pocket cost, no matter where they travel in the country. This situation represents a de facto contravention of portability, one of the five principles of the Canada Health Act. In the words of a highly respected Canadian health professional, the health system should strive to become "a good travel companion—someone to talk to, someone to share things with and, if you get into trouble, someone to rely on 24 hours a day, seven days a week."[17]

HEALTH CARE PROFESSIONALS

The professionals in the health care system are as involved in revamping the system as consumers, and their position provides a unique perspective on ailments and cures. As consumers, we should support the efforts and proposals made by these professionals, which include:

1. *Offering faster, more efficient assessment of international medical graduate (IMG) qualifications to alleviate physician shortages as long as they occur.* The media delight in carrying reports of immigrants who are fully qualified as physicians but drive taxicabs or work as short-order cooks because the provincial licensing body is slow to recognize their qualifications. Although these cases are unfortunate, accrediting health care professionals is a complex process. A simple examination of credentials from offshore medical schools does not lead to an automatic assumption that the graduate meets this country's quality-of-care standards. Nor should it. Testing is required, although substantial criticism has been raised about the necessary procedures. In the area of specialists, things really begin

to falter. In Ontario, a maximum of fifty specialist assessment positions are made available annually to IMGs, and only the top achievers are permitted to continue with their training. In the words of the College of Physicians and Surgeons of Ontario, "The criterion for selection is the availability of positions, not a standard of competence."[18] Should the fifty-first-ranked candidate for a specialist certificate be deemed incompetent even though his or her medical credentials are in order? As long as we must rely on foreign-trained physicians, we should do more to accredit them—and we can.

2. *Reviewing the relationship between the Canadian Medical Protective Association and provincial and federal governments.* Assistance in providing medical insurance for physicians and surgeons is generally helpful, but the CMPA assumes both enormous power and apparent carte blanche in defending doctos. Dragging cases through the appeals process may be an accepted strategy in civil matters, but in this field—especially when the CMPA is drawing much of its financial clout from the public purse—it strikes many people as distasteful and unacceptable.

   On a related note, the CMPA should be instructed to work closely with provincial medical licensing authorities in qualifying IMGs for essential liability coverage. The organization's inflexibility has led to charges that it is impeding the entry of qualified IMGs into the profession. In an attempt to increase available human resources and provide hands-on experience, Ontario designed a pilot project that would permit qualified IMGs to work as assistants in supervised practice situations. Despite the fact that the candidates were required to hold a valid medical degree and complete the Medical Council of Canada qualifying examination, and had received an objective assessment of their medical ability, no liability insurance was made available to them, and the project was abandoned.[19]

3. *Encourage improved communications between patients and physicians, where possible.* Patients of a certain age are not the only people who mourn the opportunity to discuss their conditions and concerns with their family doctors. A substantial number of physicians do continue to value the bond between themselves and their patients. To them, communication is not just a social chat but a clinical technique. Yet a Health Canada document noted that, on average, physicians interrupt patients about eighteen seconds into their description of their medical problems at hand, and in 50 percent of visits the patient and physician disagree on the nature of the problems. Not surprisingly, Health Canada suggests, many malpractice suits arise not from incompetence but from communication errors.[20] Clearly, this helps explain the findings of a group of U.S. doctors, who determined that 25 percent of patients do not follow the treatments recommended to them because they do not understand them, do not agree with them, consider them inappropriate, or resent the physician's attitude. As one of the article's authors explains: "Patients must be able to ask questions, voice their concerns, and collaborate with clinicians toward the goal of adherence to their health care regimens."[21]

The concept of greater exchange between physicians and patients is gaining ground. A prominent Canadian medical journal advised physicians to employ a "Four Es" approach to communicating with patients, "making it possible to perform the traditional medical tasks more effectively":[22]

Engagement—Ask open-ended questions ("What were you hoping we would accomplish today?") and give the patient sufficient time to reply in full.

Empathy—When a patient describes his or her injury or pain, express understanding ("That must have been very uncomfortable"). Physicians may see this as a waste of time, but research appears to indicate that it actually saves time because patients tend to reveal underlying issues they might otherwise conceal.

Educating—Convey information about dosage, procedures, scheduling, and other key elements in a manner that patients understand.

Enlisting—Invite the patient to become a collaborator in making decisions.

Wider use of nurse practitioners will provide physicians with more time, a luxury most will welcome. Doctors who use this resource to deepen their relationships with patients may see greater benefits for both sides than they would from using it to perform technical tasks.

WE, THE PATIENTS

Five provinces—Alberta, Ontario, Quebec, New Brunswick, and Nova Scotia—have proclaimed a patient bill of rights. Each is ripe with platitudes about timely treatment, freedom of choice, participation in decision-making, and privacy, among other concerns. Only New Brunswick articulated the responsibilities of consumers, doing so in a brief and concise manner. In that province, patients are expected to

- learn how to access health services;
- use services appropriately and wisely;
- live a healthy lifestyle.[23]

We have in our own hands the most powerful tool to control the cost of health care; to reduce wait times for surgery and other procedures; to free beds and diagnostic equipment for critical care applications; and to ensure that we live as long, as healthily, and as independently as possible. Is it unfair to suggest that Canadians who choose a lifestyle that leads to excessive demands on the health system are as responsible as underfunding and mismanagement for failings in the system? Or is it hypocritical for Canadians who make selfish choices about drinking, drug use, eating habits, and exercise to complain about inadequate health care and rising costs?

Abuses of the system by patients may no longer be as extreme as they were in a tale related to me several years ago by an ER worker regarding a Toronto family who arrived at North York General Hospital late one Friday night. The parents claimed their two young children had not been feeling well lately, refused to eat, had difficulty sleeping, and were exhibiting other symptoms. They asked that both children be admitted for observation, and the hospital agreed, promising to call the parents as soon as any diagnosis was made.

Contrary to the parents' claims, the children appeared quite healthy while hospitalized. They slept well, ate heartily, and, except for constantly asking for their parents, appeared very normal and happy. Administrators attempted to contact the parents to arrange a discharge for the children the following morning but were unsuccessful. On Sunday evening, the parents arrived for their children. Later, an outraged acquaintance of the mother and father contacted the hospital to report that the parents had taken an impromptu weekend holiday and used the hospital, at public expense, to serve as a babysitting service.

Every health care professional has a similar tale to relate, and every tale is dramatic proof that some people will fulfil the Fraser Institute's claim about consumers making excessive use of the system because no direct cost is involved.

If Canadians want our health care system to remain universal, affordable, and accessible, with or without a second tier of private insurers, they can begin by caring for the system's health. And the most effective route toward a healthy system is to create healthy consumers who treat the system as a valuable finite resource worthy of their care, attention, and respect.

Ultimately, the success of Canada's universal health care system, with or without participation by private providers, is not in the hands of doctors, lawyers, or politicians exclusively. It is in the hands of the people who fund it, use it, value it, and display deep concern about its survival.

It is in our hands alone.

NOTES

INTRODUCTION: HOCKEY, MARK TWAIN, AND McLUHAN

1. "Complete User's Guide to Private Medical Care in Canada," *Maclean's*, May 1, 2006.

2. Canadian Institutes of Health Research, *Can Canada's Healthcare Sustain the Age Transformation?*, July 22, 2002.

3. Marshall McLuhan, *Counterblast* (New York: Harcourt, Brace & World, Inc, 1969), p. 75. Actually, this is a paraphrasing of McLuhan's original statement, which has been attributed to others, including theologian John Culkin. McLuhan originated the analogy.

1: PHYSICIANS AND SURGEONS: A MATTER OF MONEY AND STRESS

1. Interview with "G. Coulter," June 15, 2005.

2. Konrad Yakabuski, "Specialists' Pay Peeve Rooted in System That Lets Them Excel," *The Globe and Mail*, September 6, 2006.

3. Institute of Health Economics, *The Burden of Osteoarthritis in Canada: A Review of Current Literature*, November 2000.

4. Canadian Cancer Society statistics. Male lung cancer cases peaked at 96.4 per 100,000 males in 1986; by 2006, the incidence had been reduced to about 70 per 100,000.

5. "Canada in Motion," COA website (www.coa-aco.org/library/health_policy/canada_in_motion.html), October 2006.

6. Federal/Provincial/Territorial Committee of Officials (Seniors), *Enhancing Safety and Security for Canadian Seniors: Setting the Stage for Action*, September 1999.

7. Institute of Health Economics, *The Burden of Osteoarthritis in Canada: A Review of Current Literature*, November 2000.

8. Posted on COA website, October 2006.

9. Quebec Medical Association news release, August 30, 2006.

10. Aaron Derfel, "Ottawa Polices Alberta and BC More Tightly Than Quebec," *Montreal Gazette*, February 12, 2005.

11. Aaron Derfel, "Emergency Clinic Plans to Add MD," *Montreal Gazette*, February 15, 2005.

12. Doug Ward, "A New Day for Healthcare," *Vancouver Sun*, April 8, 2002.

13. Yakabuski, "Specialists' Pay Peeve."

14. Ingrid Peritz, "Man Who Challenged Canada Health Acts Says His Struggle Was Similar to Ghandi's," *The Globe and Mail*, June 10, 2005.

15. "Neurosurgical Depression," *CMAJ*, October 28, 2003.

16. Sarita Verma and Leslie Flynn, "Physicians with Depression: A Need to Attend," *CMAJ*, December 3, 2003.

17. J. D. McCue, "The Effects of Stress on Physicians and Their Medical Practice," *New England Journal of Medicine*, 306 (1982): pp. 458–463.

18. Verma and Flynn, "Physicians with Depression" *National Post*, August 20, 2003.

19. Verma and Flynn, "Physicians with Depression."

20. Statistics and some viewpoints extracted from CANSTATS Bulletins, released by the Canadian Statistical Assessment Service, August 25, 2003.

21. Dorothy L. Pennachio, "Are You Sorry You Went into Primary Care?" *Medical Economics Magazine*, September 23, 2002.

22. Interview with B. Hutchison, October 12, 2006.

23. *The Medical Post*, "Parcelling Out Primary Care," May 17, 2002.

24. Ibid.

25. CBC News, "Nurse Practitioners Establish on P.E.I.," September 11, 2006.

26. Interview with D. Mercer, September 7, 2006.

27. Michael Rachlis, *Prescription for Excellence* (Toronto: HarperCollins, 2005), p. 202.

2: INFORMATION TECHNOLOGY: FIFTY YEARS BEHIND THE TIMES

1. D. Hawaleshka, "Claire Lewis Didn't Have to Die," *Maclean's*, December 30, 2002; Ken Kilpatrick, "Apology Marks New Era in Response to Medical Error, Hospital Says," *CMAJ*, March 18, 2003.

2. Richard Alvarez, quoted in Terrence Belford, "Physician, Upgrade Thyself," *The Globe and Mail*, September 14, 2006.

3. *Beyond Good Intentions: Accelerating the Electronic Health Record in Canada*, 2006 Policy Conference, Canada Health Infoway and Health Council of Canada, June 2006.

4. Alvarez, quoted in Belford, "Physician, Upgrade Thyself."

5. Canada Health Infoway, 2006 performance evaluation.

6. Jerry Zeidenberg, "Northern Ontario Launches Large-Scale Radiology Network," *Canadian Healthcare Technology*, September 2002.

7. Adelle Larmour, "Technology Saves Hospital Over 98 Per Cent on X-rays," *Northern Ontario Business*, November 18, 2006.

8. "Electronic Health Records," *Health Management Technology*, November 2005; "Few Physician Groups Use Electronic Health Records," *Association of Operating Room Nurses (AORN) Journal* news release, November 2005.

9. Interview with M. Connolly, October 12, 2006.

10. SARS Commission, *SARS and Public Health in Ontario*, interim report, April 15, 2004, pp. 12 and 119.

11. Ibid., p. 113.

12. *Beyond Good Intentions,* executive summary, p. 4.

3: PHARMACEUTICAL COMPANIES: ANGELS OF MERCY OR 500-KILOGRAM GORILLAS?

1. Karen Birmingham, "Dark Clouds Over Toronto Psychiatry Research," *Nature Medicine*, June 2001.

2. Ibid.

3. "Scientist Stands by Views of Drugs after Settling Lawsuit with U of T," Canadian Press, November 21, 2002.

4. Benedict Carey, "David Healy: A Self-effacing Scholar Is Psychiatry's Gadfly," *The New York Times*, November 15, 2005.

5. *Toward a National Pharmaceutical Strategy*, Centre for Health Services and Policy Research, University of British Columbia, May 2006.

6. Marcia Angell, *The Truth about the Drug Companies* (New York: Random House Trade Paperback, 2004), pp. xxiii–xxiv, 51.

7. University of Bristol, "Philosophy and History of Medicine" (www.bris.ac.uk/philosophy/staff/Bird/PHMed_6.pdf)

8. Arnold Relman and Marcia Angell, "America's Other Drug Problem," *New Republic*, December 16, 2002.

9. Several sources detailing the Olivieri–Apotex episode were drawn upon for this section, primarily Elaine Gibson, Françoise Baylis, and Steven Lewis, "Dances with the Pharmaceutical Industry," *CMAJ*, January 2002; CMA news release, "Hate Mail Doctor Escapes Penalty for Latest Research Misconduct," April 22, 2002; B. Bruneau and R. Wodell, "Researcher Who Sounded Alarm Nearly Silenced," *Vancouver Sun*, November 2, 2001.

10. Interview with G. Guyatt, October 4, 2006.

11. Brendan B. McCormick, George Tomlinson, Patrick Brill-Edwards et al., "Effect of Restricting Contact between Pharmaceutical Company Representatives and Internal Medicine Residents on Post-training Attitudes and Behaviour," *Journal of the American Medical Association*, October 24, 2001.

12. Interview with G. Guyatt, October 4, 2006.

13. Colleen Flood and Michelle Zimmerman, "Direct-to-Consumer Advertising: CanWest's Charter Challenge," *Research Spotlight*, Canadian Institutes of Health Research, October 2006.

14. Flood and Zimmerman, and submission of CanWest Global Communications Corporation to the Senate Standing Committee on Transport and Communications, Study of the Canadian Media, April 13, 2005.

15. Dr. Erik Steele, "Nexium—The Little Purple Cash Grab," EMS House of DeFrance, September 2, 2003.

16. Michael Rachlis, *Prescription for Excellence* (Toronto: HarperCollins Canada, 2005), p. 228.

17. Aaron Smith, "Merck: New Pain Drug Safer Than Vioxx," CNNMoney.com, November 13, 2006.

18. J. M. Wright, T. L. Perry, et al., "Reporting of 6-Month vs. 12-Month Data on Clinical Trial of Celecoxib," *Journal of the American Medical Association*, November 21, 2001.

19. Rachlis, *Prescription for Excellence*, p. 231.

20. A. Hollis, "How Cheap Are Canada's Drugs Really?" *Journal of Pharmacy & Pharmaceutical Sciences*, June 2004.

21. PMPRB, "Analysis of Research-and-Development Expenditures," Annual Report 2005.

22. Richard Gold, "Bristol-Myers Holds Canadian Patients Hostage," *The Globe and Mail*, June 21, 2006.

23. J. Gerth and S. G. Stolberg, "Drug Firms Reap Profits on Tax-based Research," *The New York Times*, April 23, 2000.

24. Suzanne Aucoin, "In 1999 They Told Me I Was Cured," *Cancer Care in Canada*, Winter 2005–06 (available at www.canceradvocacy.ca/reportcard/2005/REPORT_CARD_2005.pdf).

25. Peter Downs, "Aucoin Loses OHIP Battle," *St. Catharines Standard*, November 17, 2006.

26. Brett Skinner, *Canada's Drug Price Paradox: The Unexpected Losses Caused by Government Interference in Pharmaceutical Markets*, Fraser Institute Digital Publication, February 2005, p. 2.

27. Ibid., p. 25–27.

28. Ibid., p. 1.

29. Adam Hoffman, "Cancer Decisions," letter to the editor, *The Globe and Mail*, November 23, 2006.

30. Rachlis, *Prescription for Excellence*, p. 238.

31. Jennifer Sheepy, "Pharmacists Help Fill the Health-Care Gap," *Capital News* online, November 16, 2001 (temagami.carleton.ca/jmc/cnews).

32. Jessica Whiteside, "New Role for Pharmacists," *University of Toronto Magazine*, November 4, 2002.

33. Ibid.

4: PAYING THE PIPERS: EFFICIENCY EXPERTS IN THE MEDICAL ARENA

1. Avis Favaro, "Audits Leave Ontario Doctors Bankrupt, Demoralized," CTV.ca, November 14, 2002.

2. Letter from Irene Hsu to the Coalition of Family Physicians, June 6, 2003.

3. Barbara Sibbald, "Sixteen-Patient-an-Hour MD Loses $1 Million after Audit," *CMAJ*, June 1, 1999.

4. OHIP declined an interview on this and other topics in the preparation of this book.

5. All cases from the Association of Ontario Neurologists (www.aoneuro.on.ca/HTML/keithmeloff.htm), "Doctors Protesting Unfair OHIP Audits Stage Candlelight Vigil in Toronto," January 27, 2003.

6. "Audits Leave Ontario Doctors Bankrupt, Demoralized." Dr. Vanek did not move to the United State but accepted a position on the faculty of the McMaster University Medical School.

7. Reported in *Canadian Family Physician*, December 2003.

8. Peter deC. Cory, *Study, Conclusions and Recommendations Pertaining to Medical Audit Practice in Ontario*, submitted to the Hon. George Smitherman, April 21, 2005, p. 2.

9. Patrick Conrad, "The P4P Con Job" (www.doctorsforfreedom.com), August 2005.

10. Interview with G. Guyatt, October 4, 2006.

11. Zachary M. Seward, "A Contrasting View from the Providers," *Internal Medicine News*, April 13, 2006.

12. "What Family Physicians Need to Know about Pay for Performance" *Family Practice Management*, July/August 2006.

13. American Academy of Family Physicians, "Pay-For-Performance," (www.aafp.org/online/en/home/policy/policies/p/payforperformance.printerview.html).

14. All figures derived from Peter C. Smith and Nick York, "Quality Incentives: The Case of U.K. General Practitioners," *Health Affairs*, May/June 2004, pp. 112–18.

5: WORDS FROM THE RIGHT: THE PRIVATE ENTERPRISE OPTION

1. Interview with B. Skinner, October 13, 2006.

2. Brett J. Skinner and Mark Rovere, "Paying More, Getting Less 2006: Measuring the Sustainability of Public Health Insurance in Canada," Fraser Institute Digital Publication, October 2006.

3. Dr. Gordon Guyatt, "Money Well Spent," *Hamilton Spectator*, February 26, 2005.

4. Larry MacDonald, "The Tip of the Scandal Iceberg?" *Canadian Business*, February 16, 2006.

5. David Gratzer, "Real Healthcare Reform Begins with Choice," Fraser Forum (oldfraser.lexi.net/publications/forum/2000/02/section_03.html), February 2000.

6. David Grazter, *Code Blue: Reviving Canada's Healthcare System* (Toronto: ECW Press, 1999).

7. Robert Dreyfuss and Peter Stone, "MSAs and Medicare," *Mother Jones Magazine*, January/February 1996.

8. Montreal Economic Institute (www.iedm.org/main/content_en.php?content_id=1). Accessed December 18, 2006.

9. Norma Kozhaya, *Two Myths about the U.S. Healthcare System*, Montreal Economic Institute, Economic Note, June 2005.

10. U.S. Department of Justice, "HCA—The Health Care Company and Subsidiaries to Pay $840 Million in Criminal Fines and Civil Damages and Penalties," press release, December 14, 2000.

11. Maggie Fox, "For-Profit Hospitals Cost More—Canadian Study," Reuters News Service, June 7, 2004.

12. Ibid.

13. Interview with G. Guyatt.

14. Interview with Larry MacDonald, October 13, 2006.

15. Pushkal P. Garg, Kevin D. Frick, Marie Diener-West, and Neil Powe, "Effect of Ownership of Dialysis Facilities on Patients' Survival and Referral for Transplantation," *New England Journal of Medicine*, November 1999.

16. Free Market Medicine (www.marketmed.org), "Market Failure?" November 2003.

17. E. Schneider and A. Zaslavsky, "Quality of Care in For-Profit and Not-for-Profit Health Plans Enrolling Medicare Beneficiaries," *American Journal of Medicine*, December 2005.

18. *Nation's Restaurant News*, "Starbucks: Health Benefits Exceed Coffee Bean Costs," September 26, 2005.

19. Consumers' Association of Canada, "Four Years Later: 1998 Survey of Waiting Times for Publicly Insured Cataract Surgery in Three Alberta Health Authorities," press release, January 21, 2000.

20. The Fraser Institute, *How Good Is Canadian Healthcare? An International Comparison of Healthcare Systems* (Vancouver: The Fraser Institute, July 2005).

21. Canadian Institute for Health Information (CIHI), *Healthcare in Canada* (Ottawa: CIHI, 2002).

22. The Fraser Institute, *How Good*, p. 7.

23. Guy Caron, "The Myth of the 'European Solution,'" *Canadian Perspectives*, Summer 2006.

24. Ibid.

25. Daniel Cohn, "Voters Reject Private Hospitals in Sweden," Canadian Centre for Policy Alternatives (policyalternatives.ca/index.cfm?act=news&do=Article&call=65). Accessed October 21, 2002.

26. Jeffrey Simpson, "Health Reformed: Only in Britain, You Say—Pity," *The Globe and Mail*, April 30, 2005.

27. The pro and con comparisons are derived from multiple sources, including Peter Fisher and Jacky Davis, National Health Service Consultant's Association, "Open Letter to the Canadian Medical Association from British Doctors" (www.healthcoalition.ca/cmabma.pdf), August 15, 2005; "General Information About Treatment Centres, General PFI Question and Answer Briefing" and "Treatment Centres FAQ," U.K. Department of Health, Policy and Guidelines (www.dh.gov.uk), September 2006; "Independent Sector Treatment Centres Are Helping to Transform Patient Care," *Medical News Today*, February 17, 2006.

6: AGED CARE: THE COMING TSUNAMI

1. "Senior Dies after Being Separated from Husband," CBC News, February 22, 2006.

2. Judi McLeod, "Couple Couldn't Live without Each Other after 70 Years Together," Canada Free Press, March 5, 2006.

3. National Initiative for the Care of the Elderly (nicenet.aging.utoronto.ca/en/introduction). Accessed October 2006.

4. Statistics Canada, Analysis Series: Population Estimates and Projections (www40.statcan.ca/l01/cst01/demo23a.htm?sdi=ages).

5. National Advisory Council on Aging, *Seniors in Canada—2006 Report Card*, p. 17.

6. Canadian Association for Community Care, *Canadian Home Care Human Resources Study*, 2004 Synthesis Report, p. 10. Accessed at www.cacc-acssc.com/english/pdf/homecareresources/EngTechnic.pdf.

7. CBC News Online, "In-Depth: Health Care" (www.cbc.ca), August 22, 2006.

8. Roy Romanow, *Final Report: Building on Values: The Future of Health Care in Canada* (Ottawa: Commission on the Future of Health Care, 2002), p. 186.

9. Interview with S. Herbert, October 11, 2006.

10. On Lok (www.onlok.org/stats.html).

11. Ibid.

12. M. King, "Comprehensive Care Management: A Closer Look," *New York Doctor*, June 1992.

13. L. Bruck, "Welcome to Eden," *Nursing Homes*, January 1997.

14. Paul Willging, "The Eden Alternative to Nursing Home Care: More Than Just Birds," *Aging Today*, October 7, 2000.

15. W. Molloy and R. Russo, "McMaster Findings Support Use of Advance Directives in Long-Term Care," *McMaster NEWS*, April 2000.

16. Canadian Institutes of Health Research, *Can Canada's Healthcare Sustain the Age Transformation?* July 22, 2002.

7: FROM OPERATING ROOM TO COURTROOM: PROTECTING PATIENTS AND DOCTORS

1. Paragraph 25, page 6, *Statement of Defence, April 9, 1999*, submitted by Harper Grey Easton, per Paul T. McGivern.

2. Interview with T. Harding, October 26, 2006.

3. Paragraph 133, *In the Supreme Court of British Columbia: Morgan Beverly Bystedt by her guardian ad litem Wylie Melissa Bystedt, Plaintiff, and Richard Creighton Hay et al., Defendants,* Honourable Madam Justice D. Smith (BCSC 1735).

4. Peter Mockler, as quoted in CBC *Disclosure*, February 11, 2003.

5. Ibid.

6. Ibid.

7. Ibid.

8. Supreme Court of British Columbia, *Shobridge vs. Thomas et al.*, Honourable Madame Justice Kirkpatrick, July 23, 1999.

9. Anna Marie D'Angelo, "North Van Physician Suspended," *North Shore News*, January 17, 2000.

10. Supreme Court of British Columbia, *Emmonds vs. Makarewicz*, Honourable Mr. Justice Fraser, June 25, 1999.

11. Canadian Medical Protective Association, *Consolidated Statement of Operations*, 2005 annual report, p. 16.

12. Rita Daly, "Malpractice Costs Soar, You Get the Bill," *Toronto Star*, April 1, 2006.

13. G. Ross Baker, Peter G. Norton, et al., "The Canadian Adverse Events Study: The Incidence of Adverse Events among Hospital Patients in Canada," *CMAJ*, May 25, 2004.

14. CPSO Panel Report on Dr. Errol Wai-Ping, March 11, 2004. All patient case details, unless noted, have been drawn from this document.

15. Except where noted, all facts are derived from the investigation report by the College of Physicians and Surgeons of Ontario into charges against Dr. Sankar Vaidyanathan, November 8, 2001.

16. Melissa Leong, "Doctor Not Guilty of Incompetence," *National Post*, July 13, 2006.

17. Susan Lightstone, "Class-Action Lawsuits Medicine's Newest Legal Headache," *CMAJ*, September 4, 2001, p. 622.

18. Ibid.

19. Scot Saltstone, *The Importance of Medical-Legal Education*, Memorial University of Newfoundland, Faculty of Medicine.

20. College of Physicians and Surgeons of Nova Scotia website, November 2006.

21. Interview with D. Mercer, September 7, 2006.

22. Unnati Gandhi, "Make Doctors' Errors Public, 26 Women Say," *The Globe and Mail*, April 20, 2007.

8: HOSPITALS: DOES TOYOTA HAVE THE ANSWER?

1. The case of "Mrs. Grant" is drawn from "Unexpected Hypoglycemia in a Critically Ill Patient" by Dr. David Bates, which appeared in *Annals of Internal Medicine* 137, no. 2 (July 16, 2002), pp. E-110–14.

2. H. J. Woske, T. Roding, I. Schulz, and H. Lode, "Ventilator-associated Pneumonia in a Surgical Intensive Care Unit: Epidemiology, Etiology and Comparison of Three Bronchoscopic Methods for Microbiological Specimen Sampling," *Critical Care Forum* 5, no. 3, April 2001.

3. The daily cost of hospital beds in ICU and ward areas varies according to a number of factors. These figures, considered reasonable and conservative, were quoted by Irvin Mayers, Philip Jacobs, Jennifer Drummond, Don Sin, Peter Calder, and Brian Rowe, "Non-invasive Mechanical Ventilation for Acute COPD (Chronic Obstructive Pulmonary Disease)," Departments of Pulmonary Medicine and Emergency Medicine, Public Health Sciences, University of Alberta, September 2006.

4. Linda T. Kohn, Janet M. Corrigan, and Molla S. Donaldson, *To Err Is Human: Building a Safer Health System* (Washington: Nation Academy Press, 2000).

5. D. E. Zoutman et al., "The State of Infection Surveillance and Control at Canadian Acute Care Hospitals," *American Journal of Infection Control*, August 2003.

6. D. Wiley, "Mistakes That Kill," *Maclean's*, August 13, 2001.

7. Andrew Nikiforuk, "Hospital Scourge," *The Globe and Mail*, September 30, 2006.

8. Mark Volavka, "Hospital-Acquired Infections in Pennsylvania," *PHC4 Research Briefs*, no. 5, July 2005.

9. The Toyota Way has produced a library of books over the years, all of them insightful and informative; many of them served as a resource for an assessment of this philosophy. For links between this philosophy and the health care system, I am indebted to Steven J. Spear, "Fixing Health Care from the Inside, Today," *Harvard Business Review*, September 2005, pp. 78–91.

10. Michael M. Rachlis, *Public Solutions to Healthcare Wait Lists* (Ottawa: Canadian Centre for Policy Alternatives, December 2005).

11. Leigh Hamby and Sarah W. Fraser, "Using Patient Waiting-Time Data to Improve the Hospital Bed-Assignment Process," *Joint Commission Journal on Quality and Safety*, January 2004.

12. Karen Howlett, "So Many Patients and Too Few Dollars," *The Globe and Mail*, June 6, 2006.

13. Ibid.

14. Ibid.

15. Interview with the author, October 11, 2006.

9: TREATMENT: HOW MUCH CARE CAN WE AFFORD TO OFFER?

1. Margaret Wente, "Medical Miracles Don't Come Cheap," *The Globe and Mail,* June 10, 2006.

2. Nadeem Esmail and Michael Walker, *How Good Is Canadian Healthcare?* (Vancouver: The Fraser Institute, January 2005).

3. Michael Rachlis, *Prescription for Excellence* (Toronto: HarperCollins Canada, 2005), p. 56.

4. Ibid., p. 57.

5. National Coalition on Health Care (Washington, D.C.), "Facts on Health Care Costs," November 6, 2006.

6. N. Kates, A. M. Crustolo, S. Farrar, et al., "Integrating Specialist Services into Primary Care," *Canadian Family Physician,* December 2002.

7. I. S. Sketris and P. McLean-Veysey, "A Provincial Program in Nova Scotia to Decrease the Use of Wet Nebulization Respiratory Medications," *Journal of Managed Care Pharmacy* 6 (6): 457–62.

8. Jacques Pépin, Louis Valiquette, and Benoit Cossette, "Mortality Attributable to Nosocomial *Clostridium difficile*-associated Disease during an Epidemic Caused by a Hypervirulent Strain in Quebec," *CMAJ,* October 25, 2005.

9. Centers for Disease Control and Prevention, "Morbidity and Mortality Weekly Report," December 2, 2005.

10. Robert Miller, "Rising to the Challenge," CAR eFORUM (www.car.ca/eforum/eforum_4_1.html), November 2005.

11. Ibid.

10: OF CABBIES AND CONSUMERS

1. Rod Mickleburgh, "$1400 Buys MRI in Daytime at Public Hospital," *The Globe and Mail,* September 13, 2006.

2. Dirk Meissner, "B.C. Health Minister Launches Queue-Jumping Probe at Vancouver Hospital," Canadian Press, September 12, 2006.

3. The RCMP is understandably reluctant to discuss its immunity from charges but a report tabled by Public Safety Minister Stockwell Day in January 2007 provided protection for officers injured while performing particular activities, including investigating firearm offences, counterfeiting, and theft over $5000, "in the line of duty." Cristin Schmitz, "Report Details Offences Shielded by New Laws," CanWest News Service, February 6, 2007.

4. Paul Webster, "The Price of Health," *L'EXPERT Magazine*, December 2006.

5. Michael Rachlis, *Public Solutions to Healthcare Wait Lists* (Ottawa: Canadian Centre for Policy Alternatives, December 2005).

6. Lisa Priest, "Cheaper Knee-Replacement Clinic Gets Cold Shoulder from Ontario," *The Globe and Mail*, March 21, 2007.

7. G. Galloway, "Waiting Time Vow Delays Key Surgeries, MDs Say," *The Globe and Mail*, October 6, 2006.

8. R. B. Abu-Laban, "The Junkyard Dogs Find Their Teeth: Addressing the Crisis of Admitted Patients in Canadian Emergency Departments," *Canadian Journal of Emergency Medicine*, November 2006.

9. B. H. Rowe, K. Bond, M. B. Ospina, et al., "Data Collection on Patients in Emergency Departments in Canada," *Canadian Journal of Emergency Medicine*, November 2006.

10. Michelle Collins, "Private Health Clinics Continue to Quietly Multiply in Ontario," *The Globe and Mail*, December 27, 2006.

11. Gordon Guyatt, "Private Payment: The Zombie of Health Care," *The Globe and Mail* update, April 6, 2004.

12. Lisa Priest, "Clinics Let Cancer Patients Purchase Treatment," *The Globe and Mail*, December 8, 2006.

13. Peter C. Coyte and Meghan McMahon, *Patient Accessibility Project*, Ontario Medical Association, April 17, 2006.

11: STEAL THE BEST AND INVENT THE REST

1. Data in this section was obtained from the Organization for Economic Cooperation and Development, *OECD Health Data 2002*, Paris, and supplemented by specific sources as noted.

2. T. Woodruff, "An Ironclad Guarantee Rusts Quickly," Doctors Reform Society of Australia (www.drs.org.au/articles/2006/Woodruff2), March 2006.

3. Australian Department of Foreign Affairs and Trade, "Health Care in Australia" (www.dfat.gov.au/facts/health_care.html), 2006.

4. Embassy of France in the United States, "The French Healthcare System" (www.ambafrance-us.org/atoz/health.asp), December 18, 2006.

5. Agence France Presse, "German-wide Protests Against Health Care Reform Scheme," December 4, 2006.

6. H. Nomura and T. Nakayama, "The Japanese Health Care System," *British Medical Journal*, September 24, 2005.

7. Gerard F. Anderson and Peter S. Hussey, *Multinational Comparisons of Healthy Systems Data 2000*, Commonwealth Fund, October 1999.

8. Standing Senate Committee on Social Affairs, Science and Technology, *The Health of Canadians—The Federal Role*, Volume 3: *Health Care Systems in Other Countries*, 2002.

9. Swedish Institute, *The Health Care System in Sweden*, September 15, 2003.

10. Patricia Hewitt, "Even Nye Bevan's NHS Saw a Role for the Private Sector," *The Guardian*, July 2, 2005.

11. Don Butler, "Two-Tier Hasn't Hurt Other Nations," CanWest News Service, June 10, 2005.

12. Ibid.

13. Ibid.

14. Department of Health (U.K.), "The NHS in England: Operating Framework for 2007–08," December 11, 2006.

15. College of Physicians and Surgeons of Ontario, "Backgrounder: 2005 CPSO Registration Statistics."

16. Dr. Réjean Hébert, "Can Canada's Healthcare Sustain the Age Transformation?" Canadian Institutes of Health Research (www.cihr-irsc.gc.ca/e/10518.html), July 22, 2002.

17. Tom Closson, speech to the Empire Club of Canada, January 2001.

18. College of Physicians and Surgeons of Ontario, "Tackling the Doctor Shortage: A Discussion Paper," May 2004.

19. Ibid.

20. Health Canada, "Better Physician-Patient Communication for Better Patient Outcomes" (www.phac-aspc.gc.ca/ccdpc-cpcmc/bc-cds/pdf/ tt1_e.pdf). Accessed December 2006.

21. L. R. Martin, S. L. Williams, et al., "The Challenge of Patient Adherence," *Journal of the American Academy of Physician Assistants*, July 2005.

22. Stuart Foxman, "The Clinical Benefits of Discussion," CPSO Dialogue (www.cpso.on.ca/publications/Dialogue/JanFeb06/doctalk.htm), February 2006.

23. New Brunswick Premier's Health Quality Council, *Health Renewal: Report from the Premier's Health Quality Council*, January 2002.

ACKNOWLEDGMENTS

Among the first to offer encouragement and guidance for this book was Walter Mulkewich, and without his much-appreciated support, I would not have completed the project. Sandy Thomson shared his experience with the technical side of therapeutics. Doctors Brian Hutchison, Gordon Guyatt, and Rob Gordon provided their highly qualified professional insight, as did Kathryn Clarke and Dr. Dale Mercer at the College of Physicians and Surgeons of Ontario. Dr. Mark Bernstein preferred to keep his contribution concealed, but I am expressing my appreciation publicly. Mike Lauber and Michael Connolly at Smart Systems for Health Agency were more than generous with their time, as was Steve Herbert of Baycrest. Thomas Harding's passion for his court battle on behalf of Morgan Bystedt cut through the subject of physician malpractice like a fresh scalpel, and I hope I have portrayed the fire in his soul. Brett Skinner of the Fraser Institute proved the ideal interview subject: gracious, patient, and provocative. I am indebted to them all.

In search of a bona fide medical professional to review my draft text, only one name came to mind. During his long years of practice in Burlington, Ontario, Dr. Ian Hay displayed compassion, skill, and genuine concern for his patients, all of which made him one of the most respected physicians in his community. The generosity of his time and spirit in assisting me to ensure the accuracy of this text cannot be overestimated; any errors that may remain are strictly my own.

The people at Penguin Group continue to earn my admiration for their professional abilities. They include editorial director Diane Turbide; her assistant, Elizabeth McKay; production editors Shima Aoki and Sandra Tooze; copy editor Wendy Thomas; proofreader Janice Weaver; and publicity director Karen McMullin, among others. I am grateful, once again, to all of them.

My agent, Hilary McMahon of Westwood Creative Artists, works tirelessly on my behalf, and this is another opportunity to thank her publicly and in print. And as she has with every book produced during our marriage, my wife, Judy, remains my source of gentle strength.

INDEX